Whistling in the Dark

Whistling in the Dark

by Fred Lowery

as told to John R. McDowell

Forewords by
Art Carney and Harry James

Pelican Publishing Company
GRETNA 1983

Library of Congress Cataloging in Publication Data

Lowery, Fred, 1909-
  Whistling in the dark.

  1. Lowery, Fred, 1909-   . 2. Musicians—United
States—Biography.   I. McDowell, John R. II. Title.
ML419.L68A3 1983   784'.092'4   [B]   83-4085
ISBN 0-88289-298-3

Book design by Laura Wooten Neal

Manufactured in the United States of America
Published by Pelican Publishing Company, Inc.
1101 Monroe Street, Gretna, Louisiana 70053

To "Gracie Girl," who for more than forty years has been my chauffeur, my cook, my housekeeper, my loyal companion, my manager, my eyes, my lover, my pillar of strength, my soul mate, my wife, and—always and without fail—my best friend.

Foreword by Art Carney

Fred Lowery! What great memories the name of my room-mate from my early years in show business brings back!

That was half a lifetime ago—in the era of Horace Heidt and his Musical Knights. Life back then seemed like an endless gig. There were no yesterdays or tomorrows—just the next town, the next stage, the next performance. We didn't know where life would lead us from day to day, and we didn't really care. None of us could imagine that it would ever end.

Funny thing, though, it did!

I don't know how many music fans today remember Fred Lowery, the blind whistler who once performed at Carnegie Hall, who once whistled in the White House for President Franklin D. Roosevelt, whose lovely "Indian Love Call" enchanted millions of radio listeners across our land.

I know the very young—today's schoolchildren—know him, because Fred now travels 50,000 miles a year whistling in school auditoriums from coast to coast. And I'm sure that many of the pre–rock generation who heard Fred perform on radio, on early television, on the stage, in nightclubs, and on records remember him.

Fred was—and is—a most memorable man, not only for his rare and special talent but for his courage and spirit and his ready laughter. There were those who thought of Fred as handicapped, but I never looked at him that way. Like the rest of us in the band, Fred was a trouper. He did his job. Offstage, his blarney and his personality brightened our bull sessions and our travels. Fred and his blindness were the butt of our practical jokes more than once, but he always took it in stride and gave as good as he got.

In those days of one-night stands and an endless succession of towns and dance floors, performers lived fast and worked and played at fever pitch. And Fred kept pace with the best of us.

In later years, Fred and I went our separate ways. But we are still joined by many memories of the good and bad times of those yesterdays.

As for Fred's blindness, I remember how during our days as room-mates he would plunge into our dark rooms at night to find the light switch with unerring instinct. And once in Cincinnati when a power failure blacked out much of the city Fred spent hours leading the guests along dark corridors, getting them settled for the night by locating the numbers on their hotel doors with his sensitive fingers.

At the time, I thought how funny it was. The sighted guests were lost in the world of darkness, but Fred was never lost in whatever world he entered. Even though he may be blind, he lights the darkness of his world and ours with his rare gifts of music and humor.

Art Carney

Foreword by Harry James

Nostalgia has never been one of my strong points, even though I have a lot of living to remember. Like that ageless philosopher of baseball, Satchel Paige, I have always been reluctant to look back because somebody might be gaining on me.

But I do remember that I first met Fred Lowery back in the 1930s, when I left my father's circus band and joined Ligon Smith's dance orchestra in Texas. One of our first jobs was a tour through the Depression-stricken Southwest. It was during that tour—a tour on which Ligon's band and a collection of radio performers known as the Early Birds joined in a show optimistically named "Heads Up!"—that I met Fred.

My first memory of Fred centers on a date we played in El Paso early in the tour. After the show, a few of us ventured across the border to visit the famed *cantinas* of Juarez. Our major problem, as I recall, was that our collective bankroll didn't come close to equaling the dimensions of our thirst, not even at the cut-rate prices offered by the Mexican saloons.

During our first stop in Juarez, Fred favored the barroom patrons with a magnificent rendition of "La Golondrina"—a performance which not only brought repeated encores but also produced a continuing round of free drinks for all of us. When we finally staggered back across the border to our bus, we were all as "blind" as Lowery, without having spent a cent.

As the youngest members of the show's cast, Fred and I spent considerable time talking. We both had an intense love of music and a burning ambition to succeed. But we weren't sure what shape that dreamed-of success would take, or how we would achieve it.

Real success is a difficult goal for any musician. And I was afraid that, despite his unique talent, Fred's dreams of the big time were doomed to disappointment. It seemed to me and to others that Fred had two strikes against him before he ever got up to the plate. First, he was a whistler, and there just wasn't much demand for career whistlers. And Fred was blind. Everybody knew that blindness was a major handicap in show business. But being a blind whistler was even worse. It seemed like a hopeless obstacle that no amount of talent or ambition could overcome.

But Fred fooled me, fooled all of us. In fact, Fred beat me to the big time in Manhattan. He was a rising star with Vincent Lopez when I arrived in New York a couple of years later to join Benny Goodman.

Like me, Fred Lowery is still working, still on tour, still whistling those wonderful tunes, still in love with music after more than fifty years on the road. As I said, I'm not much for nostalgia. But I am glad that Fred has taken the time to remember those days when we were young and a talented fellow could whistle up a round of beers for his thirsty buddies.

Harry James

Acknowledgments

Many people have helped and supported me in my career and in the writing of this book. My heartfelt thanks to all those mentioned here—and to others too numerous to mention:

To my family, and especially to my son Fred, who first suggested I write a book using a tape machine to record my thoughts and recollections. His faith gave me the confidence to attempt it.

To my coauthor John McDowell of the Indianapolis, Indiana, *Star* for his tireless efforts and the long hours spent in interviews, research, and putting the story into written words. John died unexpectedly just as he was beginning the final revision of the manuscript, and my family and I deeply mourn the passing of this dedicated friend and co-worker.

To Richard Kirk of Indianapolis, John's former associate and our mutual friend, for helping prepare the manuscript for publication. His help and friendship will always be remembered.

To my longtime friend Bob Ohleyer of Indianapolis, who introduced me to John McDowell and Richard Kirk.

To Evelyn Oppenheimer of Dallas, Texas, my literary agent, for her efforts in finding the right publisher and for her unfailing support, and to Dr. Don Newbury of Snyder, Texas, who first put me in contact with Evelyn.

To Kathy Dunn, my secretary, for transcribing and typing countless tapes when I first began working on the book.

To the management and staff of Pelican Publishing Company—especially Dr. Milburn Calhoun, Frumie Selchen, and Kate Bandos—for publishing, editing, and marketing this book.

And last, but not least, to the many others who have often given me help, friendship, and guidance—Betty Carlson of Chicago, Illinois; Bob Roth of Greensboro, North Carolina; Otto Evenson of West Fargo, North Dakota; C. D. Acker of Jacksonville, Texas; Ed White of Rock Springs, Texas; Edwin Brown of Troup, Texas, T. M. Cunningham of Houston, Texas; Gordon Thrall of Jacksonville, Texas; Wayne Richison of Tulsa, Oklahoma; Elma Evans of Troup, Texas; Bing and Brownie Grunwald of Omaha, Nebraska; Evelyn and Ed Kiely of Jacksonville, Texas; and the late Matty Rosen of New York City.

Prologue

There's one thing I'd like to straighten out right at the start. It's this label I've been wearing for more than forty years: "The Blind Whistler." Horace Heidt pinned it on me even though I had always resisted trying to cash in on my lack of sight. Like most labels, it seems simple enough on the surface. But, also like most labels, when you start probing to find out what's behind it, it's not as simple as you thought.

To begin with, I am blind—but not totally blind. I'm legally blind. There are many legally blind people, some of whom see something and some nothing. I'm one who does see something. I have one artificial eye, but my other eye actually works to some extent. I can't compare what I see with what everyone else sees, because I don't know what they see. I do know that my one "good" eye isn't very good. It was seriously damaged by the same disease that destroyed the sight in my other eye while I was still an infant. And it may have been damaged even more by the uncertain medical treatment I received afterward.

Like everyone else, I've learned to do the best I can with what I've got. I can't read, and that's certainly a big drawback. But through a combination of concentration and imagination I can recognize people I know well, "watch" TV, identify colors, and tell a shapely girl from a lumpy one. I can also navigate by myself when I want to or have to, although I have trouble with curbs and other such hazards. And stairways are a serious problem.

Somewhere along the line someone said I must have about one-percent sight. That seemed like an easy way to answer questions about how much I can see, so I've used it ever since. It's really more a figure of speech than any kind of accurate measurement.

Now, about the word "whistler." Sure, everyone can whistle. But they can pick up a violin and get some kind of sound out of that, too. To become an accomplished musician—a violinist, a pianist, or a whistler—requires a great deal of work and hours and hours of practice.

People sometimes ask me what attributes make a great whistler. Well, I think they're really just the same as for any other musician. He needs good musical sense—good phrasing, good timing, good improvisational instincts—and mastery over his instrument, which in this case is his whistle. In fact, I've always tried to use the whistle exactly as I would have used an instrument if I had become a professional horn player or violinist. The main reason I didn't stick with an instrument was because they told us at the Blind School we would never be able to play in a sighted musical group anyway, since we couldn't "read" music. But fortunately I had a special knack for whistling, and it ultimately opened a lot of doors that a more conventional instrument probably wouldn't have.

I realize whistling is a kind of off-the-wall talent to base a life and a career on. No college of music offers a major in it, or even a minor so far as I know. Nevertheless, it worked for me. It was a magical gift that made a poor, handicapped boy from the Piney Woods of Texas into a headline performer with some of the finest bands in an era of great bands. Whistling has also given me a life of rewarding and exciting activity and enough financial stability to marry, own a home, raise and educate a child, pay my bills, and in general live as good a life as most fully sighted people.

So, okay, that's who I am, Horace: "The Blind Whistler." And I've long since forgiven you for hanging that label on me. In fact, maybe I owe you a little extra thanks for it. You always did have a flair for packaging, and this package has worn pretty well.

Chapter 1

I was born in the little town of Palestine in the Piney Woods area of East Texas on November 2, 1909, the fourth and last child of William and Mary White Lowery. I have no recollections of my birthplace or my parents or of the sighted world into which I was born, for I lost my home, my mother and father, and most of my eyesight before I was two years old.

My mother—her health and spirit eroded by a life of poverty and hard work—died shortly after my birth. She left my father, a wanderlustful railroadman of Irish descent, with a squalling infant son and three daughters to raise.

Bill Lowery struggled with his parental responsibilities for about a year. He even quit his job as a railroad fireman and went to work as a hired hand on nearby farms so that he could be close to home and his children. But another misfortune soon shadowed his life. I was stricken with scarlet fever, an illness whose complications left me totally blind in my right eye and with limited vision in my left.

I guess having an almost-blind eighteen-month-old son to care for was the blow that put an end to my father's reluctant attempts at homemaking. As my sisters and I learned later, Bill Lowery scrawled a hasty, apologetic letter to my grandmother, telling her he wasn't able to both work and care properly for his children. He said he was going to leave the Piney Woods in search of a better job and asked her to pick up his children at the train depot in Gould, a small East Texas railroad town near her tenant farm.

Without waiting for a reply to his letter, my father asked a friend to drive us in a wagon to Gould on the specified day. Apparently certain that Grandma Lucy White would respond to his letter, my father deposited me and my sisters—Irene, Anna Mae, and Minnie Lee—on a pile of railway ties near the station. He cautioned my older sisters to "stay with the baby until Grandma comes" and caught an eastbound train. We were still perched on the stack of ties, hungry and bawling, when our grandmother found us about an hour later.

Grandma White was understandably outraged, and through all the years of our childhood she often spoke of our father's desertion. As for us, we were bitter and hurt, but most of all bewildered. Occasionally we created fantasies about how someday he would return, rich and loving, to claim us. But he never came, in fact never even wrote a letter.

Years later, after she was grown, my sister Anna Mae set out to discover where our father had gone. After more than a year of searching, she learned he had gotten a job as a policeman in Kansas City. He had been walking a beat only a few weeks when he was shot and killed while making an arrest, leaving no record of kin on his employment file.

My grandmother and my mother's brother, Uncle Ed, were the only parents I ever knew. Uncle Ed had remained a bachelor, helping Grandma White on a dreary succession of sharecrop farms after my grandfather, Randall Hardy White, was killed by lightning in the cotton fields he had spent his life cultivating. The poverty of those early years was incredible. In fact, I sometimes think that the strongest motivation in my life, the thing that has carried me through when I couldn't see any way to get over the next hurdle, has been the memory of that grinding poverty—and the desperate wish to escape it.

Of course, most Piney Woods families were poor. Life was hard and primitive. Growing cotton was a family enterprise, and everyone, young and old, had to help. My earliest memories are of moving from one tenant farm· to another—of Grandma White setting up housekeeping· in a succession of drab sharecrop shacks, vainly hoping with each move that her family's lot would improve.

I began my apprenticeship in the cotton fields at the age of five on a farm near the village of Troup. My youngest sister, Minnie Lee, two years older than I, was my constant companion and acted as my "eyes." She led me into the fields and taught me to pick cotton. As I groped my way up and down the long, dusty rows hour after hour she followed close behind, gathering the cotton I missed and prodding me when my enthusiasm began to wilt under the searing sun. Later, during summer months away from the School for the Blind, I became an accomplished cotton picker and earned much of my spending money for the year in the hot fields.

During those days in the Piney Woods I had little contact with the world outside my family, and the few associations I did have were generally painful. When I was with Grandma White and Uncle Ed and our kinfolk, the Skillerns, no one seemed to notice my blindness. Charles and Nanny Skillern had eight children and owned their farm near Troup. Despite such affluence, their poor relations were always welcome. My sisters and I played in their big farmhouse whenever we could escape from our daily chores.

And my cousins, like my grandmother and uncle, did everything possible to help me adjust to my nearly sightless world without treating me like a helpless cripple. But when I strayed beyond our family circle I quickly learned that lack of sight set me apart from other children.

Youngsters from neighboring farms, and town kids too, were often my tormentors. One boy in particular seemed to delight in picking on me. One incident still stands out in my memory. I had accompanied one of my older cousins to a nearby swimming hole and was sitting in the shade of a big cottonwood when the bully arrived for a swim.

"Get away from here, blind boy, before I sock you!" he shouted, yanking me to my feet and shoving me down into the underbrush. "Don't you know it makes us sick havin' to keep lookin' at a freak like you?" Frightened out of my wits, I sobbed hysterically all the way home.

But the time came when the bully no longer showed up to harass me. Uncle Ed announced at the dinner table one evening that the boy had been gravely hurt in an accident.

"What happened to that no-good rascal?" Grandma White asked, no doubt remembering how his parents had laughed at her when she demanded that they stop their son's bullying ways.

"He found some dynamite caps and was foolin' with 'em when they blew up in his face," my uncle explained. "He's in the hospital, and folks in town say he'll be blind for life."

Grandma White grunted. "Serves him right. The good Lord punished him for the way he's made life miserable for poor little Fred!"

"Now, Ma, don't talk like that," Uncle Ed protested. " 'Tain't right to wish somethin' like that on anybody. You gotta feel sorry for the kid, no matter how ornery he was."

But Grandma White didn't share my uncle's forgiving heart. She was a devout fundamentalist who believed that hell and damnation awaited sinners, that a vengeful God, in the best Old Testament tradition, handed out swift punishment to mortals who displeased Him.

"Nosirreeee," Grandma exclaimed. "I ain't one bit sorry. That rascal got what was comin' to him. Now he knows what it's like to be blind. God is teachin' him a lesson!"

While Grandma White viewed the blinding of the town bully as comforting evidence of God's justice, she never could understand why the Lord refused to show compassion for her grandson. Ultimately she set the blame on my father, who she claimed put her daughter in an early grave with his wild, godless ways. She was convinced, I'm sure, that God had punished my father by burdening him with a blind son.

In later years Grandma White told me there wasn't a day that she hadn't prayed for a miracle that would cure me of my blindness. During the long, hot Texas summers, until I was well into my teens, she took me to every evangelist who set up a revival tent in the Piney Woods, hoping that somewhere, somehow there would be a laying on of hands, a divine exhortation that would produce the miracle for which she asked.

The faith-healing miracle never materialized. But another miracle did, a miracle that took me out of the Piney Woods and eventually freed me from my poverty and ignorance.

It started in the summer of my seventh year when my cousin Ruth Skillern excitedly informed me on her sixth birthday that she would be starting school in September.

"How come you're startin' school?" I wanted to know.

" 'Cause I'm six, an' all kids start school when they're six," she announced proudly.

"That ain't so," I retorted. "I'm almost eight and I ain't been to school. Bein' six don't have nothin' to do with schoolin'."

"It does, too," my cousin insisted.

"Are you sure?"

" 'Course I am. I'm six and I start in September. Mamma told me so."

"Then how come I ain't started school?" I demanded angrily. "I was six a long time ago!"

"Well . . ." Ruth faltered. "Well, maybe Grandma just forgot to send you. You'd better tell her."

There was a stunned silence at the kitchen table that evening when I interrupted the beginning of supper with the news that Ruthie Skillern would be starting school in September, now that she was six years old.

"If Ruthie can go to school when she's six, how come I'm a lot older than she is and I ain't started yet?" I asked Grandma.

Grandma White hurried to my chair and took me in her arms. "Freddie . . . poor, poor Freddie," she said softly. "Honey, I'm sure enough sorry, but you can't go to school."

"Sure I can. Ruthie says I can because all kids start school when they're six."

"Ruthie is mistaken, dear," Grandma tried to explain. "Most children start school when they're six. But you can't because you can't see. They just don't teach blind children."

"That ain't fair," I wailed. "I can do lots of things other kids do. Why can't I go to school?"

"You just can't. They won't take you, Freddie," Grandma said sadly. "Come on now, finish your supper and don't fret. It won't do no good to cry and carry on."

But Grandma White's attempts to console me were futile. In angry frustration I crashed my dinner plate to the floor. "I can see good enough, I can see good enough!" I howled, beating the table with my fists. I pushed away from the table and groped my way into the parlor, knocking over a chair. I found a book, brought it back into the kitchen, opened it, and held it up against my left eye, straining to make sense of the page. "See, I can read just like other kids!"

Gently Grandma White took the book from me and led me to bed in my room off the kitchen. She murmured a prayer and kissed me good-night before rejoining Uncle Ed at the table. Lying in my bed, I heard Grandma sigh wearily.

"It's tough on Brother," Uncle Ed said, using his pet name for me.

"My heart just plain aches for him," Grandma said. "If only there was something we could do. I feel so helpless."

"I know, I know. . . . But what can we do? Even if he could go to school he'd still be blind and helpless. Book learnin' won't help him none in gettin' a job when he's grown up. Nobody wants to hire a blind man."

"I guess you're right," Grandma answered. "It's God's will, and we must accept it. It's a cross we've got to bear."

Neither Grandma White nor Uncle Ed, nor the Skillerns, had ever heard about education for the blind. In fact, in the isolated poverty of the Piney Woods in those years even most of the sighted children got only a minimum of education. Helping the family make a living was considered more important than schooling.

I suppose I would have grown to manhood in ignorance if my uncle hadn't struck up a chance conversation with a stranger in Troup's ramshackle railroad station one day. As Uncle Ed told me years later, the stranger—an itinerant book salesman—had stopped in town to peddle encyclopedias door to door. Returning to the station to wait for the next train, he met Uncle Ed and tried to sell him a set. "Don't you have any youngsters at home?" the stranger asked after my uncle turned down his sales pitch.

"Yeah. But my nephew . . . he's blind. Books can't do him no good. He can't even go to school to learn to read."

"Sure he can," the stranger told my uncle. "There's a school for blind kids up at Austin. Don't cost nothin' for poor folks, either."

That was how my family learned of the Texas School for the Blind. But no one said anything to me about it until Uncle Ed had made a trip to Austin and determined that there really was a school for blind children. Before he returned to Troup he filled out an application, and a few weeks later a letter arrived at our farm stating that I had been accepted as a seven-year-old beginning student at the Texas School for the Blind, starting in September. It was then that Grandma White told me I would really be going to school—a very special school far off in Austin, the capital city of Texas.

Blind people live in two worlds: the sighted world and the unsighted world. As the years passed and my horizons spread far beyond the Piney Woods, I learned that there is only one bridge between those worlds, and that bridge is education. At seven-going-on-eight, however, I was not concerned with philosophical ideas as I set out for the Texas School for the Blind in September 1917. I was both excited and frightened—elated that, like my cousin Ruth and other children, I was starting school, terrified at the thought of leaving the only security I had ever known.

I made the trip to Austin alone, a daylong ride on a Missouri Pacific train that stopped at every settlement along the way. Grandma White, Uncle Ed, my sisters, and my cousins were at the station to see me off. Around my neck was a strong piece of cord and a tag inscribed with my name, address, and destination. On the seat beside me was a shoe box crammed with fried chicken, cold biscuits, potato salad, and Grandma's homemade apple pie. In my pocket was twenty-five cents that Uncle Ed had given me when we said our tearful good-byes. A quarter may not mean much today, but in those days it was a small fortune for a little boy to squander.

The strangeness of my first ride on a train quickly blotted out my loneliness. I tried to look out the window, but the outside world was indecipherable. I amused myself by listening to the clickety-clacking of the train wheels on the tracks and examining with my fingers all the "luxuries" of the coach: the softness of the plush upholstery, the cool feel of the window glass and steel trimmings, the solid curves of the seat's carved wooden armrest.

On that local passenger train to Austin, I'm sure the coaches were old and worn. But I couldn't see the stains and scars. In my imagination, I rode in a palace on wheels. I especially remember the cubbyhole toilet at one end of the coach. The conductor, who had been carefully briefed on my condition by Grandma White, led me to the toilet and explained how everything worked. It was my first introduction to the marvels of indoor plumbing. I was also fascinated by the "butcher boy"—the man who came swinging down the aisle about once an hour, selling cold drinks, candy bars, popcorn, and other goodies. By the time my trip ended I had spent my entire quarter on red pop at a nickel a bottle. I really gave the conductor a workout that day, leading me back and forth between my seat and that marvelous toilet.

I don't remember much about my arrival in Austin. I was met at the station by a teacher who collected my sparse luggage and took me out to the school in a car that putt-putted along at a brisk pace. At the school, I was given a quick supper and put to bed in a cottage which I later learned housed the first-grade pupils—girls upstairs, boys downstairs. Beyond that, I only remember the great waves of homesickness that gripped me that first night as I lay in a strange bed and wondered fearfully what the next day would bring.

I did a lot of crying during my first year at the school. As the champion crybaby of the class I soon became a favorite target for teasing, which only aggravated my loneliness and touched off new torrents of tears. I guess the school officials must have despaired of my ever fitting in.

True, I had wanted to go to school. But now I started to wonder why Grandma White had sent me away to live with strangers. I was fearful that I would never again return to the only home I had known, that once again I had been abandoned.

Fortunately I had an understanding, loving teacher, Lizzie Rutherford, who patiently helped me through those difficult and lonely days. It was Lizzie who slowly built up my self-confidence, who convinced me that my grandmother and uncle had sent me away to school because they cared about my welfare, not because they wanted to get rid of me.

Eventually I began to make friends with other children and take an interest in school activities. Gradually the teasing stopped and I became one of the gang. By the time the first year ended I had forgotten my despair. I was a part of the school and its routine; I had successfully taken a few small steps on that bridge that led from darkness into light.

Chapter 2

Although I returned to the Piney Woods each summer to work on whatever tenant land Grandma White and Uncle Ed happened to be farming, the School for the Blind in Austin was my real home for the next twelve years. There I had my useless eye removed and got a glass one instead. There I gained knowledge and self-reliance. There I found protection from the hazards and problems of everyday living until I was finally equipped to venture into the sighted world. There, too, I learned to live with people, learned to utilize my musical talent, learned the "feel" of life. Without the benefit of that schooling, I'm sure I would have been doomed to a barren, unproductive existence.

If you're blind, your education doesn't start with book learning. It starts with "life learning"—discovering the dimensions of the world around you by substituting touch, hearing, smell, taste, and imagination for the missing sense of sight, and developing memory as a storage bank of information that can further help overcome your limitations.

At the School for the Blind, our teachers patiently trained us to interpret sounds: to judge distances and locations by sound, to identify people by the sound of their voices, to become sensitive to other people's moods by recognizing changes in their tone of voice. We learned to recognize a wide variety of objects—from cups and saucers, knives, forks, and spoons, to articles of clothing—by feeling them and memorizing their shapes, sizes, textures. We played with blocks, we strung beads, we did everything imaginable to improve our dexterity and the sensitivity of our fingers, until they became reliable antennae helping us navigate through the world. Finally, we were introduced to the mysteries of braille, learning to read by skimming the index fingers of both hands across the raised dots of the alphabet for the blind developed by professor Louis Braille in the nineteenth century.

We were also taught at an early age to organize our lives systematically down to the smallest details. Each item of clothing, each personal

10

possession, had to be kept in a specific place so that we could locate it without help. We were taught to dress ourselves, to feed ourselves, to find our way between classroom and dormitory, until we gained a measure of independence.

It was a painfully slow process. Just learning to dress ourselves was an adventure. Mastering the intricacies of buttons and buttonholes, right and left shoes and gloves, shoelaces, snaps, belts, garters, flaps, zippers, shirt-tails, and neckties can be a long and bitter experience, fraught with all manner of embarrassing frustrations.

I remember I was especially baffled by the construction of my winter underwear with its itchy wool legs and sleeves and button-up flap at the rear. On more than one occasion, in attempting to dress myself, I got tangled up in those abominable long-johns, unable to separate arms from legs, front from back. Inevitably Miss Betsy Boullion, our stern housemother, would arrive on the scene, strip me like a plucked chicken, and stuff my squirming arms and legs into the right holes—a rough procedure accompanied by a lecture on dressing and my outraged howls of indignation.

By the time I was in second grade I no longer required Miss Boullion's heavy-handed help. I was learning to depend on my memory, my fingers, and on all my senses—including the faint vision in my left eye—to make my frequently fumbling way through life at school. But when it came to reading braille I was the slowest kid in the class. In later years I would listen to phonograph records hour after hour, memorizing entire musical scores, but I never seemed to have the patience to master the complex braille alphabet. Eventually I was able to read with enough proficiency to complete my classwork, but once I left school I rarely used this skill, and whatever ability I had acquired soon vanished.

I was never an eager scholar, nor did I show any aptitude for caning chairs, making brooms, repairing shoes, or the other crafts which, in those days, were deemed suitable "careers" for the blind. As I grew into my teens, that kind of practical training repelled me. To me it seemed that emphasizing these simple crafts meant such work was the best we could hope for. Today I realize my attitude was extremely narrow; those skills enabled many sightless persons to attain at least a semblance of independence as adults. But I still deplore an educational philosophy that seeks to shape everyone in the same limited mold, with no thought of his natural talents or abilities, no recognition of individual ambitions.

It wasn't that the school ignored talent or ability. Participation in sports and the arts, particularly music, was encouraged—but only for our own gratification and self-improvement, not as a stepping-stone to a career.

11

Most of our teachers and school administrators were sightless or partially so; they knew through the pain of their own experience the prejudices, disappointments, and frustrations that lay ahead for us. Blind School superintendent Bill Allen especially knew.

Bill Allen was blind, and he was also a gifted singer, a baritone of exceptional talent. During one bleak year in Chicago as a young man he nearly starved as he tried vainly to get a break as a concert singer. At last, in despair, he surrendered to his blindness and returned to a teaching position at the Texas School for the Blind. He rose from that job to head the institution. But despite his achievements as an educator he remained a bitter, frustrated performer at heart—a man completely convinced that the blind should be discouraged in all the ambitions he thought were doomed to failure in the sighted world.

Bill Allen had valid reasons beyond his own experience for his pessimistic view of show-business careers for the blind. The history of the sightless—then and now—is filled with stories of talented people whose potential careers were sidetracked by their blindness. In music even the most gifted blind artists have often ended up performing in honky-tonks or as organists, pianists, or vocalists in churches and funeral homes. Superintendent Allen and his teachers were convinced they were serving the best interests of their students when they sought to guide us toward safe employment.

If the faculty members went to extremes in trying to protect us from the sighted world's emotional bumps and bruises, they never coddled us. Lack of confidence is a chronic problem among the blind, and the school attacked the problem with both physical and cultural activities.

Roller-skating was especially popular, even among totally blind young-sters. We would line up single file, four and five deep, at one end of a long stretch of sidewalk extending down a slight grade from the broom shop to the dormitory cottages. Then, with one of us who had at least a trace of vision leading the way, the skaters would whiz along, holding on to each other's shoulders like a conga line on wheels.

Once another boy with partial vision challenged me to a roller-skating race. We scooted along lickety-split in a dead heat. Then my challenger spotted danger ahead of us and swerved off the course to safety. But I was too intent on winning to notice any shadowy perils in my path. I plunged on and won the race with a resounding thud as I crashed headlong into the tree that shaded Dormitory D.

That "win" cost me a concussion and sent me to the hospital for a week. My first day back at school I was standing on the sidewalk when a totally sightless boy ran into me and sent me back to the hospital for another stay.

Later on our gym teacher, James Durr, talked me into trying roller-skating again. I promptly lost my balance and fell, but he helped me to my feet, led me back to the beginning of our racecourse, and ordered me to skate down the long stretch of sidewalk. "This time, remember to turn off before you hit the tree," he cautioned. After all that had happened to me you can be sure I made it a point always to keep my one-percent eye focused on the path ahead.

Durr was a sightless physical fitness nut who maintained a Spartan regimen for the boys in his classes. During the winter months we had strenuous daily workouts in the school gymnasium. They began with a few brisk laps at a trotting pace around the gym floor and progressed to calisthenics, wrestling, tumbling, and other forms of exercise adaptable to the restrictions of blindness.

The real workouts, however, began in the spring, when Durr joyously moved us out to the athletic field. There we endlessly practiced such events as the standing broad jump; the hop, skip, and jump; the shot put; tug-of-war; rope climbing; and foot races ranging from 100 to 500 yards. For the races Durr rigged up a Rube Goldbergish contraption designed to keep his sightless runners on course. This device consisted of heavy wire stretched about waist-high along the left-hand edge of each running lane. Each of these taut wires was equipped with a short sliding cable fitted with a wooden handle. The contestants grasped the handles as they ran and were guided by them along the track.

"Competition is the biggest thing in life," Durr would stress in his daily lectures. "It's a tough world—tougher on you than most folks—and you've got to learn to compete, to jump into life's race and give it everything you've got." He backed up his pep talks with competition, not only among ourselves but against other schools for the handicapped.

I remember a tug-of-war we had with the School for the Deaf. Our team tugged and jerked and strained every muscle, but we couldn't budge the Deaf School tuggers a single inch. Finally, some sighted spectator took pity on us and tipped off Durr that the Deaf School coach had tied his team's end of the rope to a tree.

Another time, during my high-school years, our school competed against a number of other schools for the blind in a national athletic contest. That was my moment of glory as an athlete: I won the 100-yard dash and the basketball-throwing competition and returned to our Austin campus as a "national champion."

As much as I enjoyed sports, my big passion during my school years

13

was music. I guess my musical ambitions were born on a November morning in 1918 when Miss Emma, our second-grade teacher, rapped on her desk with a ruler to signal the beginning of lessons and announced: "Boys and girls, I have wonderful news for you. There will be no school today because at eleven o'clock this morning the armistice will be signed and the war will be over."

A World War had been raging for just about as long as we could remember. Some of the pupils had fathers, brothers, uncles, or cousins fighting in it. During the school's Sunday services we had always prayed for the safety of America's fighting men and an end to the conflict. We weren't sure just what an armistice was, but we knew it must be pretty important to bring about a school holiday.

We were at a high emotional pitch as Miss Emma led us out to the school yard to join pupils from other classes massed around the flagpole. There we stood at attention while the student color guard opened the ceremony with the raising of the Stars and Stripes. This was followed by a few patriotic remarks by school officials and the playing of the national anthem by our high-school band. Closing the program, the band's trumpeter blew a mournful tribute to the soldiers who had died on foreign battlefields. The plaintive notes of "Taps" seemed to engulf me with tides of emotion beyond my understanding.

Suddenly I felt Miss Emma's arms around me and heard her anxious voice. "Why, Fred, what's the matter? Why are you crying?"

It was then I realized that tears were streaming down my cheeks. "I . . . I didn't know I was crying," I confessed. "I wish . . ."

I stopped, feeling foolish about my outburst. Besides, I figured that no one was really interested in my wishes. But I was wrong.

"What is it you wish, Fred?" Miss Emma asked.

"Well, I wish I could play music like that."

Customarily pupils didn't begin music lessons until the third grade. I was only in the second grade, but I was nine years old, and Miss Emma convinced Henry Leiberman, the blind leader of our school orchestra, that I should be allowed to study music. Within a few days I began my formal training in the school's excellent music department.

During the next ten years I studied violin, piano, saxophone, and voice, and showed talent in all except the piano. My teachers praised my progress, saying I had perfect pitch and a natural ear for music. But they discouraged my early ambition to become a concert violinist.

"Forget it, Fred," our violin teacher Katherine Wright told me bluntly when I was in the seventh grade. She admitted I had talent and feeling, a good ear, and an amazing memory. But I lacked one essential tool—eyesight. Without it I could never play in a symphony or concert orchestra because I couldn't read the music.

After that I directed my ambitions toward the saxophone. I became a tenor saxophonist in the orchestra during my freshman year in high school, but again I was cautioned not to think of a career as a professional musician because my blindness was too great a handicap to overcome.

During a long, fatherly talk one day, Mr. Leiberman told me of the almost insurmountable odds a blind musician faced. "Talent isn't enough," he said. "Here at the Blind School we can make music together because we use a system designed for the sightless. We can't see the musical score. We can't read braille music with our fingers and play an instrument at the same time. And we can't see the orchestra leader. Instead, we follow directions by sound—by the sound of the leader's voice, by the tempo of his rapping with the baton, and by memorizing the music."

"Why can't we do the same with other orchestras?" I asked.

"Because sighted musicians are trained in a different system," our bandleader explained patiently. "They play by sight, by reading the scores, by watching the conductor. And their system and our system won't mix."

Although he discouraged my ambitions, it was Mr. Leiberman who unknowingly started me on the way to becoming a professional whistler. Around school I was known as a "whistling pest" who drove some people to distraction. It was not something I had learned in Austin, though. It was my Uncle Ed who had got me started. Every day about sundown he would trudge in from the fields. We would know he was coming long before he arrived because we could hear him whistling. It always seemed to be a happy tune, ringing clear and sharp across the countryside. I recall asking him one day why he always whistled when he came home, and he said, "Guess it's 'cause it feels so good to reach the end of another day's work."

One evening I finally got up the courage to ask Uncle Ed to teach me how to whistle. "Any ol' fool can do it," he said. "Just pucker up your lips and blow." Later, in the cottonfields, I practiced imitating the whistling of the wind and the calls of the birds. I tried whistling my own made-up tunes and the hymns we sang at Sunday services. As my whistle got louder, if not better, I began practicing in the house, but Grandma White put a quick end to that.

"For a little critter, Fred's got the loudest, most outlandish whistle I ever did hear," Grandma complained to Uncle Ed. "It hurts my ears."

By the time I started Blind School I had even discovered that by holding my tongue a certain way I could whistle two notes at the same time. Even my uncle was amazed by this odd talent. "Never heard nobody whistle like that before," he told Grandma. "It ain't very pretty, but it sure sounds like two people whistlin' at the same time."

At the School for the Blind I continued to whistle. Often I wouldn't even realize I was doing it until other students or teachers complained about the noise I was making. One day Mr. Leiberman asked me to stay after the orchestra finished its daily rehearsal. "I've been noticing your whistling," he said.

"Gosh, I hope I haven't been bothering you," I apologized. "Lots of times I whistle without knowing it."

"Not at all, Fred," my teacher assured me. "In fact, it's a most unusual whistle. Really quite musical, quite different."

"I never thought much about it," I said. "It's just something I've been doing since I was a little kid."

"Well," Mr. Leiberman said, "I think we can use your whistle in the orchestra."

I was astounded. "I've never heard of a whistler in an orchestra."

Mr. Leiberman chuckled. "Neither have I, Fred. But you're not going to be a whistler. You're going to be a piccolo!"

"A piccolo?"

"That's right. We need a piccolo player in the band and we don't have one. Matter of fact, we don't even have a piccolo. But I've been thinking that with a little practice you could learn to whistle like a piccolo and solve our problem."

That was when I turned in my saxophone and converted my whistle into a piccolo—a role in which I had many opportunities to display my virtuosity, particularly during the John Philip Sousa marches with which Mr. Leiberman heavily larded our repertoire. And that was when Peggy Richter, the school's European-trained piano teacher, first took notice of me as something beyond the worst piano pupil she'd "ever had the misfortune to teach."

Why Margaret Richter had persisted in trying to teach me piano I'll never know. Maybe she couldn't resist the challenge of a musically gifted boy who for some perverse reason couldn't even learn to play "Chopsticks." For whatever reason, she stuck by me, and—as things turned out—my entire life was enriched by her faith in my talent.

Peggy Richter was one of the few fully sighted teachers at the School for the Blind. But she had another handicap—a sorely crippled sister and aging, ailing parents. Her love for them was so strong, and her concern so deep, that she had given up a promising concert career and remained in

16

Austin to care for them. She helped support her family with her salary as a teacher—a meager income bolstered by occasional appearances as a soloist at local concerts, musicales, and church services.

Of all the music teachers at the school, Peggy, then a woman in her forties, was my severest critic. She was particularly impatient with my tendency to use my facile memory for music as a means of avoiding long hours of tedious practice and the study of braille music scores. But she was also the only teacher who didn't attempt to discourage my hopes for a career in music, and the only person who perceived a greater offbeat talent behind my freakish piccolo whistling.

"I'm stopping your piano lessons," she announced one day when I showed up in her studio.

"Why?" I demanded indignantly. I was determined somehow to master those eighty-eight diabolical keys.

"Because you'll never be a pianist if you live to be as old as Methuselah," Peggy said. "But I've been listening to you whistle in the band, and I think you're gifted with a truly rare talent. Starting today, I want to help you develop your whistling. I'm convinced you have the talent to become a concert whistler."

"A whistler! Who ever heard of a concert whistler?"

"I have," Peggy Richter replied. And she introduced me to the little-known history of whistling and the few artists who had made successful careers as whistlers. She told me of Alice Shaw, *la Belle Siffleuse*, who gained international acclaim as a whistler of classical music on the world's concert stages during the late 1800s. Later, she said, Agnes Woodward emerged as a concert whistler and, after the war, founded the School of Artistic Whistling in Los Angeles.

"And, of course, there's Bob MacGimsey, who whistled the scores of 'My Blue Heaven' and 'Girl of My Dreams,' " Peggy added, mentioning two of the nation's current hit songs.

"Sure, I've heard the records—they're great," I said. "I know Gene Austin's the vocalist, but I just figured the whistling was a background for his singing."

"Nonsense!" Peggy flared. "MacGimsey's whistling sets the special mood for those records. There are lots of good singers, but whistling—real whistling—is a rare talent."

"Maybe so. I just never thought much about whistling as music. It's just something that a lot of folks do when they're feeling good, something I seem to have a knack for."

17

"Well," Peggy replied firmly, "we're going to find out just how big a knack for whistling you've got." Having issued that manifesto, she tugged me to a seat beside her on the piano bench, rattled off Mendelssohn's "Spring Song," then had me whistle along with her until she was satisfied I could learn to work with piano accompaniment.

"That's the way we'll do it," Peggy said when the impromptu practice session ended. "I'll train you as I would a voice student, only you'll be whistling instead of singing."

That's how Peggy Richter launched my career as a whistler. Hour after hour she played the piano while I struggled through the scales and all the other musical exercises usually practiced by singers. She taught me timing and proper breathing techniques. And gradually she managed to break my habit of inserting chirping, trilling bird sounds, insisting that I stay on the melody line without fancy frills. I perfected my strange double-note whistle and learned to produce warmer, richer tones by whistling from my chest and throat rather than blowing through puckered lips as most whistlers do.

Peggy's work in directing my musical talent toward a career as a concert whistler didn't end in the classroom. She persuaded the Austin Lions Club to "adopt" me as a special talent project. A few days later, a windup victrola and a large collection of classical records were delivered to me at the school, a gift from the Lions. For the next two years, in addition to my regular classes, I spent at least two hours a day in my room listening to phonograph records, whistling along with the music until every note, every pause, every change of tempo was indelibly engraved in my memory. During those long months of concentrated study I memorized more than one hundred classical pieces, including such complex scores as the *William Tell* Overture, a number which in later years proved to be the most popular, most lavish offering in my repertoire.

Looking back across a half-century at that intense, skinny youth huddled close to a boxlike phonograph in a small dormitory room, I remember the frustrations of trying to follow the beat and keep in tune with the scratchy tones of those worn-out records. I recall my impatience when the tired old phonograph would run down at a critical point in a recording, forcing me to pause in my practice to wind it up again. But most of all I remember the magnificence of the music I was listening to—music that still echoes in my mind, untouched by the erosions of time.

But it wasn't the long hours of practice or the progress I made in my evolution from nuisance to whistler that finally convinced perfectionist Peggy Richter that I was ready to launch my professional career. It was a

18

bird whistler named Ernest Nichols. Nichols came to the Blind School to present a program at our student assembly. As a final, unexpected feature of the show, he announced:

"I've been whistling for all of you youngsters for nearly an hour. Now I want one of you to volunteer to come up on stage and whistle for me. Who's going to be my whistler?"

Nobody in the audience budged. Not even me—and I'd been sitting there throughout the program wishing I could have a chance to get on stage and prove to everybody I could whistle a lot better than that old bird-chirper. But my brave thoughts fled in fright when the opportunity actually arose.

"Do you mean to tell me there isn't a whistler in the audience—some young man or woman who can at least whistle like a sparrow, a robin, a bobolink?" Nichols roared when his first entreaty went unanswered. "Don't be bashful . . . I'm sure there's somebody out there who can whistle us a tune."

Somebody behind me hollered, "Yeah, we've got Fred Lowery. He's the best ol' whistler in Texas!" Others took up the cry—"We want Fred! We want Fred!" I tried to ignore the shouts. I slumped down in my seat, hoping to hide. For years I'd been pestering everybody in the school with my whistling. But the thought of getting up on stage and performing in front of the entire student body terrified me. I'd never been on stage except as a member of the school band. Until that moment I'd never given any thought to what it would be like to face an audience alone. Finally the boy next to me tugged me out of my seat and pushed me into the aisle, into the arms of Peggy Richter, who had been hurrying to my side.

"Come on, Fred. Show that guy how you can whistle," Peggy whispered as she marched me toward the stage.

"I can't . . . I can't . . . I'm frightened!"

"Of course you are," Peggy agreed. "Every performer is scared out of his wits before the show starts. But it goes away. Just get up there and whistle." As she led me up to Nichols, she whispered a final warning: "Don't you dare do any bird-chirping!"

I didn't. I groped around desperately and finally grabbed Mr. Nichols's arm like a drowning man clutching a life buoy. Out in front of me loomed a noisy, shadowy mass: my fellow students. After a whispered conference with Peggy, Nichols announced, "I'm delighted to introduce a splendid young chap you all know. Fred Lowery has kindly volunteered to whistle for us."

19

The kids in the audience laughed and hooted and whistled derisively, no doubt because of the struggle to get me on stage. When the razzing subsided, Nichols put an arm around my quaking shoulders and asked, "Whatcha going to whistle for us, Fred?"

Faced with such a monumental decision, I gulped nervously and blurted out the first number that flashed into my panic-stricken mind. "MacDowell's 'To a Wild Rose,' " I announced with as much bravado as I could muster.

"That's a mighty ambitious song, Fred," Nichols noted condescendingly. "Can't say I've ever heard it whistled, but good luck anyhow!"

Fortunately I had picked a classic I'd been practicing for more than a week, so it was fresh in my mind. Faintly at first, and then building steadily in volume as my stage fright vanished, I whistled the entire score without a miscue. Gripped by the splendor of the music, I forgot the audience. I forgot the bird-chirper. Without pausing, I swung into Debussy's *Clair de lune,* and from that into *William Tell.*

When the last notes of the overture faded, I suddenly realized that the applauding gray mass in front of me was the audience—my first real audience. I had successfully weathered my baptism as a performer. As for Nichols, he was lavish in his praise, and maybe a bit awed by the blind youngster who had upstaged his birdcalls with an unexpected display of the classics. He walked off the stage with Peggy and me and paused in the wings.

"This young man has a fantastic talent," Nichols told Peggy. "I've never heard whistling like that. Someday he's going to be the world's greatest whistler."

"Do you really think so?" Peggy asked. "I've been telling myself that, but I couldn't trust my judgment alone."

"Believe me, madam," Nichols assured her, "this young chap is talented. With more training and some stage experience he'll go far."

That was all the encouragement Peggy needed. She stepped up the pace of my training, expanded my classical repertoire, and even had me venture into some of the better popular music of the time to demonstrate my versatility.

At that point, Peggy talked the Wednesday Morning Music Club of Austin into sponsoring my first concert—a program that gained me considerable local publicity, but no money and no offers of follow-up performances. There just wasn't much of a demand in Texas for whistling concert artists. Peggy then decided I needed training and exposure in a more cosmopolitan atmosphere. Once again she went to the Lions Club, seeking funds to take

20

me to Chicago for professional training. And again the Lions responded, conducting a fund drive that raised $500 to finance a four-month stay in Chicago for Peggy and me.

In the face of the newspaper publicity generated by the Lions Club's "Send Freddie to Chicago" solicitation, officials at the Blind School reluctantly agreed to the trip. But, as Peggy later told me, Bill Allen cautioned her never again to interfere in the school's handling of students. He warned her to stop encouraging my musical ambitions because as a sighted person she could not understand that she was leading a blind youth down a dangerous path that could only end in bitter disappointment.

"Fred Lowery is your responsibility during this foolhardy trip," Allen told her, probably recalling his own experiences in Chicago years before. "But when he returns to school, we'll take over. And no more interference from you."

Although angered, Peggy held her temper in check, fearing that any back talk would put an end to our plans. However, when we finally stepped off the train at Chicago's LaSalle Street Station in May 1929, she exclaimed: "We've made it, Fred! Let's show that old grouch just how talented you are!"

For Peggy and me it was not a partying, sight-seeing, good-time vacation. Our limited resources eliminated such frills as shows and fancy restaurants. Instead it was a time of intense practice and study. It was also the most exciting summer of my young life—the first summer I hadn't returned to the Piney Woods to help with the farm chores.

Peggy's first step in Chicago was to get us settled at a total cost of ten dollars a week in two furnished rooms in a comfortable old house on North Kedvale Avenue. The motherly landlady also provided our breakfasts as part of her rental service. From this genteel boardinghouse I ventured—with Peggy as my guide, protector, and promoter—into a fascinating new world that I had never before imagined.

I took lessons in acting at the American Institute to develop stage presence—a sense of showmanship and timing, an ability to "sell" an audience. I took music lessons to keep up with the latest popular music and to refine my own arrangements of classical numbers. I gave private performances for several concert artists so that they could offer career advice. I gave performances at musicales and enjoyed the heady experience of being interviewed by the big-city press. But the big event of that long, hot Chicago summer came in late August when Peggy arranged a fifty-dollar radio guest spot for me on the "Farm and Home Hour," a show originating

21

from Chicago's Station WMAQ on NBC's Red Network, which had been established just two years earlier under the guiding genius of David Sarnoff, the onetime office boy at the Marconi Wireless Company.

It was my baptism as a radio performer. It also marked my first exposure to big-time celebrities: Among the guests on that day's "Farm Show" were Freeman Fisher Gosden and Charles J. Correll, a pair of former vaude-villians who were on their way to becoming the first superstars of the infant radio industry. The originators of the "Fresh-Air Taxicab Company of America, Incorpulated" staged a short skit promoting their blackface comedy show "Amos 'n' Andy," which had been gaining a mushrooming national audience since its first broadcast the previous year. My contributions to that day's show were two old-time favorites, "The World Is Waiting for the Sunrise" and the *William Tell* Overture, whistled to the accompaniment of a large studio orchestra.

Before going on the air I was certain that for once I would be free of my customary preperformance jitters. After all, in those early days of radio there was no audience—just a microphone, the performers, and sundry sound-effects apparatus crowded into a small studio. However, after listening to the slick, hilarious performance of Amos 'n' Andy, I felt like a rank amateur. As Helen Stevens Fisher, the Little Lady of the House, led me to the mike for my first number, I was suddenly overwhelmed with the realization that although there was no audience in the studio there were literally thousands of people at the other end waiting to hear me perform. For a terrifying moment I was positive I could never manage to get out the first note. But when the orchestra began to play I swung automatically into the melody, oblivious to everything but the sound of the music.

When the show ended, everyone—even Amos 'n' Andy— congratulated me on my performance. I thought maybe they were just being polite, but nearly a thousand letters of praise came in from the listening audience. Three Chicago newspapers—the *Tribune,* the *Chicago American,* and the *Daily News*—published reviews complimenting my performance. Fritzi Blocki, music critic for the *American,* went so far as to predict "a great professional future for this young and talented blind whistler who handles the complexities of the classics with such exceptional virtuosity. . . ."

It was a perfect ending for a perfect summer—and a big buildup for a big letdown.

Chapter 3

Inspired by the praises of Chicago's music critics, Peggy Richter and I returned to Texas in the early autumn of 1929 convinced that I was ready to launch my career as a concert whistler. But, like the stock market during that fateful October, our hopes soon collapsed.

The letdown came the day after our return. During our long stay in Chicago Peggy had sent Bill Allen several detailed reports on my progress, feeling the good news would soften his resistance to my musical ambitions. However, Bill quickly made it clear that he hadn't been impressed by my fledgling achievements in the outside world.

"I didn't approve of this career nonsense when you talked the Lions Club into sponsoring Fred's trip to Chicago, and I haven't changed my mind one bit," he stated flatly after Peggy and I ventured into his office seeking approval for a performance at a local musicale.

Peggy tried to reason with him, but Allen refused to budge. "Peggy," he said, "the trouble is that you're not qualified to make decisions for Fred. You aren't blind. You can't possibly understand . . ."

"Understand what?" Peggy's voice reflected her dismay. "Blindness has nothing to do with talent. Fred has talent. That's all I need to understand!"

Bill Allen interrupted Peggy's plea. "Don't get me wrong! There's no question about Fred's talent. But he's also blind. Can't you understand that he could be the world's greatest musical talent and still end up a failure? Can't you understand that outside the walls of this school nobody wants a blind musician? That's why I'm going to do everything in my power to make sure Fred doesn't get hurt."

He even warned Peggy that if she persisted in encouraging me she would lose her teaching job—a sobering thought for a woman struggling to support a household. And he told me if I had any ideas about leaving before graduation I'd better realize that the school wouldn't take me back if I failed to make my way in the outside world.

"I don't want to hear another word about a concert career," he told me.

"You may be almost twenty, but as long as you're in this school you'll do as I say!"

Superintendent Allen wasted no time backing up his words with action. My lessons with Peggy, and even my participation in band activities, were discontinued. At the same time, my off-campus trips with a sighted escort—a privilege accorded all students over sixteen—were canceled.

It was this heavy-handed discipline, this unrelenting effort to force me into the mold of the safe life-style favored by the school's administrators, that led to my rebellion against Bill Allen. After several brooding weeks of exile on campus, I finally mustered the courage to confront Allen again. I stormed into his office one November day and demanded a chance to try a concert career with no further interference.

"It's my life. I've got a right to live it like I want to!" I exclaimed.

"You're a young fool, Lowery," he shouted. "Believing all of Peggy Richter's fancy talk about a concert career is just plain ridiculous!"

"What's so ridiculous about it?"

"Good grief! Can't you get it through that thick Irish skull that there's no professional future for a blind musician? And the idea of a blind concert whistler is even more preposterous!" There was a brief pause, and then his frustration erupted once more. His words echoed like a thunderclap of doom.

"You've got to forget about a concert career, Fred—forget about show business. I couldn't make it. Lots of other talented folks couldn't make it. And neither can you. You've got to face up to the fact that you're blind. If you don't, you're going to break your heart trying for an impossible dream!"

Bill Allen's prophecy of failure lingered in my memory long after that stormy scene. Throughout my years in show business his bitter words returned to spur me on when the going was tough and failure seemed inevitable. In a very real sense, every success I ever achieved was a denial of Allen's dreadful prediction.

While I dimly realized that Allen was trying to protect me, that fact failed to cool the fire of resentment consuming me as I returned to the dormitory that day. Slamming the door, I fumbled frantically around my small room, stuffing belongings into the same battered suitcase I had brought to Austin twelve years before. I was determined not to spend another day in the school. But my frenzied rush to pack slowed to a snail's pace as I realized that I couldn't walk out alone into a strange world from which I had always been sheltered. There were no locks on the doors, no bars on the windows, no guards to turn me back. Nevertheless, I was a prisoner. I had no choice but to stay. I collapsed on my bed and wept for the first time in years. But I resolved that somehow I would find a way to shut the Blind School—and Bill Allen—out of my life forever.

Actually, my estrangement from the blind educator wasn't quite that permanent. But after I finally left the school it was more than a quarter-century before I met Allen again, at the Indiana Theater in Indianapolis while I was touring with the Stan Kenton band. Allen was brought backstage by friends he had been visiting, and we had a tearful reconciliation that reflected the emotional scars left by our bitter quarrel at the Blind School, scars we had both carried for so many years.

Reunion, however, was the furthest thing from my mind during those fading autumn days of 1929 as I struggled to devise a practical means of fleeing from the school. It seemed hopeless. There didn't seem to be anyone I could appeal to for help. The teachers and my fellow students had been advised that I was "off limits," that anyone who became involved in my problems would face severe disciplinary action. And I had no friends or family in Austin to come to my rescue.

Then, on the day before Thanksgiving, as the school emptied for the holiday, my chance to escape materialized with the unexpected arrival of my older sister Anna Mae. She was working as a stenographer in Dallas at the time and had impulsively decided to come to Austin to celebrate Thanksgiving with me. I immediately set out to enlist her aid in my escape. I suppose I hoped she might take me back to Dallas with her.

My sister sympathized with my plight, but being a practical person she also had doubts. Like Bill Allen, she wasn't impressed by my dreams of a concert career. She thought it would be foolish to abandon my education before I was ready to cope with the very real problem of making a living.

"Just what are you going to do if you leave the school?" Anna Mae asked. "How are you going to take care of yourself without a job? Where are you going to stay? How are you going to put food on the table and clothes on your back?"

"Well, maybe you could help," I ventured.

"Fred, you know I have to be back on the job in Dallas Monday morning. And I can't take you with me. I'm not making enough to support both of us."

"Okay. I know," I answered. "But my mind is made up. Just help me get away from this school. I'll get by somehow once I'm away from here. I know I've got the talent to do something with my life besides make brooms."

But Anna Mae was unswayed. "That's just wishful thinking, Fred. You have to have some place to go. Do you want to go back and stay with Grandma and Uncle Ed?"

25

"Don't be silly! They have a tough time getting along as it is. Anyway, that's my worry! Just get me out of here. I can't do that by myself!"

After Anna Mae said she couldn't take me back to Dallas with her, I really didn't know what I'd do, but finally I persuaded her to take me to Peggy Richter's home to talk about my leaving school. Peggy, like most of the staff, had already left for the holiday.

"Maybe Peggy can convince you to stick it out until you graduate," Anna Mae observed hopefully as we left the school.

Peggy, however, could see that I was beyond reasoning with, and, besides, she was in sympathy with my plight. She and her parents insisted that they had plenty of room for me in their large home. So, on Thanksgiving Day 1929, Anna Mae and Peggy Richter helped me move out of the School for the Blind. By the time my sister boarded a bus for Dallas, I was settled in the Richter home, ready to tackle the world I'd never known.

Looking back, I can readily understand my sister's doubts. There was little logic or reasoning behind my actions. But I was desperate to change my life because it had become unbearable. Unfortunately my sense of timing was on a par with my common sense, for I barged out of my haven at the Blind School into the beginning of the worst depression in the nation's history.

My memories of the early months of the depression are blurred. Listening to the radio, which had become my main source of news and entertainment, I heard all manner of reports—some wildly optimistic, others filled with gloom. But the stock market had little meaning for me. I certainly couldn't imagine that something so far removed from my world could have a significant impact on my life.

While the harsher realities had not yet caught up with us in Austin, it was a grim period in the Richter household, emotionally and economically. School officials soon learned I had been befriended by the Richters and, no doubt believing my teacher had persuaded me to drop out, notified Peggy that when the school year ended her contract would not be renewed. Faced with this disaster and the unhappy prospect of starting a new career in middle age, Peggy began the discouraging task of trying to expand her part-time piano teaching into a full-time business. As the months passed and it became evident that this was going to be a painfully slow process, I found a series of odd jobs to help support the family that had adopted me.

The most interesting of these was my interlude as the "whistling page boy"—a job that Peggy managed to arrange for me through a longtime political friend. Unfortunately it was rewarded more by publicity than financial gain. In fact, I managed to get more publicity than a colorful young

26

teacher named Lyndon Baines Johnson from Houston's Sam Houston High School. He was just then emerging from obscurity as the successful manager of Willy Hopkins's campaign for the state senate in South Texas. When that session of the legislature adjourned, I strayed from political pastures, but he went on to Washington as secretary to Richard Kleberg, congressman from Texas's fourteenth district and heir to the legendary King Ranch, and ended up . . . But you know that story.

Despite the worries and frustrations of everyday living, Peggy Richter held on firmly to her dream that eventually we would share a classical concert career combining her piano and my whistling. With that goal in mind, I continued my daily practice sessions, either with the help of phonograph records or with Peggy's accompaniment on the grand piano in the parlor of the Richter home.

But the months went by, and our dream of a concert career remained unfulfilled. Peggy did manage to keep a faint spark of hope alive by arranging occasional appearances for us in the Austin area. But in those days Texas was in no way a cultural mecca, and the opportunities for aspiring concert performers were limited even further by the onset of hard times. That old Mother Goose rhyme about "singing for your supper" proved to be distressingly true for us. Our only payment for many performances at civic, charitable, church, or club affairs—other than free publicity—was dinner prior to the program.

Ultimately we had to face the fact that a career as concert artists in Texas simply was not feasible. Our only hope lay in one of the nation's cultural capitals, preferably New York, where classical music was appreciated. But Peggy's responsibility for her ailing parents and sister bound her to her Austin household. And I was certainly not prepared to venture alone into a strange, faraway city.

So we kept scraping by in a sort of dreary limbo, while my scrapbook continued to collect glowing newspaper tributes to our performances on local programs, and the Richter household fund kept dwindling with each passing month.

For me the depression was filled with echoes and ghosts of the past—of the poverty of the Piney Woods and the dire warnings of Bill Allen. I felt betrayed by fate. But I was still young and I still had the eternal hope of youth. For families like the Richters the depression was a bitter, shattering experience. Like so many others, they had been confident that thrift, hard work, honesty, and self-reliance would always be rewarded. Then their life-style collapsed. And slowly their mood of hopeful optimism, generated by President Hoover's assurances that "prosperity is just around the corner,"

27

was replaced by quiet desperation. By the time my career as a page boy ended, even my dreams had been sabotaged by circumstances; with the loss of my job, another financial crisis loomed over our household—a crisis heightened by the death of Peggy's father, which put an end to the pension he had received as a retired college professor. Suddenly making a living— any kind of living—became my most urgent goal.

Haunted by the feeling that I was failing the family that had befriended me, I abandoned my daily practice and made my way slowly around the now-familiar streets of Austin day after day in search of a job. But at a time when college graduates and skilled craftsmen were swelling the ranks of the unemployed there were few legitimate jobs, even for men with sight.

Finally, in dismay, I sought the advice of J. J. Brown, state director of rehabilitation for the blind. He listened and then repeated the advice I had received from Bill Allen: Forget your big ideas about a music career and get into some kind of work a blind person can handle.

"Like what?" I asked, angry at hearing the same old refrain. "Like making brooms?"

"Like this," Brown replied, tossing a metal object to me across his desk.

I fingered the strangely contoured device and held it close to my one-percent eye in a futile attempt to identify it. "What in tarnation is this contraption?" I finally asked.

Brown chuckled, obviously pleased at baffling me. "It's a brand-new can opener. And before you get your dander up, let me tell you it's the greatest can opener ever invented. You mount it on the wall, and it opens all kinds of cans slick as a whistle. No housewife should be without one."

"What do they sell for?"

"Only a dollar-fifty . . . and they're guaranteed!"

"How do you expect me to sell an expensive can opener like this to a housewife who probably can't afford to buy a can of food to open? Anyway, I've never tried to sell anything in my life!"

Brown responded with the grim logic that the blind often employ in assessing their problems. "Just concentrate on the neighborhoods that seem halfway prosperous. And when the ladies find such a handsome—but tragically blind—young man at their door, they'll feel sorry for you. All you'll have to do is use your Irish blarney and whistle a pretty tune, and they'll scrape up enough money to buy your can opener."

"I don't want pity," I objected.

"You got any other ideas for making money?" he asked. "Maybe you know somebody who wants to give a blind man a job?"

28

"You know the answer to that!"

"Well, then, take my advice and start knocking on doors. Believe me, you can't miss!"

To my surprise, Brown's formula for successful salesmanship worked. White cane in hand, I whistled and spieled my way from door to door. With Peggy guiding me through the city's neighborhoods, I made as much as ten dollars a day in commissions—a veritable fortune in those times. I was ashamed of using my handicap as a sales tool, but I consoled myself with the rationalization that it was preferable to charity.

After a few months, however, my sales began to dwindle, and I learned the sad facts of life about door-to-door merchandising: No matter how good your product or persuasive your pitch, the day eventually comes when you run out of territory, when you have to move on to a new town in search of customers. For me such a nomadic existence was impossible. I was stuck with my home territory, the only territory I knew.

But fate was working overtime and a whole new career was about to open up for me. What I had been unable to do through the greatest conscious effort now happened with absolutely no effort at all. My new career began with National Business Confidence Week—an event sponsored by Lions clubs throughout the nation in an effort to boost the public's sagging morale.

The Austin Lions Club, the organization that had sponsored my early training as a whistler, joined in this national event, scheduling a local program in which I was asked to participate. I wasted no time in accepting. I was elated to have a chance to whistle for a real audience rather than an endless procession of skeptical housewives.

It was a lively, informal program featuring several optimistic speeches and entertainment presided over by Jimmie Jefferies, the master of ceremonies for a popular Dallas radio show known as the "Early Birds." Jimmie made the trip to Austin both to promote the show and to lend his prestige to the Lions Club endeavor. It was a lucky break for me, although I didn't realize it at the time.

Actually, I wasn't all that pleased with the Lions' plans for me. My favorite classical numbers had been ruled out despite my protests. The Lions felt that the "long-haired stuff" would be too dreary for a program they hoped would help cheer up a sorely depressed public. My contributions to Business Confidence Week were two hastily rehearsed popular songs: the newly published "Life Is Just a Bowl of Cherries" and "Happy Days Are Here Again," a rollicking 1929 number destined to become the theme song of Franklin Delano Roosevelt's 1932 presidential campaign.

About a week later, with the show already forgotten, Peggy and I returned home from an afternoon of unsuccessful can-opener peddling to find a letter for me in the mailbox. "It's from a radio station in Dallas," Peggy observed as she opened the letter and began to read it to me, as she did all my mail. The letter was from Jimmie Jefferies, who complimented me on my performance at the Lions Club show and offered me a tryout for a fulltime ten dollar-per-week job with the "Early Birds" on station WFAA in Dallas.

I was stunned. After all my disappointments, someone was finally giving me a chance to land a permanent job as a performer. "What shall I do?" I asked Peggy.

Peggy handed the letter to me and sighed. "Do it, Fred," she said. "It's a wonderful opportunity."

"But it's only a tryout. Maybe I won't be good enough. Maybe I'll just be wasting time and money making the trip to Dallas."

"Don't be silly," Peggy replied. "You've got to take chances or you won't get anywhere in this world. Besides, I know you'll be good enough. Don't worry about that for a minute."

Perversely, now that opportunity was finally knocking on my door I seemed to find an amazing number of reasons not to hear it. And there was something else, too. "What about you . . . and our plans for a concert career?"

That was a tough question for Peggy to answer, because if I succeeded it would put an end to the dream we had cherished through the years. But she didn't falter. "We both know there's no use fooling ourselves any longer," she said. "In times like these, there's no chance for unknowns on the concert stage. There are already too many talented, experienced musicians standing in breadlines."

"But this is radio work—pop music, not classical."

"So what!" Peggy snapped, obviously hoping to put a quick end to a conversation that was causing her deep anguish. "A person with talent can handle any kind of music. This is your big chance to get away from Austin and make a name for yourself. You've got the chance we've been hoping for. You simply can't ignore it!"

"But what about you folks? How will you make out?"

Peggy Richter's composure finally broke. She began to cry. She grabbed me and shook me like an errant schoolboy. Then, between sobs, she indulged in the only piece of profanity I ever heard her utter. "Dammit," she exclaimed bitterly, "don't you realize there's no future for you here?

You've got to think about your own life and quit worrying about us. We'll get along!"

With this unselfish blessing from Peggy Richter—the gracious, dedicated woman who had worked for so many years to help a brash, blind kid from the Piney Woods—I departed for Dallas, the metropolis of depression-blighted Texas. Maybe I would find the fame and fortune I had dreamed of for so long. But it was a whole new dream, and I had to leave an old one behind.

Chapter 4

As I was getting ready to leave for Dallas, Thurman Dobbins, an old friend from the Blind School, stopped by to see me. Thurman had switched from the tuba and taken up the bass viol when he graduated about a year after I left school. Recently he'd been playing dates around Austin with the Lester Kitchen band.

When he found out I was headed for Dallas and a radio audition, Thurman immediately wanted to go with me. "There are some good bands around Dallas," he said. "Maybe I could make some real money instead of this chicken feed. But bus fare is just about going to wipe me out."

"Me too," I answered. "Maybe we could thumb it."

In those days hitchhiking was a pretty common thing. People were more trusting, and rides were usually easy to come by. Of course, I wouldn't have tried it alone, but I figured the two of us together should be able to get by all right. Thurman was game, so we agreed to meet a couple of days later and thumb our way to Dallas.

The last thing Thurman said to me that morning was, "Radio? You're gonna whistle on the radio?"

In questioning radio, Thurman was actually giving voice to some of my own inner feelings—or maybe I should say my own inner doubts.

Of course, we were well acquainted with this new medium, and fascinated by it. In the mid-1920s the Blind School had invested in a couple of "radio music boxes" to determine if these newfangled gadgets had any value as aids for the sightless. And we youngsters had already become fans through the crude crystal sets that some of us had bought or received as gifts.

My earliest recollections of radio are of the great tides of static that crackled, roared, scratched, and hissed into the earphones of the tiny crystal set I shared with my room-mates Verdie Patterson and Elmer Pryor. As I recall, the reception on the first of the larger "radio boxes" purchased by the school wasn't a great deal better.

Despite the ear-torturing distraction—and despite the questionable quality of the programs of all-live music and news aired by the small local stations of those days—the broadcast of sound through the air from a distant station into one's home had a mystical attraction that overcame the medium's early shortcomings. Nevertheless, would-be performers still considered the stage or concert hall the best place to launch their careers, so when Thurman and I set out for Dallas I remained nervous about a job in radio. But once we settled down to serious hitchhiking I didn't have time to worry about it. Thurman's vision was a little better than mine, but it took all the concentration we could muster to be sure we had our thumbs out at the right time and to try to tell when a car might be going to stop. I've often wondered how many rides we missed because we didn't know that cars had stopped for us further on down the road.

In spite of these problems we had good luck; the fourth person who stopped to pick us up turned out to be a traveling salesman on his way home to Dallas. He told us where we could get cheap room and board and even offered to call the place for us if we wanted.

We thanked him but said we weren't sure where we'd want to stay. I knew I'd want to live near the station if I got the job, and Thurman was only going to stay a few days if he didn't find work. Actually, neither of us felt confident about being in Dallas very long.

In the end, we called a former schoolmate whose family lived in Dallas. They graciously put us up for a few days until we could get settled. Once I made contact with the WFAA people and things looked promising, Thurman decided to go on back to Austin and live with his family. I'm sure he made the right decision, because he ultimately became a very successful businessman.

When I first walked into WFAA's studio on the third floor of the Baker Hotel on an autumn day in 1931, only five years had passed since the historic broadcast of the nation's first network show. That show had originated from the ballroom of the old Waldorf-Astoria in Manhattan and had been picked up by twenty-five stations as far west as Kansas City. From that modest beginning, NBC had grown steadily to include more than 100 stations coast to coast.

One of those stations was WFAA. Like its parent network the Dallas station had prospered, mushrooming from a tiny local operation to one of the largest broadcasters in the Southwest. In those days before soap operas and disc jockeys, the station's most popular program was the "Early Birds." It was a lively early-morning variety show with an audience that extended far beyond the Dallas city limits.

That morning, Jimmie Jefferies introduced me to all the regular cast members, I was immediately impressed by their youth and their poise. There were two girls—the female vocalist Dale Evans, who hadn't even heard of Roy Rogers at that point, and the show's talented accompanist Vin Lindhe, who would soon move from WFAA to New York as arranger for Erno Rapee and his Radio City Music Hall Orchestra.

There were the Bumblebees, a musical comedy group led by Jerry Scoggins, who in later years wrote and sang the theme for TV's "Beverly Hillbillies." The other Bumblebees would also gain national fame, eventually joining the Gene Autry radio show and changing their name to the Cass County Kids.

There was Gus Levine, the show's guitar-strumming, wisecracking comic who became one of Hollywood's finest arrangers, and Norvell Slater, who later had his own Sunday network show, "Hymns We Love." Finally, there was Teddy DeHay, the boy Friday of the "Early Birds," who started out on WFAA's information desk and ultimately climbed to the executive suite.

It was impossible to remain a stranger in the midst of this pack of irreverent performers. They immediately made me feel like one of the family, including me in the unending horseplay that went on during preparations for the morning show.

"How come he's so wide awake at this ungodly hour?" Scoggins growled when Jefferies introduced me as "a whistlin' fool from Austin."

"I think he's kind of cute," Dale Evans giggled.

"Yeah, he looks like a bushy-tailed Texas redbird all right," Levine joked.

Jefferies picked up on Levine's jest when the broadcast began and introduced me to the "Early Birds" audience as The Texas Redbird, a name that became my trademark on the show.

I was nervous as we rehearsed that morning, but Vin Lindhe helped me work out some excellent arrangements. Vin was a superb accompanist and quickly became my favorite person on the show. She always went out of her way to help me with my problems, professional or personal.

As I approached the microphone for the broadcast my nervousness and self-doubts quickly vanished. With Vin at the piano, I whistled three numbers. I opened with "The World Is Waiting for the Sunrise," modulated into the soothing "Wrap Your Troubles in Dreams," and closed with my favorite showpiece, the *William Tell* Overture.

The following day Dallas music critic John Rosenfield wrote: "Fred Lowery from East Texas has made whistling a legitimate musical device. Lowery's whistle isn't like a flute or a piccolo or violin harmonics on the E string. It resembles a whistle and nothing else. But it is an instrument of

34

beauty, dramatic strength and, believe it or not, a surprising variety of tone color. Lowery can whistle two distinct notes at once, in the useful harmony of thirds. He can trill, take scale passages and toss off high staccato like few contemporary coloraturas. . . ."

The audience response was even more surprising. I had no concept of the "pulling power" of radio, no idea of the vast tides of praise or rejection a single broadcast could generate. That first performance produced more than 4,000 fan letters, my quick graduation to "regular" status, and an immediate raise from $10 to $12.50 a week. By the end of my first week on the air, Fred Lowery had been reborn. I was cocky and ambitious again, with vivid dreams of success.

If there was one thing about the Early Birds I didn't like, it was the hour we started broadcasting—seven o'clock every morning but Sunday, come rain or come shine. That meant we had to be in the studio ready to rehearse by five o'clock, which in turn meant climbing out of bed by four.

Actually, the rehearsals were fun, a time for trying out new numbers, dreaming up skits, testing sound effects, joking, gossiping, and consuming tremendous amounts of coffee. There was none of the fussing, feuding, and backstabbing that marred many of the big-time productions I was involved with in later years.

This carefree spirit took the sting out of the early-morning hours. In fact, I even felt a bit superior about the extreme demands my profession was making on me. Anyway, the demands were completely overshadowed by the fan mail, the pats on the back, the autograph seekers, the publicity, and all the other fringe benefits of being a local celebrity. The hours were long, the pay low, but I came to relish every golden minute of my early days as a radio performer.

During this pleasant time at WFAA I began dating—something I had done very little of until then. In fact, I had painfully little experience in dealing with females of my own age. In Blind School, school officials sternly discouraged romantic involvements among the students and kept boys and girls separated as much as possible.

Actually, even if the school had provided us with opportunities to develop our sexuality it would have been of little value. I soon learned that in a sighted society there are few romantic prospects for an obscure blind youth. This unhappy situation was further complicated by the prevailing hard times. I know that the female of the species is supposed to be the more romantic sex, but during those depression years no girl in her right mind would look twice at a boy who was both sightless and jobless.

So it wasn't until I joined the "Early Birds" in Dallas and became a local

35

radio celebrity that I was finally introduced to the delights of dating. Once I gained a measure of success I suddenly discovered that the two major obstacles to romance had been surmounted: First, I was no longer unemployed, and second, I was no longer a blind nobody. I was a blind *somebody,* and that made a big difference.

As any male in the worlds of entertainment or sports can attest to, females can overlook just about any kind of defect when they set their sights on a celebrity. So I soon joined my footloose friends on the "Early Birds" in evenings on the town with the star-struck girls who congregated on the fringes of show business. On a more serious level I also dated Betty Knox, the attractive and musical daughter of the family in whose large home I rented a room after several months of batching in a Dallas hotel.

But all of these romantic adventures ended after Gracie Johnston entered—or reentered—my life. I had met Gracie briefly while I was still a student at the Blind School. When Peggy Richter and I made our summer journey to Chicago, we stopped at Jacksonville, Texas, where Grandma White, Uncle Ed, and my sisters were living at the time. During that visit I accompanied my sisters to a party at the A. H. Johnston home, and there I met—and soon forgot—a small, skinny high-school coed named Gracie.

But Gracie remembered me—perhaps because I gave her a couple of jazz records. Those records had earned her an angry lecture from her father, a strict Southern Baptist, when he discovered her listening to them one day.

Gracie promptly reminded me about the records when we met again in 1932 on a "blind date" arranged by one of my friends at WFAA. After that, we dated often. She had a warm, sincere, and compassionate nature, and I soon realized that she was becoming something very special in my life.

Indeed, Gracie became—and still is—the center of my existence. She belonged to one of Texas's oldest and most honored families. Her ancestors included Gen. Albert Sidney Johnston, secretary of war in the Republic of Texas; a great-grandfather who died at the Alamo; and a maternal relative who built the first school in Jacksonville. Although not wealthy, her family was rich in the heritage and traditions of Texas. In spite of such an impressive pedigree, the Johnston family never put on airs or looked down on my humble beginnings. Most important, Gracie never seemed concerned about my lack of sight. In fact, she seemed to ignore it, except to lash out angrily at anyone who tried to make a big deal out of it. At first I thought Gracie was more considerate than most people because she was studying nursing at Baylor University. But eventually I realized she was just naturally protective.

Being a member of the "Early Birds" cast enhanced my love life, but it also had a number of other benefits. Because of our daily exposure on a popular radio show, we were in constant demand for personal appearances, a sideline that frequently brought in more money than the salaries paid by the station. Many times, after leaving the air at 8:30 in the morning, we would climb aboard a bus and drive several hundred miles for an evening appearance. At the end of the performance we would return wearily to the bus and try to get a few hours' sleep en route back to Dallas and the next morning's show. If we were lucky we would get back in time to nap for an hour or two in the lobby or studio before rehearsal.

At times several days would pass before I could return to my room for a change of clothes. Luckily the radio audience could not see our bleary eyes, unshaved faces, and rumpled clothes.

Not all our personal appearances were so hectic. Once I was booked as a solo act by the Worth Theater in Fort Worth for a single week and stayed for a twelve-week run. The Fort Worth interlude was ideal. It was a quick, easy trip from Dallas and, for depression times, the pay was good; I started out at twenty-five dollars per week in addition to my WFAA pay and ended up making an extra fifty dollars a week.

The Fort Worth booking also gave me my first experience working in a large theater. Frank Weatherford, the theater manager, was a warm, compassionate man with a keen sense of humor, but he was also a show-business professional who could be a tyrant in his pursuit of perfection. To create interest and variety he had me change my program twice a week—a chore that involved considerable rehearsing in addition to preparations for the "Early Birds" broadcasts.

On radio, we didn't have to concern ourselves with visual effects. But for the stage each routine had to be carefully choreographed, costumed, scripted, and orchestrated. And Weatherford was always on hand during rehearsals to make sure the show would go on with his special touch of showmanship. Frank was a stern taskmaster, but he taught me stage discipline.

That training came in handy in the summer of 1933 when an entrepreneur named Henry Murphy—a wheeling-dealing Irishman from San Angelo, Texas—came to lure the Early Birds away from their comfortable nest at WFAA with bright promises of big money.

Murphy showed up one morning in May with an inspired sales pitch. He had been a highly successful oil and land speculator before the crash. Like many during those lean years, he had struggled hard to survive, a struggle that had ultimately led him into show business as a carnival pitchman. It was during his carny period that Murphy got his inspiration. He got it while

37

reading in a newspaper that, according to a national study, even during the worst of times there was one luxury people would still spend money on: entertainment.

"In other words," Murphy told us as we clustered around him in the WFAA studio, "folks may not know where their next meal is coming from, but they'll spend their last thin dime for a show that'll take their minds off how hungry they are, or what they're gonna say when the rent comes due."

From that simple premise, Murphy had devised a plan. It was a plan he was certain could not fail, and he laid it out for us in a veritable storm of spellbinding enthusiasm.

"In these dismal times, folks need cheering up," he proclaimed, his Texas twang throbbing with sincerity and conviction. "Trouble is, they don't have a lot of money for entertainment. And merchants are having a tough time keeping their doors open. They need to advertise, but that costs a lotta money. Right?"

"We know times are tough," Jimmie Jefferies interrupted. "So get to the point. What do you have in mind?"

"It's simple," Murphy continued patiently. "The local merchants need a cheap way to sell their merchandise. So we'll stage a show and promote their merchandise in the local theater or auditorium or school gym—or wherever we can get a stage."

"How do you reckon to get a paying audience in times like these?" someone asked.

Murphy sighed. "By selling tie-ins to the merchants, we can cut admission prices to the bone. Say two bits for grown-ups and a dime for kids. With good entertainment and that kind of prices we'll pack the house in every town."

"You'd need something to appeal to women, because they're the ones who control the purse strings," vocalist Lois Nixon said. "Maybe a fashion show."

"I'm not spending extra money staging a fashion show," Murphy snapped. "That would take models and clothes."

"You wouldn't have to spend a cent on either one," Lois said. "The merchants would be happy to show off their fashions and accessories, and you'd have local girls standing in line to model just for the thrill of being on stage."

Murphy muttered thoughtfully.

"Hey, how about swimsuits?" one of the Bumblebees exclaimed, no doubt inspired by visions of nightly parades of scantily clad beauties.

The studio echoed with appreciative male endorsements, and Murphy

38

said, "I gotta admit you might be right, honey. Okay, we'll do it!"

"Not so fast! Where do you get this *we* stuff?" Jefferies interjected. "*We* haven't agreed to do anything, and so far—outside of a lot of fancy talk—I haven't heard any reason why we should."

But Murphy was ready for resistance. He took something out of his coat pocket and handed it to Jefferies.

"That," Murphy said, "is a contract signed by Ligon Smith. I've got his band signed for a six-month tour of Texas, Arkansas, Oklahoma, and Louisiana."

If Jefferies was impressed, he didn't show it. "So you've got Ligon's band," he said. "It'll take more than a dance band to make your idea work."

Murphy agreed. "Why the hell do you think I'm here? I need you guys. But you gotta admit that Ligon's band is a big attraction."

I guess we all agreed on that point. In those days Ligon Smith was Mr. Music in Texas. He had organized a fine dance band in the twenties, and it had been a featured attraction throughout the Southwest for years.

"How come Ligon signed with you?" Jefferies wanted to know.

"That's simple," Murphy said. "Times are tough. Ligon ran out of dates. He needs money to keep his band together."

"Well, maybe you've got Ligon Smith," Jefferies said. "But you haven't got us. Not yet, anyhow. We haven't heard any talk about money or contracts."

At that time, after nearly two years on the show, my WFAA salary had climbed to twenty dollars a week. Jefferies, the star of "Early Birds," was making thirty-five dollars a week. Our income from personal appearances was dwindling, and money, more than music or sex or anything else, dominated our conversation. So when Murphy said, "Fifty bucks a week plus a bonus from profits at the end of the tour," the Early Birds were hooked.

By early June we had packaged a two-hour program of music and comedy called *Heads Up!* And, with Murphy traveling in advance lining up dates, selling tie-in advertising, and setting up the fashion shows, we hit the road. Thus began hectic months of touring, staging entertainment, and peddling just about every kind of merchandise known to man—from hardware to corn plasters, from groceries to cars and tractors.

It was my first lengthy road trip, and before long names and places began to blur together. Boredom was our greatest problem, and we spared no effort to entertain ourselves. Since Texas had many "dry" counties, we welcomed a "wet" town and its beer as a rare oasis in a parched land. Occasionally our schedule would take us to border towns. Those stops were the most prized of all, for we could troop into Mexico for drinks at cut-rate prices. We quickly learned that our Latin neighbors were enchanted by my whistling.

That discovery came early in the tour after an evening show in El Paso. Ligon Smith suggested a venture across the border to sample the vintages of the Juárez *cantinas*. The suggestion triggered an invasion by the entire *Heads Up!* cast. Like all the larger border towns, Juárez had many bars devoted to siphoning off as many Yankee dollars as possible. Fortunately we swarmed into the first saloon we encountered, and it proved to be a back-street bistro catering to the local trade.

The babble of voices and laughter faded abruptly as we moved up to the bar and ordered a round of beers, a bottled Mexican brew that proved to have the kick of an ornery mule. The silence made it clear that this *cantina* was unaccustomed to catering to tourists and that Yankee strangers were about as welcome as a protesting humane society delegation at a bullfight.

We might have fled after finishing our drinks if it hadn't been for the marimba band performing on a platform at one end of the bar. It was a typical neighborhood band playing with much gusto and little finesse, but it had a vibrant Mexican flavor. The sound appealed to our own road-weary mood, and we stayed on for another round despite the chilly reception.

Midway through my second beer the band began to play one of mv favorites, "Cielito Lindo." Without realizing what I was doing I found myself whistling the sad refrain. At the end, the *cantina* erupted in an outburst of clapping and shouts. Suddenly I was besieged by backslappers urging me to whistle another tune.

The customers soon determined that we were American musicians, and they insisted we help out with the entertainment. Ligon Smith explained that the band's instruments were on a bus in El Paso. "But Lowery carries his instrument with him at all times," he said. "He'll be happy to join the band for a few numbers."

The "few numbers" turned out to be a lengthy stint. And my pay was a continuing round of free drinks for myself and all the *Heads Up!* cast. After that, whenever we ventured into border towns, my assignment was to whistle up free drinks. It always worked. The Mexican bar patrons seemed to delight in my whistling.

Of all the happenings on the road with *Heads Up!* one night in particular stands out sharply in my memory.

It was in the Arkansas hills somewhere between Fayetteville and Fort Smith that our arthritic chartered bus gasped, coughed, and died on a dusty, hot summer evening. Our driver poked and kicked and cursed and finally hiked to a nearby town. He returned with a mechanic who looked at the engine and announced that we were stranded until he could fetch a new carburetor from an automotive supply store at Fort Smith in the morning.

"Any hotel or boardinghouse in these parts where we can stay?" Ligon Smith asked.

"Nope," the mechanic replied. "Nearest is probably twenty miles from here."

So there we were, stuck in the middle of nowhere, wedged into the hard, narrow seats of the stalled bus and wondering just why on earth we'd ever agreed to this crazy one-nighter existence.

There was groaning and grumbling and a lot of indelicate language. But Ligon Smith produced some corn lightnin' from his luggage, and before long everyone was feeling a lot better. Then a young trumpet player from Ligon's band jumped up and shouted, "Hey, let's jam!"

There was general approval, and the boys in the band got out their instruments and set up shop for a jam session on the shoulder of the narrow mountain road. With the scene lighted by a full moon so bright that even I could see it the eighteen-year-old trumpet player wailed away, and the band followed him into the mournful strains of "St. Louis Blues."

That jam session under the stars lasted for at least two hours with the young trumpet player leading the way. For a youngster who had been playing trumpet in his father's circus band until about a year before, it seemed to me that this kid had a real talent for jazz. Obviously the other musicians thought so too, because they followed his lead without question. Harry, his name was. As the youngest members of the *Heads Up!* troupe, he and I had a lot in common, and I'd got to know him fairly well on the tour. Harry was always ready to swing into a jam session, always ready to play any time of the day or night, always practicing, even on the bus.

When the last notes had echoed back into the hills and the band members began to straggle back to the bus, Harry grabbed my arm. "Hey, Fred," he said. "Let's take a walk and unwind."

"Just happens I haven't got anything else planned. No heavy dates tonight," I joked. So, with Harry guiding me, we hiked up the winding road and finally stopped to rest on a broad, flat boulder at the crest of the hill.

"You know, Freddie," Harry said solemnly, "you're good. I mean *really* good . . . the way you handle some of those tricky arrangements."

It's never been my style to turn down a compliment, so I didn't bother to contradict Harry's extravagant praise. But I did reciprocate, assuring him that beyond a doubt he was the finest trumpet player I had ever heard.

41

Suddenly Harry laughed derisively. "Yeah, we're mighty good, all right. That's why we're sitting on top of this damned mountain.

I laughed too. "Stands to reason," I said. "If we weren't great, we wouldn't be making all this money."

Harry groaned. Salaries were a chronic sore point among the band's sidemen. As anonymous musicians, they made less than we Early Birds, who were the stars of the cast. "Did you ever stop to think that we could spend our lives out here in the sticks and never make a cent more than we do right now?" he asked.

"Sure, but at least we're working," I answered. I meant it. After all, *Heads Up!* was a big improvement over the "Early Birds." And in a nation where 19 million were unemployed a fellow was lucky if he had any job, let alone a job he liked.

But Harry had his sights set on bigger things. "I don't know about you," he said, "but I've got to get out of here one of these days pretty soon. New York's the town. That's where the opportunity is—and the money. And that's where this good ol' boy is heading before long!"

"Oh, I get fed up with Texas sometimes," I said, "but I never thought seriously about leaving, even though I gripe about the money and the hours."

Harry considered. "Yeah, well maybe it's different for you. I suppose being blind makes a guy see things differently. . . ." Harry's voice faded awkwardly as he realized what he was saying. "Hell, Freddie, I didn't mean it that way."

"Forget it, Harry," I said. "I'm not sensitive. Besides, it sure as hell wouldn't stop me from going to New York if I decided to go."

"Then you're out of your mind to stay here," Harry said.

Suddenly Bill Allen leaped out of my subconscious to reecho his dire warning. "But how can anybody who's just starting out really know if he's good enough? How can you be sure?"

There was a pause, so long I thought he wasn't going to answer. Then Harry replied, "You know, Fred, a lot of the guys think I'm a smart-aleck kid, too big for my britches."

"Well," I allowed, "you ain't exactly a shrinking violet."

"Listen, I *know* I'm a good musician. I may be young, but I've worked damned hard to get this far. I started blowing a horn in my dad's circus band when I was ten. And my dad made me practice hour after hour. I hated it then, but now I m glad he did. He made me a musician. And I'm going to make my talent take me just as far as it can!"

Listening to Harry, I remembered my own life at the School for the

42

Blind—the long hours practicing in class and in my room. "Sure, Harry, I know what you mean," I said. And all of a sudden I did.

It definitely was one of those nights that stick with you for a lifetime. For me, it was the beginning of a new ambition—to go to New York. Listening to Harry, I got a sudden insight about self-confidence—that being good enough is half just believing in yourself. Sure, you had to have talent. But you had to have the determination to make that talent work for you.

And Harry . . . well, he would prove he was good enough, all right. Harry James was a kid with a king-sized ambition, and a lot of salesmanship too. At least, I bought his dream of Manhattan. Ultimately we both realized that dream.

Harry eventually joined Ben Pollack on tour somewhere in Pennsylvania or Ohio. The Pollack band never made it really big, but during the twenties and thirties it produced several musical giants, including Glenn Miller, Benny Goodman—and Harry James. After Pollack, Harry hit the big time with Goodman's band and the "Camel Caravan" radio show. From there he went on to his own band, movies in Hollywood, and marriage to one of America's sweethearts, the beautiful Betty Grable.

Even as Harry and I were talking about New York, changes were in the wind. *Heads Up!* had already hit its peak and was on the downhill skids. We continued our one-nighters along the lonesome roads of the Southwest for a few more weeks, but by late October our wayward musical bus was running out of gas. Our summer success faded with the shortening days of autumn. As the nation's economy got worse, merchants turned to other, cheaper promotional ideas, or just gave up advertising altogether. Unable to sweet talk any more promotional dollars out of the hard-pressed small-town store owners, Henry Murphy announced one day in Oklahoma that he was broke and couldn't meet the payroll. And he went scurrying off in search of another pot of gold at the end of another rainbow, leaving us stranded.

In shock, we "Early Birds" refugees glumly watched Ligon Smith's band depart for a hurriedly arranged engagement at a Tulsa hotel. A quick accounting disclosed that our total cash reserve was less than five dollars. But Jimmie Jefferies saved us from starvation with a collect telegram to Station WFAA in Dallas:

STRANDED BROKE IN ENID OKLAHOMA STOP SEND HELP OR WILL HAVE TO EAT THE REDBIRD STOP CAN EARLY BIRDS RETURN TO NEST STOP.

Fortunately for my well-being and the digestion of my fellow performers, the management of WFAA took us back. We'd only been gone a few months and still had a strong following. A week later we were on the air once more, renewing our "Early Birds" routines and shuddering with painful memories every time we got near a bus. We had learned a little bit about the hazards of show business and a *whole lot* about promoters. And we had lived to tell the tale.

There had been a time not long before when I could have readjusted comfortably to the familiar routine of WFAA and felt satisfied that I had found my niche in life. After all, how many kids from the School for the Blind were making a living as radio performers? For that matter, how many were making any kind of a living? But now New York was constantly on my mind. I knew without doubt that New York was where I had to go if I was ever going to put old Bill Allen down for the count. But I had no idea how I would get there or what I would do if I went. And then I got the answer—or at least I thought I did.

"Here, let me get that for you," a voice said. I was startled, because I didn't recognize it, and at five in the morning there weren't many strangers standing around in front of WFAA to help you with the door.

"Thanks," I said, continuing to fumble clumsily in the dark, self-conscious because a stranger was watching. "I usually don't have any trouble opening the door."

"No offense," the stranger replied. "Just trying to be useful. I'm Morton Downey."

"Are you kidding?" I said, trying to get my one-percent eye focused. After all, Morton Downey—radio's premier singing celebrity of the thirties—was just about the last person I expected to meet at the station entrance on a Tuesday morning before the sun was up.

"No, I'm not kidding," Downey said. "That's who I am. And who are you?"

"Fred Lowery," I stammered. "The Texas Redbird?" I put it as a question since I was sure Morton Downey had never heard of me.

"Why, sure," Downey said. "The whistler! I caught your act on the hotel radio over in Fort Worth yesterday." He reached out and grabbed my hand in greeting.

"That's right, I'm the whistler," I answered in amazement, shaking his hand.

"Say, you're really good. Never heard anyone whistle double notes like that before."

It turned out that Morton Downey was in town on a national personal appearance tour. To everyone's surprise he had decided to participate, unannounced, in our "Early Birds" broadcast. He did it without fanfare, or even rehearsal, which made it a bit tough on the band. But, all in all, both he and the band did a thoroughly professional job.

Midway through the show, after "Wearing of the Green" and a couple of the other Irish ballads for which he was famous, Downey turned to me and asked if I could whistle "Mother Macree."

"Sure and that's a silly question to ask a man named Lowery," I said, hamming it up with an inept Irish brogue heavily laced with a lifelong Texas twang.

"Then let's whistle a duet," Downey said.

I was flabbergasted. "You want to whistle with me?" At that time I had whistled a lot of music in accompaniment with vocalists, but I'd never attempted a duet with another whistler. However, I couldn't very well refuse an invitation from Morton Downey, so I found myself in front of the microphone with radio's most illustrious tenor. To my surprise, Downey proved to be a talented whistler, and we harmonized our way through "Mother Macree" and several other sentimental Irish ballads in a manner that was sure to bring tears to the eyes of the hardest-hearted sons of Erin.

After the show Downey took me to one side, clamped a fatherly arm around my shoulders and complimented me on my performance. "You have real talent, Fred," he said. "Did you ever think about going to New York?"

Did I? "I've been giving it some thought," I admitted cautiously. "But it's an awfully big step, especially for a cow-town whistler like me.'

"Nonsense!" Downey exclaimed. "Why, just about everybody in show business originally came from some tank town. Most of the stars are small-town folks who had the nerve to tackle the big city."

"Well, maybe I'll think about it," I said.

Downey was expansive. "That's the spirit! And when you get to New York, be sure you look me up. If I'm not in town, see Hugh Ernst, my manager. We'll help you get started."

Looking back across the years, I realize that Morton Downey—a friendly, bighearted man—probably handed out the same well-intentioned but soon-forgotten encouragement to lots of talented unknowns during his travels through the hinterlands. At the moment, however, I was floating on clouds of inspiration. Encouragement from a young trumpet player in Ligon Smith's band was one thing, but Morton Downey was something else.

The last thing I said to Morton Downey that day was, "Thanks for the whistling lesson . . . and for opening the door!"

Despite my newly bolstered resolve, leaving Texas wasn't easy. Bill Allen kept popping up in my troubled dreams like a jack-in-the-box. And many of my friends echoed his gloomy sentiments, if in milder and and kinder language.

Alex Keyes, WFAA's manager, tried repeatedly to dissuade me. "You're an established celebrity here in Dallas, Fred," he reminded me every time we met. "But in New York you'll just be another nobody." Hyman Charninsky, conductor of the Palace Theater orchestra, agreed. "Man, you're a great whistler—the greatest. But how many jobs are there for whistlers in New York? None, and you know it!"

But in spite of all these warnings, or maybe because of them, I became more and more determined. It really became an obsession. After all, I had been warned many times before, and I had gone ahead and followed my instincts—and succeeded. Perhaps because of those experiences I increasingly trusted my instincts.

However, there was one big problem I couldn't get around, one big question mark that stood squarely in my path and kept me from doing anything about New York. That problem was my feelings about Gracie Johnston and her feelings about me. I was in love with her, and I thought she might be in love with me. I certainly didn't want to leave Gracie just now. And she might not want me to go.

I hadn't dared to think about marrying her. In fact, I had purposely put the thought out of my mind. How could I ask a lovely young woman—a woman with no handicap—to share my life? And what about children? How could I possibly think about tackling the responsibilities of a family?

These were not casual concerns. They were questions that went to the very core of my being. They reflected my very real doubts about who I was, who I could become, and what I could ever hope to accomplish in life. It was one thing to bang my own head against a wall. But the thought of asking someone else to help me do it scared me out of my wits.

So it came as a great shock to me when I actually did the very thing I had thought I was determined not to do—ask Gracie to marry me. It wasn't a romantic setting. Gracie and I were sitting in a downtown Dallas cafeteria having the fifty-cent blue-plate special when I reached across the table, groping for her hand, and knocked over a glass of water. "Maybe you've heard that I'm thinking of going to New York," I blurted, trying to mop up the water with my napkin.

Gracie clasped my dripping hand and laughed. "I guess you've told just about everybody in town but me."

"I know, I know," I groaned. "It's just that when I'm with you I'm afraid if I open my mouth I'll hear what I don't want to hear."

46

"What's that?" Gracie asked.

"I want to go to New York. I want to give it a try. But I know that if you don't want me to go, I might not. And I'm afraid that's what you'll say . . . that you'll be like everyone else, telling me to stay here in my own backyard where I won't get hurt."

"Why should I tell you not to go?" Gracie exclaimed. "What right do I have to dictate what you should or shouldn't do? Fred, you've got to do what *you* think is right for you and not worry about what others think or say."

"It isn't that simple," I said, finally giving vent to my deepest feelings. "You must know by now how I feel about you. What you think, what you feel is more important to me than what anyone else thinks or feels . . . maybe even more important than what *I* think or feel. Because, more than anything, I'd like us to be together for . . . well, for the rest of our lives."

Gracie did the unthinkable. She giggled. "Fred, are you proposing?"

"Oh, at this point really I don't know. I reckon I am," I confessed miserably. "I've wanted to for a long time, Gracie. But I was afraid . . ."

"Afraid of what, for heaven's sake?"

"Gracie," I said desolately, "I don't think I've got the right to propose marriage. It just isn't fair to ask you to marry a blind man and . . ."

Gracie's temper flared. "Fred Lowery," she exclaimed, "I don't want to hear any more of that nonsense. You're a good man, a talented man. I love you, and of course I'll marry you!"

That's how Gracie and I became engaged, holding hands on a wet cafeteria table. Even more miraculous than her saying "yes" was her insistence that I should go to New York. "You'd never forgive me if I kept you here in Dallas," she said. "You've got to try, or you'll never be happy. You'd always wonder about what might have been." But she rejected my plea for us to tackle New York together.

"We're young," Gracie said. "You go to New York and see what happens, and I'll finish nursing school. However things turn out, you can be sure I'll be here waiting for you."

Once again I got the right reaction from the right person at the right time. Gracie, who meant more to me than anyone else, had given me the motivation I needed to keep moving ahead. She had told me to take a chance—that, win or lose, she'd be waiting for me. It was a rare gift, and only she could have given it.

A few weeks later, on the morning of January 2, 1934, I made my final appearance on the "Early Birds." In that last broadcast, after my customary show opener, "The World Is Waiting for the Sunrise," I whistled several numbers my listening audience had favored, including Gracie's favorite,

"Indian Love Call," and my traditional sign-off melody, "Look Down That Lonesome Road."

Indeed, it was a lonesome road I was looking down. Somewhere deep inside me a chorus of voices led by Bill Allen had started chanting a dirge in memory of the late blind whistler, sometimes known as The Texas Redbird, who had tried his wings in the treacherous updrafts and downdrafts of New York and perished ignominiously in the attempt.

I seemed to hear that dismal chorus day and night. It swelled to incredible proportions as I lay alone in the blackness of my room that last night in Dallas. And I tried to drown it out the only way I knew how. I began to whistle in the dark, and I whistled louder and louder until at last my whistling silenced all the doubting voices inside me.

Chapter 5

I believe that fear is everybody's worst enemy. At least I know it has always been mine. I was certainly apprehensive as I boarded a Greyhound bus for New York on the third day of January 1934. Some friends had come along to give me a festive send-off. But a cold, wet norther was blowing through Dallas on its icy path from the Panhandle, and I just couldn't get my spirits up.

Not that I wasn't ready to go—and loaded for bear. In my new pearl-gray stetson hat, my best Sunday suit, and hand-tooled cowboy boots, I cut as fine a fashion figure as Dallas's ready-to-wear emporiums could produce. And I had $500 in traveler's checks safely tucked in my pickpocket-proof money belt. That tidy nest egg was made up of $200 I had managed to save over a three-year period and $300 the Salesmanship Club of Dallas had magnanimously contributed as an expression of their good wishes and faith in my talent.

But as the bus pulled out of Dallas and headed north to Oklahoma, the enormity of my gamble really hit me. "Dear God," I silently prayed, "don't let me fail." I could imagine the humiliation of returning to Dallas empty-handed. I could hear the chorus of I told-you-so's. And I vowed that I would starve before coming home in defeat as Bill Allen had done years before.

On the bus that morning I soon realized that my doubting friends had a point when they cautioned me against leaving familiar surroundings. When I had traveled before, it had mostly been with friends and fellow performers who were part of my life. Now, surrounded by strangers, I got that old abandoned feeling again. And I felt isolated in a way that was unalterably tied to my blindness.

A sighted person can ease the boredom of travel by reading, watching fellow passengers, or gazing out the window. But a sightless person sits alone in the darkness, feeling the miles rumble endlessly by, wondering about the sights of cities and towns and countryside. He tries to forge a link with the world of sight by listening to the chatter of other passengers—tries to picture in his mind what kind of people they are and weaves fanciful stories about them, his imagination prodded by their voices and comments. So, for example, when I heard a passenger on the bus remark that we were crossing the Red River, I found myself wondering if the river was really red.

I had three days and two nights ahead to do nothing but eat, sleep, and play the listening game. So I listened. A man toward the back of the bus talked endlessly about the farm he'd lost in Oklahoma's dust bowl. A weary mother across the aisle continually hushed her crying baby. An indignant woman somewhere up front proclaimed at length that the recent repeal of Prohibition would lead the nation down the path to damnation. A giggling girl in the seat in front of me flirted with a sailor who entertained her with improbable tales of his exploits in far-flung ports.

At one stop a woman boarded the bus and settled down in the vacant seat next to me. "Do you mind if I sit here?" she asked.

I assured her that I welcomed her company. I sensed in her soft, cultured voice a lively and compassionate nature. "I'll be happy to have someone to talk to," I said. "I've got a long trip ahead of me, and I was feeling kind of lonely."

My new companion's name was Dorothy Colton. She told me she was returning home to Long Branch, New Jersey, after the funeral of her husband in his native Texas. I told her I was on my way to New York. Except for these brief amenities and some small talk about the weather and the long trip ahead, we didn't converse much at first.

It wasn't until the bus stopped for our evening meal that Dorothy Colton realized I was blind. As she told me later, she thought it was odd that I was wearing sunglasses on a sunless winter day. But when she saw me carefully groping my way off the bus she realized my problem. In those days, and in later years, I scorned the use of a cane as an admission of my handicap.

My lack of sight didn't seem to dismay her. She immediately took over and helped me locate the men's room and then the lunch counter, where she read the menu to me. She didn't say much about my blindness until the next morning, when we stopped for breakfast and a chance to freshen up after a restless night.

"I feel I'm imposing on your good nature," I protested as Dorothy Colton again helped me down the bus steps.

"Don't be silly!" she replied. "My brother and my uncle have severe sight problems, so I know what you're going through making a long trip like this all by yourself. I'm just glad I can be of some help. It takes my mind off my own problems."

Later, as the bus continued eastward, its big tires hissing along the rain-drenched highway and windshield wipers thumping like giant metronomes,

50

Dorothy succumbed to her curiosity about a blind young man traveling such a long distance alone.

"Are you going to school in New York?" she asked.

"Not exactly, ma'am, unless it's the school of hard knocks," I chuckled. "I'm in radio, or at least I was back in Dallas. Now I'm going to try my luck in New York."

"Radio!" Dorothy sounded both impressed and puzzled. "What do you do?"

"I'm a whistler."

There was an awkward silence—the same sort of pause that seemed to occur every time I told a stranger about my profession.

"A whistler," Dorothy finally managed to echo weakly. "But I didn't know anybody whistled for a *living*."

"Well," I admitted, "There aren't many, that's for sure. In fact, I'm one of the few professionals around. But there have been some pretty famous whistlers."

"Really? I guess I just never heard of them."

Given that opening, I wasted no time in displaying my knowledge of esoteric whistling lore. I told Dorothy how a couple of years previously a New York University professor named Charles Shaw had touched off a storm of indignation when he wrote in a highbrow book, *The Road to Culture,* that whistling was the unmistakable sign of a moron and that no great or successful man ever whistled.

"Well," I said, "that professor really stirred up a hornet's nest. Newspapers around the country reported that all kinds of famous people— including Teddy Roosevelt, Woodrow Wilson, Albert Einstein, Charles Lindbergh, Henry Ford, and John D. Rockefeller—liked to whistle."

"Of course," Dorothy said. "I know lots of people who like to whistle. But *professional* whistlers? I just haven't heard of any."

At that time, such famous whistlers as Elmo Tanner, Muzzy Marcellino, Gene Conklin, and Lou Halmy had not yet emerged. Dorothy had never heard of the talented pioneers Peggy Richter had taught me about, but she was familiar with Bob MacGimsey's hit recording of "My Blue Heaven."

"That's my point," she said. "I love the record, and the whistling is lovely, but I never knew the name of the whistler. I always associate the record with Gene Austin. The whistling just seems like background music—you know, like a piano or violin."

"Whistlers don't get the recognition they deserve," I acknowledged. "Take Andrew Garth, for example. I'm sure you've never heard of him either. Still, he's pretty well-known in Philadelphia, like I am in Dallas. He calls himself a 'whistlist,' and he specializes in classical music. But outside the Philadelphia area I guess nobody but musicians has ever heard of him. As far as I know, Garth, MacGimsey, and a few bird imitators are the only full-time professional whistlers now."

"Don't forget Fred Lowery," Dorothy laughed.

"Well, yes . . . but right now he's looking for work!"

Dorothy Colton seemed fascinated by the thought of a grown man actually being paid to whistle. She insisted on hearing details about my technique.

"There's a lot more to whistling than just puckering up and blowing," I said. And I explained that I had taught myself to whistle without puckering after I discovered how blowing through puckered lips cuts down on the flow of air, giving a harsher tone to the whistle. I also explained how I could whistle two tones at the same time and raise or lower one without changing the pitch of the other by curling my tongue back and letting the air flow over and under it.

"That's absolutely fascinating, Fred," Dorothy exclaimed. "I can hardly wait to hear you whistle!" She paused, then clasped my arm excitedly. "Fred," she said, "I just had a wonderful idea. Why don't you whistle a song or two right here on the bus to help brighten the trip for everyone?"

I was flattered but hesitant, because I certainly wasn't in the mood for performing. "I don't know," I said. "I haven't practiced for a couple of days, and this isn't a very good place for it."

"Oh, go ahead, Fred," she urged. "Just one song. I'm so anxious to hear you whistle." Dorothy scrambled to her feet and, before I could stop her, voiced an appeal to the other passengers. "Folks, Fred Lowery—this young man sitting beside me—is a professional whistler from Texas. Wouldn't you like to hear him whistle? Give him a hand!"

There was a smattering of applause from the bored passengers, all of whom would no doubt have welcomed any kind of diversion to break the monotony. Dorothy's well-intentioned interest had me on the spot. I was trapped in a situation that most professionals dread—forced into an unrehearsed, unpaid, impromptu performance before a strange audience. I was tired and anxious, dispirited and homesick. I just wasn't in the mood for whistling. But with the attention of everyone in the bus focused on me I couldn't back down. So I stood up, braced myself against the back of the seat to maintain my precarious balance in the bouncing bus, and told my fellow passengers that I would whistle one of my favorites, "The World Is Waiting for the Sunrise."

It was fortunate that I announced the title of the number in advance, because the tune that emerged was scarcely recognizable. The notes were weak, unsteady, and off-key. When I finally collapsed in my seat, clammy with what entertainers today call "flop sweat" and burning with humiliation, there was a stunned silence followed by a brief flurry of polite clapping.

"Dorothy," I whispered hoarsely, "I'm sorry it turned out so bad. I tried to tell you I didn't feel up to whistling today. I know it was terrible, and I'm sorry to disappoint you."

Dorothy Colton patted my clenched hands. "It was my fault for pushing you into something you didn't want to do," she said. "Anyhow, it really wasn't that bad, Fred. Don't worry about it." Several years later, however, she confided that after my inept performance she was overwhelmed with pity for the poor blind boy who was traveling all the way to New York thinking he had a chance to become a big-time entertainer.

Despite my flop, Dorothy managed to lift my sagging spirits with her sense of humor and her optimistic views on life. She must have been in turmoil over her husband's death and the prospects of widowhood, but she never permitted her feelings to intrude on our talk. By the time we finally reached New Jersey I felt a whole lot better and ready to tackle whatever obstacles might lie in my path.

At Newark, as she prepared to leave the bus to transfer to the Jersey Shore train, Dorothy gave me her address and telephone number in Long Branch and asked me to keep her informed about my progress in New York.

"Don't forget now," she said, "my family and I will help you any way we can. Just give us a call and we'll come running!" That was the beginning of a priceless friendship with a lovely lady—and her family. It was a friendship that helped sustain me through many difficult times during my early days in New York, a friendship that endured through the years.

Even as I waved good-bye to Dorothy, another woman was taking her place in the seat beside me. My new seatmate was a flirtatious young lady with a merrily tinkling laugh. She confided that her name was Jenny Morgan and that she was starting a new job clerking in Macy's basement, but that she really expected to get her big break in a chorus line before long, and didn't I think that New York was just about the peachiest town that ever was?

It was only about a fifty-minute ride from Newark to midtown Manhattan, but my new friend, chattering at marathon pace, managed to pack a lot of information into that brief time. I learned that she was a really-truly redhead, five-foot-four, 112 pounds, who just adored dancing, and lived with her parents in a big house in Newark. But she was going to find her own apartment in New York to be close to the action.

Between her runaway recitals of vital statistics and fanciful daydreams, Jenny managed to learn that I was a radio performer from Dallas, Texas, that I hoped to get a chance to perform on network radio, and that I was determined not to let my sightlessness stop me.

When she learned I was blind, Jenny moved a bit closer and whispered, "How awful to be young and handsome and not be able to see. But," she assured me, "it doesn't make any difference to me. I think you're swell, and I want us to be good pals in New York."

"Who said New York is an unfriendly place?" I asked myself as I stepped down from the bus with tangible proof of the Big City's hospitality firmly clinging to my right arm. "You just can't find a warmer welcome anywhere—not even in Dallas!"

The bus station was packed with weekenders on the move. Everyone was in a hurry. In the noisy chaos I could sense a supercharged urgency that I had never before encountered, and I was glad I had chatterbox Jenny to help me through those first frantic moments.

But even with Jenny as guardian angel, my arrival quickly deteriorated into near-disaster after she guided me to a vacant seat on a bench and hurried away to claim my baggage. "Now, don't you budge until I get back with your things," Jenny cautioned as she left. "You'll get trampled in this crowd."

I had scarcely gotten settled in my seat at one end of the long wooden bench when a hurrying commuter tripped over my boot-clad feet and sprawled in my lap.

"Get your damn boots out of the aisle," he snarled, pushing himself onto his feet and rushing off without pausing to pick up my hat, which he had knocked off. I edged off the bench, dropped to my knees, and began to grope for my prized stetson, trying to ignore the caustic comments of passersby as they swerved around me in their rush through the station. Suddenly I clutched a slender, silken ankle—a find that touched off a shrill, indignant female shriek followed closely by an echoing whack as a woman's purse bounced sharply off my head.

In a daze, I heard the woman shout hysterically, "This maniac tried to assault me!" I could hear mutterings from a gathering crowd, and the next thing I knew I was being hauled roughly to my feet by one of New York's finest.

"Okay, young fellow, what's going on here?" the policeman demanded, clutching my arm in a viselike grip. "What you got to say for yourself?"

"There's been a mistake," I protested before the woman's voice squealed once more, "He attacked me!"

The accusations continued as Jenny bulldozed her way through the crowd with my suitcase. "What's the matter, Fred? What's happened?" she cried.

"There's been a horrible mistake," I managed to croak once again before my burly captor interrupted.

"You know this man, lady?" the policeman roared.

"Of course I do," Jenny said. "He's my friend. . . . What are you doing to him?"

"He's a sex maniac," the female voice wailed anew.

"That's ridiculous!" Jenny stormed. "This man just got off a bus from Texas. He's blind, and he was waiting on the bench while I got his suitcase."

"He's *what?*" the policeman exclaimed. He pulled off my dark glasses, which miraculously had remained in place throughout the melee, and took a close look at my eyes.

"By God, he is blind!" the officer said. Then, puzzled, he asked, "What the hell were you doin'?"

"I've been trying to explain," I said. "I was sitting on the bench and somebody knocked my hat off. I was just trying to find it when I accidentally grabbed the lady's ankle. I'm terribly sorry, but I didn't mean anything."

Suddenly people in the crowd began to laugh, and the tension eased. The policeman gave me a pat on the back and departed, and the young lady came up and apologized. But it soon became clear that I had suffered a terrible loss. My precious new stetson had vanished during the excitement.

"Good grief," Jenny giggled as she led me toward the exit, "don't you know better than to go around grabbing women's legs?"

"Never again," I vowed. "No hat is worth that kind of trouble." I tenderly patted the top of my battered head. "I don't know what that woman was carrying in her purse, but it felt like cement."

At the big revolving doors leading out to Seventh Avenue, Jenny paused. "Fred," she said. "I've got to hurry. I'm late for a date. Do you have a place to stay?"

"Sure. Some friends in Dallas made a reservation for me at the Chesterfield Hotel. They said it's a place where a lot of musicians stay when they're in New York."

"Never heard of it," Jenny said. "But I'm sure it must be okay. Wait here. I'll catch a cab for you. And this time don't even move your big toe. I've had enough excitement for one night!"

Jenny Morgan plunged through the door and returned a few minutes later to lead me across the icy sidewalk to a waiting taxi. After getting me settled in the cab and promising to call me "real soon," she planted a quick kiss on my cheek and scurried off into the night. I was alone in the Big City.

"Where to?" the cabbie asked.

"The Chesterfield," I said, trying to sound suave. "It's near here, I think."

"Yeah . . . yeah . . . I'll get you there. Just keep your shirt on!" And the taxi scooted out into the Manhattan traffic amid the screeching of tires and the blaring of horns.

The cabbie paid no attention to the din around us. "What you wearing them cheaters for?" he asked. "The sun ain't very bright tonight."

"Cheaters?" I said.

"You know—them dark glasses you're wearing."

I was suddenly embarrassed and defensive. "Frankly," I said, "it's none of your business. But it happens that I wear them because I have a sight problem."

"Oh, blind, huh? I got a buddy who lost . . ." The cabbie's musing was interrupted by traffic. He jammed on the brakes, shifted gears, rolled down his window, and hurled a stream of invective into the night. "You ain't the only one who's blind," he shouted at me over his shoulder. "So are half the drivers in this stinking town!"

About ten minutes—and countless ticks on the meter—later, the cabbie pulled over to the curb and announced that we had arrived at the Chesterfield. "That'll be two-sixty, counting the suitcase."

"It was sure a longer ride than I figured," I said as I paid him.

Following the bellhop into the hotel lobby, I complained about the long ride from the bus station.

"Long ride, nothing," the bellhop replied. "The bus station is less than two blocks from here. You just got taken for a ride."

The cabbie may have fleeced me, but the bellhop proved to be a real friend. I don't know if he had any experience with the sightless. He never said. But he did seem to sense the special problems facing a blind person getting settled in a strange place. Maybe the ability to size up a new guest and anticipate his needs is part of being a bellhop. After I checked in, paying a week's rent for a room with private bath at $1.75 per night, he introduced me to my new home away from home. It was the first of a long succession of hotel rooms that I would occupy during the next few years—a comfortable, high-ceilinged room with a window facing Forty-ninth Street.

The bellhop—Herman was his name, I learned—led me up and down the third-floor corridor between the elevator and the door to my room four times so that I could make an accurate count of the steps. Inside the room, he showed me where the light switches and lamp were located. He guided me to the bed, the dresser, the desk, the telephone, the radio, three chairs,

56

the closet, and the bathroom, until I had the makeup of the room and its furnishings firmly fixed in my mind. He unpacked my suitcase, hung up my two extra suits, and laid out my toiletries. He showed me the hot and cold water taps and the bathtub and shower. In fact, as a one-man hospitality committee, he did just about everything but give me the combination to the hotel safe.

"Anything else, sir?" he asked after I gave him a fifty-cent tip—an extravagant gratuity in those hard times, but one that won me a loyal friend during my stay at the Chesterfield.

"Well, I am kind of hungry. Is there a restaurant in the hotel?"

"No, but there's one practically next door—the Rialto. It's a kosher joint . . . nothing fancy, but the food's good."

"Sounds great," I said. "Can you get off long enough to show me where it is and let me treat you to a sandwich and coffee?"

Herman led me back downstairs, out to the street, and about half a block to a Jewish delicatessen-restaurant where the air was heavy with tantalizing aromas. We had pastrami on rye with big dill pickles and coffee and cheesecake for a total tab of one dollar. As we ate, Herman briefed me on the location of the hotel: the Chesterfield, I learned, was on Forty-ninth between Sixth and Seventh avenues, just a couple of blocks from NBC, the RCA Building, and other important bastions of the entertainment world.

Back on the street Herman guided me to the corner of Sixth and then to the corner of Seventh so that I could pinpoint the intersections in relation to the hotel entrance. This was important as a starting point in learning to find my way around Manhattan. Outdoors as well as indoors a blind person moves about using a mental blueprint, memorizing the number of steps between the key points in his daily routine. His ears are also vital, for the sounds of traffic starting and stopping and the movements of other pedestrians nearby are like signals telling him when to stop and go.

However, I soon discovered that Manhattan presented a special problem. Just as they do today, New Yorkers blithely ignored traffic signals, crossing streets at all angles in a hazardous game of "chicken" with the city's endless flow of traffic. During my early weeks in New York I was knocked down twice by cars as I recklessly followed in the wake of jaywalking pedestrians. Fortunately, I escaped injury, and after my second mishap I put aside my pride and began asking passersby for help in crossing the streets. I may have been foolhardy, but I wasn't crazy. Or was I?

Chapter 6

When I returned to my room that first night in New York I flicked on the radio and eased myself into the chair by the window. I was exhausted, but too excited to sleep. The radio poured forth a soothing tide of music courtesy of Glen Gray and his Casa Loma Orchestra. From outside, despite the tightly closed window, the perpetual humming, buzzing, and pounding of the city invaded my room. I leaned back in the easy chair, listening. And thinking. Would I ever be able to make my way through this bewildering metropolis?

If Stafford Chiles hadn't shown up at my door that first Saturday morning, it might have taken me weeks to find all the places and people I needed to find in the city. Before leaving Dallas, I had written my old friend and former Blind School classmate. He was teaching at the Maryland School for the Blind at the time, but he had lived in New York and prided himself on being an expert in the perilous art of sightless "sight-seeing" in Manhattan. I had told him where I'd be staying, and he came unannounced to help me find my way around.

Stafford's sight was about on a par with mine, so it was really a case of the blind leading the blind as we set out to explore midtown Manhattan. Stafford proved that he really knew his way around New York. He soon determined that everything I required—Radio City, the major talent agents, and the theater district—was within a six-square-block area surrounding the Chesterfield Hotel. For the next two days he marched me up and down the wintry sidewalks until I had memorized the streets and buildings, the particular hazards, and the larger landmarks that I could distinguish with my feeble vision.

About noon on Sunday Stafford led me over to Fifth Avenue en route to Radio City. "Well, Fred, what do you think about the big town now?" he asked.

"I think it's pretty amazing that a couple of kids from the school in Austin are strolling along Fifth Avenue," I said. "Here we are, walking around like we own the town. I sure didn't think I'd have the nerve to move around the city like this so soon."

"The point is, Fred, that two of us can do what one wouldn't dare to do. It took me a long time to get to know New York because I was afraid to go out alone. That's why I wanted to help you break the ice. Just remember, if you get lost or the traffic gets too bad, don't be afraid to ask for help. You'll find most people here are just as nice as in Dallas, even though they're always in a hurry."

Stafford Chiles was right. After my weekend indoctrination I ventured out of the Chesterfield by myself day after day, asking for help whenever I became confused. Eventually I came to know the feel of the streets, the sidewalks, the buildings, the shops, and the restaurants as well as I knew the layout of my own hotel room.

On Monday morning I tucked my scrapbook under my arm and strolled out of the Chesterfield ready to conquer the world. I still had a lot to learn, but at least, with Stafford's help, I had summoned the courage to plunge into the mainstream of life in Manhattan. Out of the hotel, I turned smartly to the left, stepped off nineteen paces, and turned left again. My nose told me I was right on target at the entrance to the delicatessen. After a quick cup of coffee and two doughnuts I left the deli and turned right, heading for the offices of Petrie and Associates, the New York representatives for Station WFAA in Dallas. I followed the course charted for me by Stafford during our two days of exploration: two blocks straight ahead, one block to the left, turn right half a block, enter a narrow marbled lobby, take an elevator to the fourteenth floor, and ask for directions.

"It's at the end of the corridor to your left," the elevator operator told me. Sure enough, at the end of the hallway was the Manhattan citadel of Mr. Petrie.

As I pushed through the large glass doors I found my way barred by a desk and a receptionist with a soft voice that seemed to hold the promise of unmentionable delights.

"Good morning, sir. May I *help* you?" she asked.

Overwhelmed by musky perfume and seductive vibrations, I hurriedly tried to focus my one-percent vision. "Er . . . I'm looking for the Petrie offices," I stammered.

"Then you're in the right place."

Nervously, I held out a letter of recommendation from the manager of WFAA. "I'm Fred Lowery from WFAA in Dallas," I said.

The receptionist gave my letter a quick reading and realized that my dark glasses weren't camouflaging a celebrity. The enchanting tones hardened abruptly. "So, what do yah need?" she demanded, in what I later learned to identify as pure Flatbush, the native tongue of a legion of Manhattan receptionists and secretaries.

"I'd like to see Mr. Petrie," I explained.

She picked up a phone, whispered briefly, laughed, then banged down the receiver.

"Mr. Petrie's not in," she announced.

"Well, who can I see?"

"Everybody's busy this morning. Mr. Petrie's secretary says to leave your letter of introduction and your phone number. We'll get in touch with *you!*" That was the last I would hear from WFAA's New York representative.

The next stop on my first-day itinerary was more important, though—the nearby offices of Hugh Ernst, the talent agent who managed Morton Downey and several other established stars. Here, I was sure, I would find the help the famous tenor had promised that morning in Dallas.

Ernst's offices were housed in a building near CBS. The waiting room proved to be small, crowded, and filled with cigarette and cigar smoke. It was presided over by a woman who apparently served as phone answerer, typist, stenographer, receptionist, and errand girl combined. Her voice was tired but pleasant.

"Can I help you?" she asked.

"I'm Fred Lowery from Station WFAA in Dallas. Is Mr. Downey in?"

"Morton Downey?" She sounded puzzled.

"Yes, he told me to stop by and see him when I got to New York."

"I'm sorry, but Mr. Downey hardly ever comes here."

"Well, how about Mr. Ernst? Can I see him?"

"Have a seat," Ernst's girl Friday said wearily. "You'll have to wait."

When I turned and started fumbling my way around the smoke-filled room, she apparently realized for the first time that I had a problem. She hurried to my side and helped me locate an empty chair. "I'm so embarrassed," she said. "I didn't realize you couldn't . . ." Her voice trailed off awkwardly.

"There's nothing to be embarrassed about," I assured her. "I'm blind, but I don't let it get me down."

Before she could reply, a door creaked open and a man's voice boomed, "Hey, Polly, quit gabbing and come in here and take a couple letters."

Polly vanished into the inner office for what seemed an eternity. The smoke thickened as several more unemployed performers entered the waiting room and started grumbling when they found all the chairs occupied.

60

"Where's everybody coming from?" one of the newcomers growled. "Every place I've been today it's packed."

"Keep your shirt on, brother," a man seated to my left advised. "I've been here going on two hours, and Ernst hasn't seen anyone yet."

"How come you keep waiting then?" another voice across the room wanted to know.

"Same reason you are. I've got a seat, and it's warm in here... and maybe something will come up."

An uneasy silence descended as the inner door opened again and Polly's heels clicked across the uncarpeted floor. She stopped by my chair, leaned down, and whispered, "I told Mr. Ernst about you. He says he'll see you for a few minutes."

A storm of irate protests erupted as Polly guided me across the room toward Hugh Ernst's office. "How come Ernst is seeing *him?*" a man said. "He just got here, and I've been waiting since the office opened."

"It's not fair!" a woman wailed. "How does he rate?"

"You gotta be blind," someone observed coldly.

I was trembling and sweating as Polly ushered me into the safety of Ernst's office. After helping me to a chair she left me facing a shadowy form behind a large desk.

"What's the matter, kid? Did those palookas outside scare you?" Ernst asked in a deep voice that filled the office.

"You ain't just whistlin' Dixie," I replied. "I thought they were going to jump me."

Hugh Ernst snorted. "Don't let it get you down, kid," he advised. "Their trouble is they're out of work and mad at the world. They really aren't sore at you. They just took it out on you because I keep 'em sitting out there." The talent agent sighed. "Hell, I can't help it. I feel for 'em, but I can't help 'em. Polly says you know Morton. What's your name and what're you doing in this lousy town? You broke?"

I assured him I wasn't broke and told him how I had met Morton Downey during an "Early Birds" broadcast in Dallas. "Mr. Downey told me to see him or you when I got to New York to help me get started."

Hugh Ernst, I learned, liked to punctuate his rapid-fire monologues with a variety of snorts, grunts, sighs, and belches. This time he grunted. "Well, what do you do? Piano? Singing?"

"No," I confessed self-consciously, "I'm a whistler."

"A *what?*" Ernst exclaimed.

"A whistler."

"Holy mother!" the talent man bellowed. "Now that crazy mick is sending me whistlers. What'll it be next?"

"I'm a pro," I said defensively. "I've been on radio in Dallas for more than two years." I suddenly remembered the scrapbook I had brought with me from the hotel and pushed it across the desk. "Here are some press clippings."

Ernst belched. "Look, kid," he said. "I know you've gotta be talented or Morton wouldn't have told you to come here. But a whistler! What the hell can I do with a whistler?"

"I'm good, and I can prove it if I get a chance," I retorted. "There's nothing wrong with whistling!"

"Sure," Ernst chuckled. "I whistle in the bathtub every day. But who'd pay to hear it?" He paused as if at a loss for words, then plunged ahead with his customary bluntness. "Besides, kid, you've got another big strike against you—"

I know. But that sure as hell doesn't interfere with my talent. I've proved that in Dallas, and I've proved it on the vaudeville circuit.

Another gusty sigh emerged from the far side of the desk. "I didn't make this world," Ernst complained. "I just try to get along in it. And I'm not gonna kid you. My advice is go back to Texas where you've got friends and a job."

"I'll damn well never go back," I shouted furiously. "I'll starve first!"

My outburst apparently startled Hugh Ernst. He pushed back his chair and came around the desk to where I was sitting. He helped me to my feet and tossed a comforting arm around my shoulders. "Hell, kid, don't take it personal. I could be wrong. Anyhow, I can't do anything till Morton gets back in town. Give Polly your phone number and we'll get in touch. Maybe Morton and me can work something out for you."

Ernst ushered me back to Polly's desk, paused long enough for me to leave my phone number at the Chesterfield, and then accompanied me through the sullen silence of the waiting room. "We'll be getting back to you, kid," he said as the elevator door hissed open.

Ernst kept his word. One morning about a week later Polly phoned me at the hotel. Morton Downey was back in town and he and Ernst wanted to meet me for drinks at six o'clock at Charley's Tavern on Seventh Avenue and Fifty-first Street.

In ensuing years Charley's Tavern became my favorite bar, a preference I shared with a lot of other musicians. It had first gained a loyal clientele as a Prohibition-era speakeasy, and after the repeal of Prohibition in December 1933 Charley kept doing legally what he had been doing illegally for a long,

long time. It was a relatively small bar, and it was always crowded. But I knew nothing about Charley's as I made my way through a noisy crowd on the appointed evening. I was edging along cautiously when Hugh Ernst grabbed my arm and pulled me over to a table. "We've got a big surprise for you," he exclaimed above the babble of the crowd.

In the dim light, my vision was almost zero. A shadow rose before me and clasped me in a quick hug. The sweet scent of perfume, the softness of feminine flesh, and a tingling kiss on the cheek told me that this definitely wasn't Morton Downey.

"Fred, how wonderful to see you!" a familiar voice said. "Why didn't you let me know you were in New York?"

"Gosh . . . I sure know your voice, but I can't rightly place it," I stammered.

"Fred, honey, it's Vin . . . Vin Lindhe. Remember me?"

Did I remember Vin—my first accompanist on the "Early Birds"? How could I ever forget? But I had lost track of her after she left WFAA for a job as an arranger for the Radio City Music Hall Orchestra.

This time I did the hugging. "Lordy, Vin, I should have known your voice. But you were the last person on earth I expected to run into."

Vin giggled and guided me to a chair. "I saw Morton at the studio and he told me he was meeting a fellow from Dallas for a few drinks. When he told me who, I almost died! I simply had to tag along and surprise you."

"Well, you sure succeeded," a voice at the far side of the table chuckled. "I thought Fred was going to faint when you kissed him." It was Morton Downey. The nation's favorite balladeer reached across the table and grabbed my hand in greeting. "Great to see you, Freddie boy! How's whistling these days?"

"Nothing doing so far," I admitted. "I'm looking every day, trying to make contacts. But it takes time I guess."

"Hugh tells me he thinks you should go back to Texas," Downey said.

"Fred may be a great talent," Ernst put in. "But the odds against him are too big."

I cut him off quickly. "I told you once, Mr. Ernst, and I'll tell you again. I'm not going back!"

"That's telling him, Fred," Vin agreed, clasping my hand. "Don't let these New Yorkers buffalo you!"

Morton Downey's hearty chuckle rang out again. "The trouble with you Dutchmen, Hugh, is that you just can't understand Irishmen like Fred and me. Tell us we can't do something and we'll die trying."

Ernst grunted and summoned the waiter.

"Tell Charley I'd be obliged if he'd stop by our table," Downey told him after he took our order. "If you want a music career in New York, you've got to know Charley," he said. "All the musicians hang out here when they're in town. And you get more leads here than you do at agents' offices or the union hiring hall. Charley loves musicians. If you're short, he's usually good for drinks on the tab or even a loan."

Before long Charley arrived at our table with a round of drinks on the house. He welcomed me warmly when Morton introduced us. "It's an honor to meet you, Mr. Lowery," he said. "I hope we'll have you as a regular guest. Remember, you're always welcome."

And I always was. Through the years, Charley's Tavern was a place where I could always find companionship, encouragement, and a helping hand if I needed it.

In the beginning Morton Downey made an effort to keep the promise he'd made in Dallas. At the close of that evening at Charley's he assured me again that he and Ernst would help me get started. About two weeks later he arranged a spot for me on his sustaining NBC program—an appearance that brought me my first paycheck in New York, a fifteen dollar fee. But soon afterward he left for the West Coast on another tour, advising me to keep in touch with Ernst. And every time I'd contact the agent he'd repeat his advice to "get back to Texas."

As it turned out, Vin Lindhe had many connections in New York, including some that were pretty high up in radio network management. Shortly after our reunion at Charley's Tavern Vin and her husband, a New York manufacturer, invited me to Sunday dinner at their Greenwich Village apartment.

"I've arranged a talent audition for you," Vin said as we sipped coffee and brandy following dinner.

"What kind of talent audition?" I asked.

Vin explained that the networks held periodic auditions to screen would-be performers. "Usually you have to wait about six months for an audition, but I've managed to arrange one for you next Friday," she said. "And I'm going to play the accompaniment for you."

Promptly at 3 P.M. on the following Friday, Vin and I arrived at the designated NBC studio for the audition. During the cab ride we'd had a brief dispute over the number I would whistle. I was in favor of the *William Tell* Overture.

"That's too highbrow," Vin protested. "Give 'em something simple like 'Waiting for the Sunrise.' "

So I ended up whistling "Sunrise," and everything went beautifully.

Afterward the technicians and studio judges crowded around and congratulated me.

"We don't have the final decision. That's up to the front office," one of the judges confided. "But I suspect you'll be hearing from us soon."

Two weeks later, we had heard nothing. With Vin running interference for me through a seemingly endless chain of corporate buck-passing, I invaded the NBC offices in search of information. We finally ended up in the office of the network's director of talent.

"I'm afraid I haven't heard anything about Mr. Lowery," the talent director said. "Let me get a copy of the report on his audition." He summoned his secretary, and within minutes the report was on his desk. After scanning it he said, "The committee rates you high on talent, but low on audience appeal. Their recommendation is negative."

"That's ridiculous," I protested. "I had the highest audience rating on the 'Early Birds' program on WFAA in Dallas. That rating stood up for more than two years."

"Mr. Lowery, just because you had a big radio audience in Texas doesn't mean you'll be able to attract a big audience in New York, or on network radio. In fact, our people feel that whistling probably has too much of a rural flavor for metropolitan audiences."

"I never heard such nonsense," Vin stormed. "I'm going to take this up with some other folks here at NBC!"

The talent director apparently knew that Vin and her husband had connections and seemed suddenly fearful of getting trapped in a politically uncomfortable situation. So, like all experienced climbers of the corporate ladder, he hedged. "I was merely explaining the thinking of our committee," he said. "In fact, no final decision has been made on Mr. Lowery. I think we may be able to place him on some local shows and analyze the audience reaction."

So I was worked into several spots on local shows during the next few weeks. And I also landed a spot on a Major Bowes program called "Capitol Family," which originated from a studio in the basement of the Capitol Theater on Sunday mornings. But these were small successes that ultimately led nowhere.

During the icy winter of 1934 I struggled continuously to get my stalled career moving. I managed to meet a number of important people and get invited to some memorable shindigs. It was an exciting time of making new contacts, rubbing elbows with the famous, the near-famous, the influential— and with other hopefuls. But as time passed my economic condition rapidly deteriorated. Everyone I met seemed to accept me. At practically every party I was called on to perform, and my hosts invariably praised my whistling effusively. But no one seemed to take me seriously as a professional entertainer.

The annual get-together of the Texas Club of New York was a typically frustrating experience. Early in February Vin telephoned me at the hotel and told me to be sure to be available on the evening of the fifteenth.

"What's doing?" I asked.

"That's the night of the Texas Club's big powwow," she explained. More than 500 expatriated Texans, including quite a few show-business stars, belonged to the organization. "You've got to be there. There'll be a lot of folks you should get to know."

That year the Texas Club's dinner-dance was held in the RCA building's Rainbow Grill—a room that seemed almost as big as the state of Texas once Vin started table-hopping, introducing me to people as "the newest Texan in town."

One of the first people Vin introduced me to was Mary Martin from Weatherford, Texas. Mary said her father was a judge back in Weatherford. She was a divorcee with a young son and she was bouncing back and forth between Manhattan, Texas, and Hollywood trying to get a break. Several years later she got that break with her first big role—in the musical *Leave It To Me*. And her singing of that show's hit song, "My Heart Belongs to Daddy," catapulted her to stardom in movies and on the stage in such musical extravaganzas as *South Pacific, Annie Get Your Gun, The Sound Of Music, Hello Dolly!, I Do! I Do!,* and, of course, *Peter Pan*.

Mary was one of the few people I had met in New York who didn't seem surprised to discover an oddball who harbored dreams of becoming a famous whistler.

"I just love to whistle," she said. "I could whistle better than any kid in Weatherford." To prove it she puckered up and tootled a tune complete with fancy bird-chirping trills.

"How was that?" she asked.

"Nice chirping," I replied, "but it's not really whistling."

"What do you mean? What's wrong with it?"

I responded with a portion of my own special arrangement of an old Stephen Foster favorite, "I Dream of Jeannie With the Light Brown Hair."

"That's whistling," I said.

If Mary Martin was angered by my bad manners, she didn't show it. Like so many talented people, she had a quick and gracious appreciation of talent in others. "That was fabulous," she said. "I've truly never heard whistling like that before. Someday I want you to teach me how to really whistle."

In 1954, when she first undertook the starring role in *Peter Pan,* Mary came to me for those whistling lessons. As her performance proved, she was an exceptional student.

I still shudder when I remember the end of that Texas shindig. Tex Ritter was one of my heroes, and I had asked Vin to be sure to introduce me to him. By the time the how-de-dos were finally exchanged, Tex was mighty well fortified against snakebite. He was seated at a crowded table where his raucous storytelling was provoking roars of laughter.

As soon as he learned I was a blind whistler out of the Piney Woods, Tex ceased his monologue and started smothering me with fatherly advice. "I don't usually stick my nose into other folks' business," he said. "But I sure enough think you made a big mistake leaving Texas."

I sighed wearily, anticipating another lecture on the futility of a blind person seeking a career in show business. "You left Texas a few years back, and you're doing mighty well for a poor ol' country boy," I said.

"Yeah, kid. But you gotta realize I ain't had the handicaps you've got."

"Being blind didn't make any difference back in Dallas," I insisted, becoming angrier by the second.

"Of course not. Folks back home know you and love you and appreciate your talent. That's why you ought to head back to Texas where you belong. Here, you're just another nobody—a blind nobody. . . ."

"Take it easy on the kid, Tex," somebody in the crowd around us protested.

But in his bourbon-coated determination to play big brother, Tex didn't heed the protest. He plunged ahead with his lecture, no doubt convinced he had my best interests at heart. "You've gotta realize that seeing blind people makes a lot of folks feel sad or uncomfortable or guilty. That's why it's so hard for a blind person to land a job as an entertainer. In show business you've gotta leave 'em laughing, not crying. Believe me, kid, this is a cold, cruel city, and you're bound to get hurt if you stick around."

A few weeks earlier, Tex Ritter's star status would have awed me into silence despite my anger. But by then I had been exposed to the celebrity partying circle. I had rubbed elbows with many entertainers. I respected their talent and professionalism, but I didn't want to be an admiring fan. I wanted to be one of them. Besides, I had had several doses of snakebite medicine myself that night. Angrily, I shrugged off the protective arm my fellow Texan had clasped around my shoulders. "Tex," I roared, "I'm sick

67

of that speech." And I proceeded to broadside the famous singer with a barrage of good old Texas cussing.

My outburst touched off a wave of shocked gasps; subjecting a public idol to such abuse was unthinkable. Fortunately, as I prepared to let loose another angry barrage, Vin Lindhe grabbed my arm and hustled me out to the cloakroom, leaving Tex sputtering indignantly.

"Where are we going?" I stormed. "I've got more to say to that cowboy crooner!"

"You just hush that whiskey talk," Vin snapped. "You've said too much already. You're going home before you get in any more trouble."

The next morning I telephoned Vin and apologized.

"I hope I didn't embarrass you," I said. "I didn't mean to blow my stack, but when he went into that same old song-and-dance about me being blind and going back to Texas, I just couldn't take it!"

"I know, Fred," Vin sympathized. "But you've got to learn to grin and bear it, at least while you're breaking in. You need all the help you can get. If they start saying you're a troublemaker, your goose will be cooked in this town."

I knew Vin was right. And I assured her I'd curb my temper and apologize the next time I met Tex Ritter.

As it turned out, no apology was necessary. When I met him at another party a few months later, Tex had no recollection of our previous meeting.

"Man, I sure enough don't remember much about that Texas party," he confessed after I told him what had occurred. "That's what I get for stickin' my nose in your business."

During the next couple of weeks, with Vin Lindhe's help, I concentrated on a long-standing goal—an appearance on the Rudy Vallee "Variety Hour." Right from the start I had figured that was the one show that could give me the national exposure I needed. Since lesser achievements seemed beyond reach, I naturally decided to go for the top.

It was difficult for unknown talent to discover the procedures that led to the microphones airing the major network shows. By myself I might eventually have made the necessary contacts, but I'm sure it would have been a long and blundering process. But it took Vin only two phone calls to discover the behind-the-scenes route leading to the Vallee show.

"We have to start at the Thompson agency," she informed me.

"I never heard of that talent agency," I observed.

"It's not a talent agency. J. Walter Thompson is a large advertising agency that handles the Fleischmann Yeast account. Fleischmann sponsors the

Rudy Vallee 'Variety Hour.' So the Thompson agency acts on behalf of Fleischmann in screening talent for the show."

"You mean to say Vallee doesn't select the talent he uses on his own show?" I asked.

"It's not really Vallee's show. It's Fleischmann's show; Fleischmann pays the bills. Vallee and his Connecticut Yankees are permanent performers, but they work for Fleischmann just like the one-shots."

Two days later I was sitting in the Madison Avenue office of the Fleischmann Yeast account executive at the Thompson agency, making my pitch for an appearance on the Rudy Vallee "Variety Hour." I recited my dramatic account of the Life and Times of Fred Lowery, and when I finally ran out of words I handed him my scrapbook.

Hugh Ernst hadn't even bothered to open it. But the account executive was basically a salesman. While talent was an intangible, he did trust figures, market reports, press clippings. They were his yardstick for decision-making. He pounced eagerly on the scrapbook. "Very impressive," he said after flipping through it. "I'd like to keep this book for a few days to give it a closer reading. It's apparent the critics feel you have a unique talent— the sort of thing we're looking for on the Vallee show. But . . ."

There was a silence, and my elation at finally finding someone who took my clippings seriously began to fade. Here it comes, I told myself—the big brush-off. But the silence proved to be merely a pause while the account executive lighted his pipe. After a couple of puffs, he continued ". . . but I don't want you to expect quick action. You still have to be screened by NBC's Talent Board before you can appear on a network show. And that may take a little time."

I was overwhelmed with relief. "You mean you aren't concerned about my being blind?"

"Of course not," the account executive said. "In fact, I think it's definitely a plus . . . gives the show a human-interest flavor."

"Then you don't have to worry about the Talent Board," I said. "I was screened weeks ago."

"Well, in that case," the account executive said enthusiastically, "we may find a spot for you in a few weeks. Keep in touch."

Keep in touch? For two weeks I phoned or dropped by constantly, making a real pest of myself. Finally, one morning when I telephoned I wasn't given the customary runaround. Instead, my call was quickly switched to the Fleischmann account executive's secretary.

"Mr. Lowery, would you be available to appear on the Rudy Vallee show on March fifteenth?" the secretary asked.

It was a call I had literally waited a lifetime to receive, but for some perverse reason I impulsively said, "Just a minute, please. I'll have to check my calendar."

As soon as I said it I regretted my idiotic impulse. The agency secretary, I was sure, hadn't been fooled one bit. But I had no choice. I had to go through with the charade. So I leaned back in my chair, frightened out of my wits that she might hang up, and waited. After a few seconds that seemed like an eternity I picked up the phone again.

"Are you there?" My voice squeaked with anxiety. To my vast relief, the secretary was still on the line, no doubt amused by my childish pretensions.

"Yes, Mr. Lowery. Will you be available?"

"Oh, yes," I exclaimed. "That will be fine. There's nothing on my calendar for the fifteenth.

"Very well, Mr. Lowery. Be at NBC studio 8-H at 8:30 on the morning of March fifteenth."

"In the morning? But the Vallee program broadcasts in the evening," I said inanely.

"Yes, Mr. Lowery. But *rehearsals* start at 8:30 sharp. Please be there on time."

"Don't you worry," I assured her. "I'll be there on the dot!"

Chapter 7

On the morning of March 15, 1934, I showed up at NBC's huge Studio 8-H ninety minutes before the start of rehearsals. The studio was empty, and I took an aisle seat at the foot of the broad stage. I had not arrived at that ridiculous hour because I was fearful of being late, but because after a sleepless night I couldn't tolerate my hotel room for another minute.

Sitting there in the empty studio, I thought about all the letters Vin Lindhe had helped me write to my relatives and friends in Texas, telling them to be sure to tune in the Rudy Vallee program that evening. Similar letters had gone to Stafford Chiles in Maryland, to Dorothy Colton in New Jersey, and to a few other friends in various parts of the country. And Vin had telephoned newspaper and magazine people, music critics, and various show-business executives, urging them to listen to my performance. I realized that in addition to the regular Vallee audience a lot of special people would be tuned in when I stepped up to that NBC microphone. Chills went jitterbugging up and down my spine every time I thought about it.

I tried to bolster my courage by telling myself that this was just another show. But my common sense wouldn't let me buy that kind of self-delusion. The Rudy Vallee "Variety Hour" was by no means just another broadcast. At that time it was the hottest variety show on the networks, with the largest audience. It was a program that had become a national showcase for talent—a program that could make or break a young performer's career.

Today, the fame that surrounded Rudy Vallee and his band has faded. His music, unlike that of contemporaries like Benny Goodman, Glenn Miller, Duke Ellington, Harry James, Guy Lombardo, Lawrence Welk, and the Dorsey brothers, has not endured the test of time. But in 1934 Rudy Vallee and his Connecticut Yankees were the biggest money-makers on the American band scene even though many critics panned Vallee's gimmicky music and his nasal crooning. Some musicians disliked Rudy personally. He was called variously an Ivy League snob, a penny pincher who paid miserly wages, and an opportunist who would do anything to advance his career. Nevertheless, no one could dispute the fact that from the time he graduated from Yale and joined the Johnny Cavallaro band at New Haven as a saxist Vallee's rise had been spectacular. By the early thirties his adenoidal vocalizing through a megaphone had made him the twentieth century's first major singing idol. He was a bigger-than-life celebrity who, like later superstars Bing Crosby, Frank Sinatra, and Elvis Presley, attracted huge crowds of fanatical young fans wherever he appeared.

Rudy was also one of the first bandleaders to crash the Hollywood scene. In fact, on the day I showed up at NBC for rehearsals, Vallee's movie *George White's Scandals* was opening its New York run at Radio City Music Hall. It was a movie that starred not only Vallee but also his orchestra; his featured vocalist, lovely Alice Faye; and comedian Jimmy (The Schnoz) Durante, and boasted such songs as "Hold My Hand," "Sweet and Simple," "You Nasty Man," and "So Nice"—tunes the whole country was humming. Despite such competition as Clark Gable in *It Happened One Night* and Humphrey Bogart in *Midnight,* Vallee's *Scandals* proved to be an immediate smash hit.

My mood that morning was further affected by my rapidly dwindling bankroll. Despite the fees I had picked up for local radio performances, and despite my efforts to economize, I had less than forty dollars left of the funds I had brought with me to New York in January. I was therefore painfully aware that if I flopped during rehearsals and was taken off the program I would lose the $300 fee I was counting on to finance my continuing pursuit of a career. There was simply no way I could convince myself that this would be just another show. Too much was at stake.

My melancholy thoughts were suddenly interrupted by the slamming of a door and the clatter of footsteps down the aisle leading to the stage. The footsteps stopped beside my seat, and I detected a tall, shadowy figure.

"Hello, I'm Rudy Vallee," the figure announced in brisk, no-nonsense tones.

Startled at finding myself unexpectedly face-to-face with the Great Man, I stammered and finally managed to announce my name.

"Oh, yes. Fred Lowery, the whistler." Vallee grabbed my hand in a brief greeting, dropped it after a couple of pumps, and turned to dash up the stairs leading to the stage. "I'll get back to you later on," he shouted over his shoulder. "We've got to get together on an arrangement for your number."

Within minutes of Vallee's arrival the musicians began to straggle into the studio, cursing the uncivilized hour. By 8:30 sharp the entire band was on the scene, noisily arranging chairs and music stands and tuning instruments.

A sharp rapping from the stage above my head put an end to the clamor. "Our sound last week was lousy," Vallee announced. "I've heard better music in kindergarten bands." His voice boomed eerily, and I suddenly realized that he was talking through his megaphone. "The big trouble is in the brass. You cats with the horns are messing up the tempo. There isn't enough beat to rock a goddam cradle . . . ."

Section by section, with eloquent profanity, Rudy Vallee ripped into his musicians. He roared at the trombonists. He ranted at the string section. He raved at the percussion. I was beginning to truly appreciate why Vallee was so disliked by musicians when a soft, vibrant female voice bewitchingly accompanied by an expensive scent distracted me from his assault on the band. "Mind if I sit here beside you?"

I hurriedly stood to let the lady wriggle past me to the adjoining seat.

"I never could say no to a beautiful girl," I joked, trying frantically to focus in, even though it didn't require eyesight to recognize that she was something special.

"Flattery will get you everywhere," the melodious voice responded. "I'm Alice Faye. Who are you? One of the guests on tonight's show?"

I realized that my instinct was correct. This talented beauty was already becoming famous across America as a vocalist with Vallee's band.

"I'm Fred Lowery. And you're right, I'm on tonight's show. I've just been in New York a couple of months, and this is my first good shot."

"Oh, yes, Rudy told me about you. You're the whistler."

"Yeah, and right now this whistler is scared as all get-out," I admitted.

"Don't let Rudy scare you," Alice Faye said. "He likes to make people think he's tough, but he's really a softy behind all that shouting and cussing . . ."

Alice's reassurance was interrupted by another thunderclap from the stage. "Hey, Alice, what the hell are you doing down there? We're waiting for you!"

Alice Faye's giggle rippled anew. "I'm a-comin'. I'm a-comin', massah," she said as she pushed past me once again. "Don't beat me, massah, I'm a-comin'!"

Alice's flip response touched off a flurry of guffaws on the bandstand, an outburst punctuated by another roar from Vallee. "Dammit, Alice, since when have I been paying you to be a comedian?"

Despite Vallee's Simon Legree treatment of his band, in his dealings with the show's guest performers he was entirely courteous and considerate. I was one of four guests on that Thursday's show. The others were big-name celebrities—Broadway actors Walter Huston and Billy House and a shy

73

teen-age musical prodigy, violinist Yehudi Menuhin. Vallee sat with us for nearly an hour, discussing the roles we would play in the show's format. Through it all he was an Ivy League gentleman. He learnedly discussed the classics with young Yehudi, and they finally agreed on two violin pieces. He exchanged views on acting techniques with Huston and House before sending them off with the show's writers to develop a couple of dramatic skits. Then he got around to me.

"You've been mighty quiet, Fred," he said. "What's the trouble? Got the heebie-jeebies?"

"Worst jitters I've ever had," I admitted.

Vallee chuckled. "Don't let it get you down. You wouldn't be worth a damn if you weren't nervous."

During the next few minutes Vallee quietly put me at ease, getting me to talk about my early days at the Blind School, about my radio career in Dallas, about my experiences in New York, and about my musical repertoire. "Any particular number you'd like to whistle?" he asked.

I told him I considered "The World Is Waiting for the Sunrise" my best popular number.

"That's fine. It's a good number," Vallee said. "We'll work up an arrangement and go through it with you a few times later in the day." He paused, as if something had suddenly occurred to him. "By the way," he said, "I feel kind of awkward about this, but how can you . . ."

"About my being blind?" I said.

"Yes. I've never worked with a blind musician before. We can write an arrangement, but it's just dawned on me that you won't be able to read it."

I laughed. "I've been involved in music most of my life. I learned a long time ago to memorize it as easily as your musicians can read it."

"Okay, I'll take your word for it," Vallee said, apparently relieved to drop the subject. "We'll get together with you on the number in a couple of hours."

It was midafternoon before Vallee and his Connecticut Yankees got around to rehearsing my number, but I didn't mind the long wait. Sitting in the midst of what at times seemed complete chaos, I relished the knowledge that at last I was part of some big-time action.

The band quickly polished up the week's new arrangements, Rudy crooned and perfected various hit lyrics, Alice Faye half-sang, half-hummed her way through several numbers, and some big-name visitors dropped in to watch rehearsals from time to time. Alice Faye brought a couple of these VIPs over during one of the breaks in rehearsal. She introduced me to comedian Joe ("Wanna Buy a Duck") Penner and to Eddie Cantor, the famed song-and-dance man who had been rehearsing his own "Chase & Sandborn Hour" show in another NBC studio. Cantor chatted briefly, wished me luck, and dashed back to his studio, but Penner, apparently enjoying a day of leisure, plopped down in the seat next to me.

Like many comedians, Joe Penner turned out to be a rather serious-minded fellow, at least during our conversation that day. He was the one who tipped me to the fact that Vallee's bandstand tirades were deliberately designed to provoke his musicians into a creative frenzy.

"It's kind of hard for musicians on radio to be inspired by a mike," Penner explained. "When a band's playing in a ballroom, it has the dancers and the customers at the tables to put them in the mood. Musicians are like all entertainers—they've got to have an audience to bring out the best in them. But in a radio studio they're playing to an unseen audience."

"How about the studio audience?" I asked.

"That's not an audience. That's a bunch of claques herded into the studio to provide a crowd atmosphere," Penner replied. "Radio entertainers don't pay much attention to studio crowds. They know the real audience is far away at home, listening to their radios. It's kind of scary sometimes when you think about it, knowing that your career depends on whether or not all those millions of unseen people like your music or laugh at your jokes."

"You mean to tell me that's what makes Rudy Vallee act like a madman during rehearsals?"

"That's how I've got Vallee figured. He keeps riding his musicians hard just to get 'em fired up. Can't be any other reason for all his ranting and raving."

Penner was equally blunt in discussing my blindness. He was particularly intrigued by the fact that I could sit in the studio hour after hour enjoying myself even though I couldn't see what was going on around me.

"Just like meeting Cantor and me," Penner said. "If Alice hadn't brought us over and introduced us, you probably wouldn't even have known we were in the studio."

"Well, maybe that's one of the bonuses I get for being blind," I said. "She knew about my sight problem, so she made a special effort to introduce me to you, knowing I would enjoy it. If I could see, I'm sure she wouldn't have bothered. She would have figured that if I wanted to meet you I'd walk up and say howdy."

"I see what you mean," Penner said, then hurriedly corrected himself. "I mean I *know* what you mean."

75

"Don't worry," I assured him. "Folks just naturally say 'see' and 'look,' and it always seems to embarrass them when they say them to a blind person. They seem to think we'll feel they're making fun of our blindness. But that's not so. As a matter of fact, we use the same words and don't think anything about it."

"I still don't know how you can sit here hour after hour without being able to see what's going on. It would drive me nuts," Penner said.

Once again I found myself trying to explain the world of the blind to a person with sight. "Our imaginations become our eyes," I said. "*You* see what's going on around you. *We* imagine what's going on, based on what our other senses and instincts tell us. It's kind of like listening to the radio. You get a mental picture of what's happening even though you can't see it. . . ."

My explanation was cut short when Alice Faye tapped me on the shoulder. "It's time to rehearse your number, Fred," she said, helping me up the stairs to the stage and seating me on a chair on the bandstand facing Rudy Vallee, who was perched on his stool like a schoolteacher confronting unruly students.

"Okay, Fred, the band will run through your number a few times," Vallee said. "Let us know when you're ready to give it a whirl."

Vallee tapped his baton and the Connecticut Yankees began to play my song—the band arranger's version of "The World Is Waiting for the Sunrise." It was a lively arrangement full of the musical flourishes that Vallee delighted in, an arrangement custom-designed for whistling.

After concentrating during four run-throughs I was ready. The last traces of jitters vanished as Alice Faye led me to the microphone. The music began, the sun came up, and all was right with the world. There wasn't a flaw in my whistling during that rehearsal. Alice gave me a quick hug, and even Vallee came down from his throne to congratulate me on my performance. "I told you there was nothing to worry about," the maestro said.

The hour-long network broadcast that evening went just as smoothly, from the moment sugary-voiced announcer Jimmy Wallington opened the show until the notes of the band's closing number faded. I was all spruced up in a rented tux, enjoying the best seat in the house—right beside Alice Faye on the front row of the bandstand. My great moment came midway in the program when the Connecticut Yankees swung into "Whistling in the Dark."

The music ended, and Vallee spoke into the mike. "Friends," he said, "the music you just heard was a number titled "Whistling in the Dark." It's not very well known, but it's appropriate because one of our special guests tonight is a young man from Texas who has spent his life doing just that. It's my privilege to introduce Fred Lowery, who comes to us from one of our NBC affiliates, station WFAA in Dallas. Fred was educated at the Texas School for the Blind, and he brings us a most unusual sound, that of a caroleer, a whistler. I'm sure you'll find his music a very unique, a very special treat."

Alice Faye had told me that every seat in the large studio was filled, but I didn't let that bother me, remembering Joe Penner's philosophy that the only audience that mattered was at home. I don't believe I would have noticed the crowded studio even if I could have seen it, for every fiber in my being was concentrated on the music. Once it started I didn't even think about the people who were listening to me across America. My mind was too occupied with remembering every note of the arrangement.

Fortunately my memory didn't falter. Just as they had in rehearsal, the band's music and my whistling blended perfectly. I felt that I had never been in better form. Applause thundered through the studio as I finished.

"At last," I told myself as I stood at the mike clutching Rudy Vallee's arm. "At last I'm on my way!"

My elation was still at a high pitch the next day. By noon I had tangible evidence of my success. I had been to the bank and cashed my $300 check, and the money was carefully tucked away in a dresser drawer. It was comforting to be back in the chips again, but the overnight recognition generated by my performance was even more rewarding.

I had been awakened early that morning by a phone call from a friend at NBC who wanted to cheer me with the news that my whistling on the Vallee show was already producing a favorable—and sizable—response from the show's audience across the country. In addition I had received telegrams of congratulation from Gracie, from my sisters, from Grandma White and Uncle Ed, and from other relatives and friends back in Texas.

The telephone in my room continued to ring all morning. Vin Lindhe called from Chicago, where she was on tour with the symphony. Stafford Chiles called from Baltimore. Dorothy Colton called from New Jersey. Morton Downey and some of my acquaintances in New York called too, as did Hugh Ernst and several other talent agents. But despite their flattering words, the agents carefully avoided any discussion of signing me as a client.

Joe Penner's agent was one of the "flesh peddlers" who telephoned. He explained that Penner had urged him to listen to the Vallee broadcast. "Like Joe said, you've got talent, Fred," the agent told me. "I'll be keeping an eye on you. Maybe we can talk business one of these days."

But my biggest thrill was provided by Walter Winchell, the "king" of show-business gossip whose spicy tidbits and dramatic exposés were avidly awaited by millions of newspaper readers and radio listeners across America. As I sauntered through the hotel lobby that morning on my way to the bank, one of the bellhops called out, "Hey, Fred, congratulations on making Winchell's column!"

"Winchell's column? What are you talking about?"

"You mean you haven't read Winchell this morning?"

"No," I said sarcastically, "I've been too busy reading the dictionary!"

The bellhop, who had frequently read my mail to me, realized his blunder. "I'm sorry, Fred. For a minute I forgot that you can't read. I was so excited I just forgot."

"Hell's bells, man!" I exclaimed. "What did Winchell say about me? Hurry up—get the paper and read it to me!"

The bellhop scurried off across the lobby and quickly returned, crackling *The Mirror* open to the page featuring Winchell's syndicated "Broadway Beat." "Here it is, Fred. Just listen to this."

I still have that newspaper clipping in a scrapbook. It says, "Guest stars appearing on the Rudy Vallee 'Variety Hour' last night included the famous actor Walter Huston, Billy House and violinist Yehudi Menuhin. But an unknown whistler by the name of Fred Lowery stole the show. . . ." Those words sound like a routine plug for a radio show and its guest performers. But back in that era getting your name in Winchell's column was a notable milestone, especially for a newcomer like me.

A few hours later, while I was still basking in Winchell's praise, there was a knock at my hotel door.

"Hi, Fred, remember me? Jenny Morgan. You know, the girl on the bus."

A subtle perfume and a mile-a-minute girl's voice indeed stirred memories of the bus ride from Newark and my harsh introduction to Manhattan in the bus station's crowded waiting room.

"Yeah, you're the girl who was going to call me in a day or two, the girl who was going to be my friend in a strange city," I said. "Where have you been?"

Jenny, the marathon chatterbox, was not without an excuse. "I'm truly, truly sorry, Fred," she said contritely. She had often started to telephone me, she explained, and had even come to the hotel a couple of times, only to leave without seeing me because she was too embarrassed.

"Embarrassed? About what, for pete's sake?"

"Because I talked real big on the bus about my dancing career, about how I had a chorus-line job coming up. I'm nothing but a silly little salesgirl, and I didn't want you to laugh at me or feel sorry for me. . . ." Jenny's

78

explanation disintegrated in a shower of tears, and I hurriedly pulled her in from the hall and shut the door before her sobs could arouse the curiosity of guests in nearby rooms.

"That's a stupid excuse," I scolded after I finally managed to stop her crying. "There's no need to be embarrassed because you haven't been able to break into show business. Gosh, look at me. I'm in the same boat you are. But I'm not bawling about it. Sure, you get tired and get the blues. But you've got to keep trying."

"There's no reason for you to be blue," Jenny sniffed. "You're not a nobody like me. You've been on the Rudy Vallee show. You're going to be famous one of these days. And I'm afraid you'll pity me, or think I'm some kind of a hussy throwing myself at you."

I was exasperated by what I considered cockeyed female logic. "If you feel that way, why did you come here?"

"Because I just had to see you, to let you know how thrilled I was to hear you on a big broadcast like that."

In later years, after much exposure to the female fans who flock adoringly around entertainers, I probably would have shrugged off Jenny's melodramatic words as an invitation to trouble. But in those days, although I wanted to view myself as a man of the world, I was actually an innocent. I was touched by Jenny's tears, flattered by her praise, and perhaps excited by the unexpected attention from an attractive female. However, the telephone rang before I could say anything more. A man at the other end of the line introduced himself as Mr. Vanderhoff, a talent agent. He said he had heard my performance on the Vallee program.

"Quite frankly, Mr. Lowery, I was awfully impressed by your whistling. You have a very unique talent, and I'm sure I can arrange some bookings for you," he said.

A talent agent who wanted to talk about bookings! It was a call I had been hoping for all day, but it couldn't have come at a more inconvenient time. "I really do appreciate your kind words," I said. "And I'm certainly interested in talking about bookings. Give me your address and I'll get in touch with you first thing Monday."

Mr. Vanderhoff wasn't about to accept a delay. "I had hoped to see you today, Mr. Lowery. I was so impressed by your performance that I called NBC this morning and got your address. In fact, I'm calling from the hotel lobby right now. I hope I haven't made the trip in vain."

"Mr. Vanderhoff, I do appreciate your interest in my career, but I'm kind of busy right now."

"Just give me a few minutes of your time," the tenacious Vanderhoff insisted. "Come down to the lobby and we can talk business here. You'll never regret it, I promise!"

I clamped a hand over the mouthpiece while I briefed Jenny on the call. "There's a talent agent in the lobby. He wants to talk about setting up some bookings for me. Says it's important."

"Go ahead and see him right now, Fred," Jenny urged. "It could be a big break for you. I'll wait here. I won't run away. Cross my heart!"

"Okay," I told the stranger at the other end of the line, "I'll meet you in the lobby in a couple of minutes. Just ask one of the bellhops to guide me to where you're sitting. But remember, I can't give you much time today."

"My friend, a few minutes is all I'll need," Mr. Vanderhoff assured me.

The bellhop led me to a leather divan in a quiet corner of the lobby. Vanderhoff leaped to his feet, grabbed my hand, and got me settled next to him for our business talk.

"It's a privilege, a rare privilege, to meet you, Mr. Lowery," he gushed. "I'm sure you'll find our meeting worthwhile."

"I sure hope so," I said, trying to size up the stranger. Although I couldn't see his face clearly my ears sounded a warning as he began describing his plans for my career. The words were impressive—a series of late-spring and summer bookings in the resort hotels of the Adirondacks, a veritable borscht-belt bonanza at $150 per week. But it dawned on me that Vanderhoff wasn't talking like a talent agent; he talked too much, too fast, too glibly. Still, I figured, I had nothing to lose by listening. I could always check him out later.

When he finally paused for breath, I hastily rose from the divan, hoping to make a break for my room and the interrupted reunion with Jenny Morgan. "Really, I've got to run along," I said. "Your proposition interests me, and I'll be glad to get together with you again next week. Just give me your card and . . ."

But Mr. Vanderhoff tugged me back down on the divan. "A few more minutes, please, Mr. Lowery," he said. Then, midway through a description of the delights of performing in the mountains, he stopped abruptly, scrambled to his feet, and pushed a calling card into my hand. "I'm afraid I've taken up too much of your time," he said with a nervous chuckle. "Here's my card. Get in touch next week and we'll work up a contract." With that, Mr. Vanderhoff hurried out of the lobby. Vastly relieved to be rid of him, I speculated about his sanity as I made my way back to my room.

The room was empty. Not a trace of Jenny Morgan except the lingering scent of her perfume. In her wake, however, were dresser drawers stacked on the floor, their contents scattered. Frantically I pawed through the tangle of clothing and papers. My money—the $300 in crisp new bills I had brought back from the bank that morning—was missing. I telephoned the desk clerk in a daze. Had he seen a red-haired young lady leave the hotel? I remembered she had told me she was a "really-truly" redhead.

"Yes, sir, Mr. Lowery. A young lady—a redhead—came out of the elevator while you were in the lobby talking with that gentleman."

I hung up the phone in despair. It was hard to believe, but Jenny was a thief. She was gone, and so was my money—the money I had counted on to finance my continued stay in New York. Slowly I picked up the phone again and asked the operator to connect me with the police.

It was late afternoon when a Manhattan detective arrived. He listened without comment as I told my story: Meeting Jenny on the bus in January and not hearing from her again until today, her sob story, the phone call, my weird encounter with Mr. Vanderhoff in the lobby, his abrupt departure, and my return to an empty, looted hotel room.

"Do you have the business card this Vanderhoff character gave you?" the detective asked.

I retrieved the card from my jacket pocket. The detective studied it briefly and snorted. "It's a business card from this hotel. He must have picked it up at the desk while he was waiting for you, and he handed it to you when he left figuring it would keep you from getting suspicious until they could get away. It was a pretty safe move, seeing as how he knew you were blind."

"Are you telling me that Jenny Morgan and this Vanderhoff guy were in cahoots?"

"You'd better believe it," the detective said. "From your description, I'd say these two are veteran bunco artists."

"I still don't understand," I said. "It doesn't seem possible. On the bus in January, Jenny seemed like such a nice girl. She even helped me out when I got in trouble in the waiting room. How come she and her partner didn't try to fleece me then?"

The detective theorized that when Jenny first saw me on the bus with dark glasses, a sharp new suit, and a fancy stetson hat, she probably sized me up as a well-heeled rancher heading for a wild time in the big city—a sagebrush playboy ripe for the plucking. When she learned I was only an unknown blind whistler hoping to break into show business, she tossed me back and went casting for bigger fish. But a couple of months later, when she happened to hear me on the Rudy Vallee show, Jenny and her boyfriend realized I might have a bankroll and dreamed up the talent-agent story to get me out of the hotel room long enough for Jenny to search for hidden treasure.

"Being blind made you too easy a mark to pass up," the detective explained. "We'll try to pick them up, but chances are they're long gone. I'll call you if there are any developments."

I sat by the telephone the rest of that long, bleak weekend, but the detective didn't call. On Sunday afternoon I finally phoned the police station. The detective was off duty. I was shunted to various extensions, until a weary voice finally informed me that there were no breaks in the case. "We'll call you if there's anything to report," it said.

At that point I knew I would never see my $300 again. But a philosophical acceptance of my loss did not ease the pain of being betrayed by a girl I had accepted as a friend. Nor did it erase the humiliation of knowing I had been a gullible and easy mark. And certainly it didn't relieve the fright that accompanied the realization that I was once more jobless and almost broke.

Chapter 8

I have no idea how many times I counted my depleted resources that weekend. The figures always came out the same: $9.73 in cash and a $20 traveler's check. I had no job prospects, and my weekly $12.25 hotel rent was due. At best I figured I had only enough money to survive for a couple of weeks.

One thing was certain: I didn't have enough to finance my return to Texas, even if I were inclined to run back home with my tail between my legs. So I forced myself to climb out of bed on Monday to confront the world.

My first stop that morning was at the hotel desk where I presented my last traveler's check to pay my rent. There I immediately encountered yet another problem. "Mr. Lowery," the desk clerk said, "I'm afraid I can't cash this check."

"Quit your kidding," I snapped, convinced the desk clerk was having some fun with the hotel's prime sucker.

"I'm not kidding. I'm sorry, but I can't cash this check. It's endorsed wrong."

"What do you mean? How could I endorse it wrong?"

The deskman sighed. "I know you have a sight problem, and I know you've been upset. The fact is, Mr. Lowery, the check is made out to Fred L-O-W-E-R-Y, and you've endorsed it Fred L-O-O-W-E-R-Y.

I snatched the check and held it close to my left eye. In the bright light at the desk I could faintly make out the large, crudely scrawled printing of the signature I had developed at the Blind School. The desk clerk was right. In my agitated state I had signed the check exactly as he said, L-O-O-W-E-R-Y.

"You're right, I've made a stupid mistake," I admitted. "But what can I do about it? How can I get my money?"

"Try the bank. Maybe they can help you," the clerk suggested.

At the bank where I had cashed my $300 check the previous Friday I showed a teller the traveler's check and explained my error.

"I'm sorry, sir, but I'm not authorized to cash an improperly endorsed check," the teller said.

"My God!" I exclaimed frantically. "Can't something be done?"

"Well, you can send it back to the bank in Dallas that issued it and explain what happened. I'm positive they'll issue you a new check."

"But that will take weeks! I can't wait that long. Without this check I'm broke—It's the last of my savings!"

Apparently the teller felt sorry for me. "Why don't you talk to Mr. Buckley?" he said. "He's one of our vice presidents. He handles customer relations; maybe he can help you."

I seriously doubted it. Like many Americans during those depression years I harbored a deeply rooted suspicion of bankers, a distrust caused by the breakdown of the nation's banking system in the early thirties, when untold thousands of families lost their life savings in the collapse of banks across the country. Squirming impatiently on a hard bench as I waited to see Mr. Buckley, I recalled that Grandma White and Uncle Ed had also seen their meager savings wiped out. I had no reason to trust bankers, I told myself, wondering why I was wasting my time.

"Mr. Lowery?" A man's quiet voice intruded on my gloomy thoughts.

"That's right."

"I'm Jere Buckley. I understand you've got a problem." Somehow the friendly voice seemed incongruous in the austere precincts of a bank. "Let's go in my office and see what we can do about it."

The banker led me into a room off the lobby and helped me get settled in a soft leather chair in front of a desk. Seconds later a match flared briefly at the other side of the desk as Buckley lit a cigarette. "Okay, now tell me about it," he said.

The man at the other side of the desk wasn't conforming to my idea of an uncaring, nay-saying, banker. I told Buckley my tale of woe—from cashing the Vallee check to being fleeced to the mistaken endorsement to the economic disaster I was facing.

After listening patiently Jere Buckley finally observed, "It's too bad you didn't put the $300 in the bank."

"I've never had a bank account," I replied. "With my sight problem it's more convenient to keep my money where I can get to it easily when I need it without having to fill out checks and deposit and withdrawal slips. Besides . . . "

"Besides, what?" Buckley prompted.

"I guess I just don't trust banks," I blurted recklessly. "My folks and a lot of other people I know lost everything when the banks failed."

84

Buckley chuckled and said jokingly, "That's not a very diplomatic thing to say when you're asking a banker for help."

"I guess you're right, but that's how I feel."

"I understand," Buckley said. "But nowadays, with Roosevelt's new banking laws, our depositors are protected." Abruptly, Buckley changed the subject. "But I'm sure you aren't interested in banking laws. Let's see what we can do about this confounded traveler's check.

Buckley wasted no time in dispensing with that problem. He crossed out the offending endorsement, had me endorse the check properly, initialed the correction and handed me a ten and two fives.

Apparently he was intrigued by the way I handled the money, holding the bills close to my eye to determine the denomination, then carefully folding them and putting them in my wallet.

"It must be difficult keeping track of your money," the banker said after I tucked my wallet back in my jacket pocket.

I explained that like many legally blind people I possessed some vision, enough to make out the markings on a bill if I held it close to my eye. "Beyond that, I fold bills of different denominations in different ways and keep them in different parts of my wallet. That way I can find them by touch."

"It's amazing," Buckley said. "All the people around me handle large amounts of currency every day, and I never give much thought to it. But when I watched you put away your money, it suddenly occurred to me that such a simple thing can be a vastly complex problem if you've lost your sight."

"Mr. Buckley," I said, "you people try to shut us out of the everyday world. You think about us as helpless and useless if you think about us at all."

Jere Buckley was understandably shaken by my vehemence. "Mr. Lowery," he stammered, "I didn't mean to upset you. Really, I didn't mean to imply that I looked upon the blind as helpless human beings. . . ."

For some reason I had focused all my pent-up rage and frustration on the hapless banker. "You're like most people, Mr. Buckley. You look upon blindness as a physical problem. But it's not! The real problem is the attitude of the people around us. We can overcome our blindness. We can compensate for our loss of sight, just like you'd learn to compensate for the loss of a leg or an arm. But we just can't seem to overcome the prejudice of people who are determined to shut us out . . . people who try to bury us in pity . . . people who think we should be grateful for the few crumbs society tosses out to us . . ."

"Mr. Lowery . . . Fred . . . What can I say except that I'm terribly sorry I've offended you with my thoughtless prying. You have every right to be angry."

At that point my anger suddenly ebbed. "Mr. Buckley," I said, drained by my emotional outburst, "forgive me for blowing my stack. It wasn't your fault. It's just that I've had some bad problems lately. And all my life I've been beating my head against the same old wall, having people tell me I can't do what I want to do because I'm blind. Why can't people understand that the blind are just like everybody else?"

The bitter tirade with which I responded to Jere Buckley's concern should have infuriated him. But instead of ordering me out of his office Buckley invited me to join him for a midmorning coffee break at a nearby hole-in-the-wall cafe.

"You don't have to buy me coffee," I said in stubborn resistance. "You don't have to feel sorry for me."

It was Buckley's turn to be irked. "Fred," he exclaimed, "it's plain to see that you're a pigheaded Irishman. Who said anything about pity? Did you ever think that I might enjoy talking with you, that I might want to get to know you better?"

"I can't imagine why!"

"It happens that I have a number of friends in show business," Buckley replied in exasperation. "I'm also a big radio fan. That's how I happened to be tuned in on the Vallee show last Thursday and heard you whistle. So, you see, you weren't exactly a stranger when you came into my office today. You have talent, and I'd like to help you if I can."

So I ended up sipping coffee in a small Manhattan restaurant with banker Jere Buckley. I recounted my early years in the Piney Woods, my Blind School education, my beginnings in radio, and my struggle to survive since coming to New York. When I was finished, he asked me to return to his office the following day. "It seems to me that the first step is to solve your immediate financial difficulties," he said. "Let me give the problem some thought between now and tomorrow."

As I waited to see Jere Buckley the next day, it seemed that the bank had changed overnight from a cold, hostile fortress to a warm, friendly haven. And my new friend soon provided tangible proof that it actually had.

Buckley had a plan prepared for my financial rehabilitation, a plan that included not only a $300 loan to replace my stolen bankroll, but also a blueprint for establishing a more economical lifestyle until I could get my stalled career off the ground.

"For a fellow who's looking for work, you've been living much too extravagantly," Buckley said. "Staying in a hotel, eating out all the time,

86

barhopping, and partying. That sort of high living is okay if you can afford it, but it just doesn't make sense when you don't have a steady income."

"But how am I supposed to make contacts if I don't get around and meet people?"

"What good have your contacts done?" Buckley objected.

"Well," I said, "I did get on the Vallee show and a few other broadcasts."

"Sure. But you still don't have any stability."

"So what do you want me to do?" I asked.

Jere Buckley proceeded to itemize the ground rules for the new Fred Lowery. First, I was to deposit my $300 loan in an interest-bearing savings account and draw from it once a month for living expenses. Second, any money I earned would also be placed in the savings account, to replenish funds I had withdrawn. Third, he would help me set up a budget and teach me how to live by it. And finally, I should find a cheaper place to live—a small apartment with cooking facilities so that I wouldn't be wasting my money eating in restaurants.

"I'd prefer an apartment, but it isn't practical for me," I said.

"Why not?"

"Because, like it or not, I do have problems that require help. I can't cook. I can't read my mail or newspapers or magazines. I can't see who comes knocking at my door. I need people around me, and I can find that in a hotel."

"I didn't intend for you to live by yourself in an apartment," Buckley replied. "What you need is to share an apartment with another young man."

"And where am I going to find a place like that in Manhattan?" I countered. "Who wants a blind room-mate?"

Amazingly Jere Buckley had an answer for that, too. He knew a young bachelor, another recent arrival from Dallas, who was looking for someone to share his apartment in the West Seventies. By doubling up, the banker explained, I would cut my weekly rent from $12.25 to $3.50, a saving that would more than pay my share of food costs.

By the end of that week in March—a week that had started on a such a desperate note—I had a bank account, a budget, and a financial adviser. I also had a lively young room-mate with an impish sense of humor and a king-sized ambition to someday become publisher of the *New York Times*, a lighthearted companion who casually accepted my blindness as a fact of life that didn't have to interfere with our daily routine. His name was Irvin Taubkin. He was a native New Yorker who had ventured to Texas to serve his apprenticeship on the *Dallas News*. Although he had lived in Dallas for only a couple of years, Irvin had acquired a true Texan's thirst and a vast appetite that never seemed to add an ounce to his short, scrawny frame.

Irvin and I shared a parlor, bedroom, and sink in a large, crumbling brownstone on West Seventy-sixth Street. The apartment had what Irvin described as "very early" Victorian furniture, two narrow beds with lumpy mattresses, a communal bathroom in the hall, a tiny sink, a two-burner gas plate, and an ancient icebox that was serviced three times a week from late spring through autumn by a loud and profane iceman who made his rounds in a horse-drawn wagon. With the onset of winter, the noisy ice deliveries stopped, replaced by the banging, clanging, and hissing of steam radiators that managed to produce a minimum of heat with a maximum of sound.

At that time Irvin worked in the promotion department of the *Times*, a job from which he eventually rose to become promotion director (later he started his own public relations business in Manhattan). He seemed to have an inexhaustible supply of energy. He rattled around the city on endless explorations and delighted in joining heated public debates in taverns, in parks, or on street corners. In his spare time Irvin handled our shopping and did all our two-burner cooking, relegating me to the more menial chore of dishwashing.

Without making a big deal out of it, Irvin also seemed to find time to serve as my eyes whenever I had to make a complicated trip through the city. In fact he became the first "brother" I had ever known, setting himself up as my protector and confidant. He helped me write letters and read me my mail, the newspapers, and magazines. At the neighborhood tavern on Columbus Avenue we discussed philosophical and moral issues over many a stein of beer. And together we ventured often through New York—from Harlem to the Bronx, from Flatbush to Queens—on Irvin's impetuous adventuring.

Between Irvin and Jere Buckley, I soon found that my time was fully occupied. After putting my financial affairs in order, Buckley set out to light a fire under my career. "It seems to me your big problem now is to define clearly what you want to do, what your talents are best fitted for," Buckley said one evening when he dropped by our apartment.

"That's easy," I replied. "I want to be a performer. I want to make a name for myself in show business."

Buckley pounced on my reply. "Doing what?" he asked. "That's your problem. Ever since you arrived in New York you've been running around trying to break into show business. But as far as I can determine you've never really taken the time to think about the big question."

"What big question?"

"The question of just where your talent as a whistler can be used. And I'm not talking about one-shot appearances like the Vallee show. I'm talking about a full-time job as an entertainer, a steady, creative job that will build your reputation and put you back on your feet financially. Just where can a whistler hope to find that kind of a job? That's the big question!"

"Well," I said hesitantly, "I never thought about it that way. I guess I'm thinking about a full-time spot on a network show, sort of like the 'Early Birds,' only a lot bigger."

"That's wishful thinking," Jere Buckley said. "The big network shows use guest talent to fill in around the established stars that head their programs. They have different performers every week to give their shows variety."

"Well, what do you suggest?"

Buckley spent some time reflecting. "Did you ever consider trying for a job with one of the bands?" he finally asked.

"No. Not really."

"I feel it's worth thinking about," Buckley said. "Even in these hard times the bands are getting bigger and better all the time. Prohibition's ended, there are more and more cabarets and nightclubs and hotels hiring bands, and radio is using more and more music in its programming. And there are more and more record companies, too."

I had to admit that what Jere was saying made sense. The popularity of dance bands was undoubtedly mushrooming, and an increasing number of talented musicians like Benny Goodman were starting to form their own orchestras. But I pointed out one major problem. The dance bands hired instrumentalists, not whistlers.

"Don't be so sure about that," Buckley said. "I was in Pittsburgh a few months ago and heard a whistler with the Ted Weems band—a young fellow named Elmo Tanner. He didn't do any solo numbers, just whistled background. But he was good. It might be the start of a trend. The bands are always looking for something different."

"Well, it's worth considering," I agreed. "But I don't know anybody in the bands in New York. How am I going to get to know the right people? Who do I see?"

Buckley quickly pointed out that I was falling into the same old unproductive rut, wanting to devote my time and energy to making contacts. "Getting to know people in show business—the performers and the talent agents—isn't going to help you as much as you think," he said. "Show-business people aren't about to go out of their way to help unknown talent when they aren't even sure their own jobs are safe. You've got to have the support of a friend with real clout, someone who's important enough to influence the right people—like Vin Lindhe, only bigger. And I think I know just who that person is."

"Who is this miracle worker?" I asked.

But on this point Buckley was secretive. "Just be patient, Fred. Let's see what can be done."

A few days later he answered my phone call with terse instructions: "I'll pick you up in front of your apartment at 6:30. We're going to a party, so dress up."

"Where's the party?"

"I'll tell you when I see you." He hung up before I could ask any more questions.

When Buckley arrived at Seventy-sixth Street that evening Irvin Taubkin and I had been sitting on the front steps of the brownstone for at least half an hour, waiting anxiously for the fairy godfather's coach that would whisk me away to fame and fortune. When it finally arrived, though, it was a wheezing, rattling taxicab, and my banker friend was calling to me impatiently through a rolled-down window. "Hurry up, Fred. I got stuck at the bank on some last-minute business, and we're late for Clara Bell's party."

"Who's that?" I asked as Irvin hustled me into the cab. Before Buckley could reply, the cabbie's voice interrupted. "Where to now, mister? I ain't a mind reader!"

"To the Plaza," Buckley replied. "And make it fast!"

"Speed, speed, speed. Everybody's in a hurry," the cabbie grumbled. "Who am I—Barney Oldfield?"

I was too astounded by Buckley's pronouncement to pay much attention to the cabdriver. In all my wanderings around New York I had never ventured into the Plaza. Even in those depression days the Plaza was a different world. It was the queen of New York's high society hotels—a fabled hostelry for the very wealthy, the very distinguished, and the very powerful.

"What's at the Plaza?" I ventured timidly.

"That's where Clara Bell lives. We've been invited to her party tonight."

"And just who is Clara Bell?" I asked again.

"Clara Bell Walsh," Buckley replied, evidently assuming the name would mean something to me. "You know—the wealthy widow with the racing stable."

"Never heard of her," I confessed. "I've never paid much attention to horse racing."

My banker friend chuckled. "You're in for a surprise. Whatever happens tonight, one thing's for sure. Once you've met her you'll never forget Clara Bell Walsh!"

During the remainder of our taxi ride Buckley briefed me on the legend of the daughter of D. D. Bell, one of Kentucky's most famous horse breeders. The onetime southern belle had become one of the more memorable members of New York's social set after inheriting her father's fortune and his racing stable.

Buckley explained that Clara Bell Walsh was one of the celebrated "thirty-nine widows of the Plaza," the multimillionaire ladies who had retained their large town apartments at the hotel even after the more modern Waldorf-Astoria opened its doors in 1931. Clara Bell had lived in the same elegant seventh-floor suite since the day the Plaza opened for business on October 1, 1907, when she and her husband, industrialist Julius Walsh, were among the hotel's exclusive set of first-day tenants.

"Even after her husband died in the early twenties, Clara Bell continued to live at the Plaza," Buckley said. "She's lived in the hotel longer than any of the other original tenants, and she's famous for the parties she gives and the guests she attracts from all walks of life."

Minutes later we were welcomed at the door of Clara Bell Walsh's apartment and ushered into a foyer. I could hear voices, laughter, and the sound of someone playing "Kitten on the Keys" on a piano. Then above the noise a woman's voice boomed joyously, "Hey, friends, look who's finally made it. It's Jere Buckley!"

A tall, Junoesque figure burst into the foyer and grabbed my slender banker friend in a bear hug. "It's wonderful to see you, Jere," she roared delightedly. "I was afraid you weren't coming."

Even as Buckley was voicing his apology for our late arrival, our hostess turned her attention to me. She seized my hand in a hearty greeting and exclaimed, "You must be Fred—the boy that Jere's been raving about."

I later discovered that Clara Bell Walsh referred to all males under the age of thirty as boys, but at that first meeting I was completely taken aback. "Yes, ma'am, I reckon I'm Fred Lowery," I said, struggling to collect my wits. Never before had I encountered a female like Clara Bell Walsh. It was difficult to realize that this large, friendly woman was a wealthy widow who had moved in the rarefied circles of high society all her life. She possessed a common touch, a sincere enjoyment of living, that attracted people of all kinds. I quickly sensed that she was a person without pretense, a person who would be equally at home in the Piney Woods or at Buckingham Palace.

"Come on in and meet everybody," Clara Bell said, leading me into a huge living room where the guests were clustered around a massive grand piano.

"We're getting the piano warmed up," Clara Bell said. "John Charles Thomas is going to sing us a couple of songs."

I couldn't believe my ears. "John Charles Thomas—he's here? He's going to sing?" The famed baritone was an artist I had admired for years.

"Oh, yes," Clara Bell casually assured me, "John always sings whenever he drops in for one of my parties. He's a lovely, lovely man. I'll introduce you later on, after he's finished. And don't forget, we want to hear you whistle. We've heard so much about your talent from Jere."

After handing me a glass of champagne Clara Bell Walsh turned me over to Jere Buckley, instructing him to make sure I met the other guests. When she hurried off to tend to her duties as hostess I grabbed Jere by the arm. "You didn't tell me I'd have to whistle," I said indignantly. "I'm not prepared. I don't know what these people would want to hear."

"There's nothing to be nervous about," Buckley whispered. "It's just a party. I've been telling Clara Bell about your amazing memory for music. So show her what you can do. Whistle something classical. That's sure to impress everybody."

"How about a Chopin *Polonaise?* Is that highbrow enough?" I asked, recklessly naming one of the classics from my Blind School repertoire, a number I hadn't whistled in years.

"That will be splendid. I'll tell Clara Bell," Buckley replied, leading me into the crowd around the piano just as John Charles Thomas began to sing a medley of songs from Jerome Kern's *Show Boat.* It was an unforgettable experience hearing that magnificent voice in person. And it was an even more unforgettable moment when I was introduced to the great singer a short while later. He was one of about fifteen guests I met at that party. In the excitement of the evening I quickly forgot many of their names, but there were a few, like Thomas, that I couldn't possibly forget. Among them were Fanny Brice, the onetime Ziegfeld star and exwife of racketeer Nicky Arnstein; Jimmy Durante; Ed Wynn, the "Texaco fire chief"; sex symbol Mae West, who I later learned was a close friend of Clara Bell Walsh; and Ethel Merman, the singer who had become a Broadway star in George Gershwin's *Girl Crazy.*

As I recall, much of the conversation that evening was centered around the Plaza and the scheduled opening of the hotel's new Persian Room. The former Rose Room had been redone in an Arabian Nights motif by Joseph Urban, gifted designer of Flo Ziegfeld's fabulous sets.

Clara Bell Walsh and her guests seemed especially excited about plans for a glamorous cocktail dance that would commemorate the debut of the Persian Room—a soiree that, I gathered, promised to be the city's biggest social event since the twenties. They speculated on who would be coming to the opening, exchanged inside information on Urban's latest inspirations for the decor and expressed satisfaction that society favorite Emil Coleman and his orchestra had been engaged to provide music for the dance.

It was party chitchat to which I could contribute nothing. But for once I was content to remain silent, eavesdropping on the gossip and hoping desperately that our hostess would forget to ask me to whistle. To my dismay, Clara Bell Walsh eventually got back to me and made it clear that she hadn't forgotten. "Jere tells me you're planning to whistle Chopin," she said.

"Perhaps you'd rather hear something lighter . . . a couple of popular numbers," I suggested hopefully.

"Oh, no; we're thrilled by your choice," Clara Bell enthused as she led me to the piano and the young lady who had volunteered to accompany me.

So I whistled Chopin for a party of celebrities on my first visit to the Plaza. There was never a more reluctant whistler, but fortunately for my society debut I still remembered the complex *Polonaise* score from the long hours of listening to my windup Victrola, and I managed to get through without mishap. For a special flourish I rang down the curtain on my performance by whistling a dreamy Chopin nocturne.

The applause and the kind congratulatory remarks from such a distinguished audience were gratifying, but the biggest honor of the evening came when Clara Bell informed me that John Charles Thomas wanted to whistle a duet with me.

"Mr. Thomas wants to whistle a duet!" I exclaimed.

"That's right," Clara Bell said. "He'd like to whistle 'Home on the Range' with you. It's his favorite song."

"Good grief, I can't do that!"

"Don't be a silly boy!" Clara Bell said. And, ignoring my protests, she marched me over to the piano where Thomas was waiting. "Fred says he'll be honored to whistle with you," she said.

"I'm afraid I'm not in your class as a whistler," Thomas confessed. "But I love to whistle."

His down-to-earth attitude put me at ease. And Thomas proved to be a fine whistler, although he cluttered his music with bird trills and chirps. When we finished we did an encore—"Red River Valley," another cowboy ballad favored by the famous singer, who admitted a bit sheepishly that he was addicted to country music.

Warmed by a new round of congratulations, I was starting in on another glass of champagne when Jere Buckley nudged me. "I think it's about time for us to be going, Fred," he said.

"So soon?" I said. "I'm just getting in the partying mood."

Buckley laughed. "I think you're just a frustrated playboy. But this isn't the time or the place to become the life of the party," he added more seriously. "Your whistling has been a big hit, and after that duet with Thomas anything will be an anticlimax. It's time to go home while you're still on top."

I heeded my friend's advice. After all, this was his ball park and he knew the rules. Reluctantly abandoning my champagne I said my thank-yous and good-byes. In return, Clara Bell Walsh surprised me with a traditional show-business kiss on the cheek and whispered in my ear, "I'm so glad you were able to come. And don't you fret, boy. You'll be hearing from me!"

In the taxi on our way back to the brownstone I told Jere Buckley what Clara Bell had said. "What on earth was she talking about?" I asked in honest puzzlement.

"You've just taken a big step forward, Fred," Buckley replied. "That was Clara Bell's way of letting you know that she likes you, that she's impressed with your talent, and that she's going to help promote it."

Jere Buckley was never more correct. Clara Bell Walsh wasn't just making polite conversation. Soon after that party at the Plaza she began to influence my career. She was a wonderful, big-hearted woman who became and remained my true and wise friend for the rest of her life.

Chapter 9

Spring came, and I was still jobless. I had sincerely believed that an appearance on the Rudy Vallee show would be a guarantee of instant success. I soon learned that Vallee's fame didn't rub off. After the first flurry of publicity and congratulations no one had beaten a path to my door.

The only tangible result of my performance on the Vallee show was the renewed interest of "Air Breaks," an NBC talent show. After hearing my network broadcast, the producer arranged several spots for me, including one novelty act in which I had to provide bird-chirping sound effects for a trio as they sang a couple of melodies about a mockingbird and a red, red robin that came bob-bob-bobbin' along. I hated it, but I needed the ten-dollar fee and the illusion that I was part of the show-business scene in the big city.

I continued to receive commonsense guidance from Jere Buckley. And Buckley's wife Doris all but adopted me, providing a motherly warmth and concern that I treasured. My friendships with the Buckleys and Irvin Taubkin had come along at a critical time, for Vin Lindhe had embarked on an extended orchestra tour in Europe.

I hadn't heard from Clara Bell Walsh since the party in her Plaza suite. But whenever I began fretting Buckley would assure me that the onetime Kentucky belle never forgot a promise. As usual, he was right.

This time opportunity didn't come knocking at my door; it used the telephone. My room-mate was impatiently awaiting a call from his newest girl friend one morning when our communal pay phone rang. Irvin dashed into the hall to answer. A minute later he slammed back into our apartment. "It's for you, Fred. Some doll's on the line," he announced in the Damon Runyon vernacular to which he was addicted at the time.

The doll on the line was Clara Bell Walsh. She didn't waste time with casual chitchat; she simply told me to meet her in the lobby of the St. Regis at two that afternoon. Then she hung up without bothering to tell me why I should meet her. She hadn't even asked if I could make it. As I later learned, to my frequent frustration, that was the way Clara Bell Walsh was. She took it for granted that people could always find time to respond to her impulsive summonses, and she was rarely disappointed.

On that particular morning, however, I was not yet attuned to Clara Bell's idiosyncrasies, and her terse instructions left me bewildered. A quick phone call to Jere Buckley didn't help. He said he had no idea what Clara Bell was up to, but he emphasized that it was a summons I couldn't ignore. "You can be sure it's something important," Jere said. "Clara Bell wouldn't go to the trouble of meeting you at the St. Regis just to pass the time of day."

I knew very little about the St. Regis except that it was one of New York's finer hotels. I wasn't even sure where it was located. But that afternoon Irvin escorted me on a quick ride on the elevated, led me to Fifth Avenue and Fifty-fifth and got me settled on a leather lounge in the hotel lobby before he scurried off to his job at the *Times*.

As usual, I was early. And, as usual, I found that impatient solitude was often the unjust reward for punctuality. Clara Bell wasn't just a little late that afternoon. Long after two o'clock she still hadn't made an appearance. I sat in the St. Regis lobby for what seemed an eternity, surrounded by the subdued comings and goings of that era's "beautiful people." Finally I decided that I had been stood up. But just as I began contemplating the mechanics of finding my way back to West Seventy-sixth Street from an unfamiliar neighborhood a human tornado whirled into the quiet lobby and touched down beside me with a gusty sigh.

"Lordy, the traffic in this town's getting worse all the time." Clara Bell was panting as she grabbed me in a quick hug. "Thought I was never going to get here. Mary Pickford's in town. We had lunch down in the Village, and it seemed like I'd never get back uptown. Hope I haven't kept you waiting long, dear boy."

Before I could find an opening to reply, she tugged me to my feet and convoyed me at a brisk gallop into the nearest elevator. "The Roof!" she snapped to the elevator operator.

As the elevator began its slow climb Clara Bell clutched my arm in an iron grip as if she feared that I might somehow stray out of the creeping conveyance. "I do hope that Vincent won't be furious," she said. "He's such a stickler about being on time." Returning her attention to the elevator operator she demanded, "Can't this contraption go any faster?" When he assured her that was out of the question she snorted with unladylike disgust. "Everything in this town goes fast except taxicabs and elevators!"

At last I was able to find an opening in Clara Bell's monologue. "Who's Vincent?"

"Good heavens!" Clara Bell exclaimed, "I forgot to tell you. You've got an appointment to audition with Vincent Lopez!"

"Vincent Lopez, the orchestra leader?"

"That's right, dear boy. Vincent is an old, old friend. I've told him about your marvelous talent, and he's arranged to audition you at today's rehearsal."

"This is terrible!" I protested. "Why didn't you let me know ahead of time so I could get ready?"

Clara Bell's robust chuckle filled the small elevator. "Freddie, boy, please do forgive me. It's just that I dearly love to surprise my friends!"

As soon as the elevator jerked to a stop after its long climb to the Roof, she hustled me to a plushly carpeted foyer lighted by glittering crystal chandeliers that dazzled even my faint vision. From somewhere near us music surged in a rising crescendo. Entranced, I stopped in the middle of the foyer, resisting Clara Bell's insistent tugging at my arm. "My gosh," I half-whispered, not wanting to shatter the mood, "that's Vincent Lopez. It's got to be Lopez at the piano!"

"Oh, are you familiar with Vincent's music?" Clara Bell seemed surprised that I could identify an unseen pianist.

"Every musician in the world knows the Lopez sound—especially when he's playing 'Nola.' "

"Well, let's not stand here mooning. Let's go and meet the great Lopez in person!" Clara Bell resumed the march into the hotel's famed supper club–ballroom, towing me in her wake.

As we pushed through the leather-covered doors, the music was punctuated by an irritable crashing of the ivories. "Aren't you ever on time, Clara Bell?" a high-pitched masculine voice wanted to know. A short, pudgy figure approached us.

"I just knew you'd be furious, Vincent." For a change Clara Bell's voice was humble in apology. "I'm truly, truly sorry, but don't blame Freddie. He's been waiting for me in the lobby for hours and hours. It's all my fault." And before the maestro could reply, Clara Bell introduced me.

Vincent Lopez acknowledged the introduction with a quick handshake. Then he popped a question that almost floored me.

"What month were you born?"

"November," I managed to reply.

"When in November?" Lopez seemed impatient with my slow-wittedness. "What year? . . . What day? . . . What hour?"

I was flabbergasted. "Well, the year was 1909, and the day was

97

November 2," I explained, trying to humor the great man.

"What about the day and the hour? Was it a Monday, a Tuesday? Was it in the morning or at night?"

"Mr. Lopez," I replied, "I just don't know. I was kind of young at the time!"

Ignoring my flippant response, Lopez apparently decided to accept the fact that I had no further details to offer and noted regretfully that I was obviously not a believer in the stars.

For a frightening moment I was convinced that Lopez hired only true believers in astrology, a faith far removed from my Southern Baptist upbringing. "I'm afraid I don't know much about it," I managed to explain.

Lopez sighed. "Well, at least you're a Scorpio. That's something in your favor. I think we'll be in harmony."

I later learned that Vincent Lopez was a fervent follower of the mystic dictates of numerology and astrology and consulted the stars and charts each day, seeking guidance. Once he had determined my basic astrological roots, he quickly got down to business. "Clara Bell tells me you're a talented whistler. Let's see what you can do."

With no further preliminaries Lopez led me to his piano at one side of the bandstand and introduced me to the band. "This is Fred Lowery, the whistler I was telling you about—the guy that's kept us waiting for so long." A derisive, off-key fanfare blared briefly from the trumpet section as Lopez adjusted the microphone for me. The satirical fanfare had scarcely faded when a couple of sidemen contributed an outburst of raucous off-key whistling.

Lopez ignored his noisy musicians, waiting patiently for the hilarity to subside. "Okay, Fred," he said finally, "do you have any special number in mind?"

"How about 'The World is Waiting for the Sunrise'?" I suggested, falling back on my lucky song.

"Why not? Let's give it a whirl." Lopez announced my selection to the band. "Don't be nervous. Just relax and follow us," he instructed as he sat down at the piano and rippled the keys with his nimble fingers. Before I had time to think, the orchestra was playing. And I began to whistle.

"In the groove, man!" somebody in the band hollered as I finished the number. Lopez seemed to agree. "Sounded good from here, Fred. Now let's hear it from out on the floor." The bandleader summoned another musician to take over the piano, introduced him as Lou Bring, and hopped off the bandstand. "Okay, let's try it again," he called from somewhere in the distance. Once again the music started; this time I was feeling a lot more confident.

"Sounds just as good out there in customer land," Lopez said when he returned to the bandstand. With no further auditioning or conversation, he asked me, "Would you like to join our group?"

"I sure would, Mr. Lopez," I said, trying to believe that I had landed a job with a famous band. "I sure would."

"Okay, you're hired. But on one condition."

"What's that?"

"That you stop calling me Mr. Lopez. It makes me feel too damned old!"

When I joined the Lopez organization in 1934, Lopez was already one of the landmark names in popular music. The Brooklyn-born son of a music teacher, Lopez had pioneered dance music on radio, had played the first popular music heard in Carnegie Hall, had helped make the first "sound" movie, and had led the way in demonstrating the dramatic potential of radio promotion that eventually resulted in the big broadcasts.

Although Lopez had formed his first dance band in 1917 it wasn't until 1921, when he moved from the obscurity of the Pekin Restaurant on Broadway to the swank Grill Room of the Pennsylvania Hotel, that his fame as an orchestra leader began to grow. On the night of November 27, 1921, his band made the first remote broadcast of live dance music. That historic ninety-minute program was sent by telephone wire from the Grill Room to the broadcasting facilities of station WJZ in Newark, thirty miles to the west. During that broadcast Lopez urged the audience to let him know how they liked his music, and he offered a free autographed picture of himself to everyone who responded. This first known radio promotion generated a flood of replies that quickly exhausted the supply of photographs; the success of the broadcast catapulted the Lopez orchestra to fame. He played in London's Hippodrome and when he returned to America his orchestra became a regular feature of early radio in New York. It was during these years that the opening words of his broadcasts—"Hello, everybody. Lopez speaking"—became his trademark.

On the evening of November 15, 1926, Lopez participated in another historic broadcast. Playing for some 2,000 guests in the Grand Ballroom of the old Waldorf-Astoria, the Lopez orchestra provided the music for the first network broadcast by the newly formed NBC.

In 1922, between those landmark broadcasts, Vincent Lopez and his orchestra teamed with Eddie Cantor, George Jessel, and the vaudeville

99

team of Weber and Fields to produce the first experimental "singing" movie for Dr. Lee de Forest, who in later years became the "father" of television. And in 1925 Lopez was invited to conduct the first jazz concert at the Met— a controversial event that rocked Manhattan's culture buffs.

Of course, it took me several months to learn from some of the old-timers the legends that lay behind Lopez and his music. On that first day I was much too busy and too excited to be concerned with past glories. After quickly accepting Lopez's offer of a $50-per-week starting salary, I went with Clara Bell Walsh to a nearby tailor to get fitted with a rented tuxedo for that evening's show. That errand completed, Clara Bell rushed me back to the hotel for a meeting with the band's arranger, a gifted trombonist named Glenn Miller.

Glenn Miller is a legend now, his fame as one of the giants of the big band era enduring long after his tragic death during World War II. But when I sat down with him at the piano in the St. Regis before that evening's show to work up a couple of quick numbers for my debut with the band, Miller was an obscure musician, a onetime sideman with the Ben Pollack band. He was quiet and soft-spoken, deeply dedicated to producing the perfect tone, the perfect mood, the perfect tempo. I'm sure a less talented arranger would have given as little time as possible to the task of collaborating with a mere whistler. But Miller seemed fascinated by a new sound and spent many hours helping me create a whistling repertoire and style adapted to the distinctive Lopez style.

In the beginning Lopez wasn't exactly sure how to utilize my special talent. Dance orchestras rarely included whistling in their arrangements. When used at all, it was usually restricted to a few bars of background. In an organization loaded with talented instrumentalists and singers, I wondered where I would fit in. Before the start of rehearsal on my second day I asked Lopez what he had in mind.

"I don't know just how it will work," Lopez told me, "but I've got a feeling that whistling could be a big thing." He explained how it had occurred to him that whistling was something everybody could do, something everybody could relate to. "When they hear someone like you make beautiful music, they're going to compare their whistling with your whistling. And they're going to marvel at how you sound so great and they sound so lousy. They're going to love every note, because it's the music of the common man."

During my first night on the bandstand—and for the next few weeks—I performed only during intermissions, whistling Miller's initial arrangements with a piano accompanist. The routine never varied. As the band left the stand the lights were dimmed and Adam Carroll, our intermission pianist, led me from a seat at the rear of the bandstand to a microphone beside a piano that had been pushed to the center of the dance floor. By the time the spotlight zeroed in on us we were ready for the show to begin. I didn't leave the mike until the lights were dimmed again at the end of the intermission.

"I don't want to make a big thing out of your blindness," Lopez explained. "If I have somebody lead you to the floor mike while the lights are on, people will say I'm using you to build myself up as a do-gooder who's giving a blind man a job. And I don't ever want that to happen. I'm hiring you because you have talent, and I think that talent can become a big asset for my orchestra. That's the *only* reason I'm hiring you." Lopez broke off his lecture with a chuckle. "Plus, of course, you had the good sense to be born a Scorpio!"

Never once during the four years of our association did Vincent Lopez mention my blindness in public, nor did he in any other way try to capitalize on my handicap. In the beginning he told me bluntly that I would be expected to carry my share of the load, that I should never expect any special treatment. In setting these standards he gave me a priceless gift of dignity for which I will be eternally grateful. Vincent Lopez had his faults. He was vain, stubborn, and in many respects a tyrant on the bandstand. But he wasn't a bigot, a hypocrite, or a phony. For me, his virtues more than made up for his shortcomings.

Camouflaging my blindness during the intermission performance was no great problem. But when Glenn Miller finally completed his tedious arranging task and announced that I was ready to start working with the full orchestra, the problem was more complex. Miller's revised arrangements made me a working member of the dance group. I whistled at least one chorus of each number, provided special musical flourishes from time to time, and presented three solos each evening. My new status as a whistling sideman—a promotion that boosted my pay to $75 per week—required my full-time presence on the bandstand. I was assigned a front-row seat at one edge of the stand, and Lopez installed a microphone with an off-and-on control button beside my chair. I had only to stand, flip the "on" switch, whistle my tune, flip the "off" switch, and sit down again.

Lopez didn't attempt to keep my blindness a secret. That would have been impossible, because as my reputation as a featured artist grew there was a continuing flow of publicity. But from the first note of a performance to the last I was just another musician on the bandstand, with nothing but dark glasses hinting at any difference.

The Lopez style of music was particularly well suited to my talents. It was strictly popular dance music emphasizing sweet sounds and melodies, mood music, waltzes, and occasional Latin rhythms. It was the music that had made him a successful big-time New York dance orchestra leader with a popular weekly network radio show. While the new sounds of swing were beginning to capture the public ear at that time, Lopez was content to let others experiment while he stuck with his own proven formula.

I recall one afternoon before the start of rehearsal at the St. Regis when Glenn Miller showed Lopez a newspaper review filled with lavish praise of the "excitingly different" sound of the newly formed Benny Goodman band at Billy Rose's Music Hall—a sound that, according to the critic, had "the whole town jumpin'."

"No question, Benny's a fantastic talent," Lopez said. "It's great music. But I learned a long time ago that to make it in this business you've got to play music the public likes, not music that the critics and other musicians like."

For a whistler, Lopez's dance music was far more suitable than the upbeat swing arrangements. His emphasis on waltzes and mood numbers gave me opportunities that didn't exist with the more frenetic music of the swing bands. And the strict discipline of the Lopez orchestra provided me with priceless basic training for a lifetime career as an entertainer.

The hours of rehearsing and performing were long and arduous. As a leader Lopez was a tyrant, particularly during performances. He was constantly at war with Larry Tice, our lead saxophonist, over a union rule that required at least a ten-minute break after every thirty-minute session on the bandstand. Lopez, apparently endowed with a cast-iron bladder, was always reluctant to stop the music. Frequently he would try to stretch the time between breaks to more than an hour. On the other hand, he favored a twenty-minute intermission.

These marathon sessions were often enlivened by the spectacle of sidemen putting aside their instruments and rushing off the bandstand to the nearest rest room in the middle of a number. Finally, Lopez's defiance of the thirty-minute rule became so flagrant that Tice reported the matter to the union, touching off a bitter dispute which our tireless leader ultimately lost. Lopez didn't accept his defeat graciously. He refused to talk to Tice for months and continued to fudge on the union rule whenever he thought he could get away with it.

Despite the rigorous regimen there were few dull moments in the Lopez orchestra. Though the music was sweet, the life-style of the men and women in the orchestra was far from serene. At no time during my years with Lopez was the group what you'd call a "happy family." It was an organization honeycombed with cliques and split into two camps—those who smoked the "weed," as we called marijuana in those days, and those who preferred liquor. There were a few married men with families, but a large contingent of young bachelors dedicated to tireless pursuit of the fair sex. Lopez himself was a confirmed misogamist whose distaste for marriage was, according to legend, the result of an early and disastrous venture into matrimony. His distrust of marriage wasn't limited to his own life. He extended it to all members of his orchestra except a few of his veteran sidemen, like drummer Johnny Morris, who had been married long before they joined his organization. He tolerated and even occasionally joined in the romancing of the fun-loving females who clustered around our band, but when it came to wedded bliss Lopez tried to discourage everyone from indulging. He was particularly opposed to marriages within the orchestra, believing that while such unions might be forged in heaven they could only lead to hellish complications on the bandstand.

Once in my memory Lopez relaxed this ban. In a weak moment he gave his blessing to the union of our top trumpet player Ernie Mathias, and pretty vocalist Lois Still shortly before we embarked on a long tour.

A few weeks later Lopez's fears were justified. During an evening's dance session an inebriated customer pinched Lois while she was crooning a love song into the mike. Lois shrieked. Alerted by his bride's cry of distress, Mathias leaped from the bandstand and battered the pincher over the head with his trumpet. By the time order was restored, the offending customer was en route to the hospital with bumps and lacerations and Mathias was lodged in the town jail with his battle-dented trumpet impounded as evidence.

Lopez bailed Mathias out of that assault-and-battery rap, but he warned the couple he would tolerate no further outbreaks of violence on the bandstand no matter how serious the provocation. In an organization in which no secrets survived for more than a day or so, details of Lopez's angry confrontation with Ernie and Lois quickly filtered back to the members, giving us first-rate conversational material as our musical caravan continued its tour.

According to reports, Mathias had agreed to hold his temper in check when Lois encountered the inevitable dance-floor Romeos. And his resolve to behave lasted almost a month. Then, during a one-night gig in the Midwest farm belt, the scenario was repeated: a pinch, a shriek, and an enraged roar as Mathias charged from the bandstand brandishing his trusty trumpet. Again Lopez had to bail out his trigger-tempered trumpeter. Again he reluctantly forgave the newlyweds, for pretty vocalists and talented trumpet players were hard to find. But after several more incidents, Lopez sacked the volatile lovebirds. His nerves and his pocketbook just couldn't stand the strain. After Ernie and Lois had departed he pointed out to us that this experience proved he was right in all his warnings about the perils of matrimony.

With our newlyweds finally offstage, life on the bandstand should have quieted down. But serenity was not one of the characteristics of the Lopez organization. There was always some sort of fussing and feuding going on.

Since his early years in the business, Lopez had always featured a Latin dance team. Like "Nola," it was one of his trademarks. These dancers invariably thrived on conflict, fighting with each other, with Lopez and his sidemen, or with anyone else unfortunate enough to encounter them during rehearsals or performances.

During the stormy Ernie and Lois interlude—and after—our dance team was Florence and Alvarez, a pair of talented hoofers whose precision teamwork on the dance floor was equaled only by their intense mutual hatred. They were not married, although the violence of their battling at times suggested that they were.

It didn't take much to set Florence and Alvarez off. A missed step, a bruised toe, a wrong tempo could ignite a knock-down, drag-out dressing-room battle after the act was completed—a battle that frequently disrupted the orchestra's music-making. It was rather difficult to "wrap your troubles in dreams and dream your troubles away" with shouts, screams, and obscenities reverberating from backstage.

Florence and Alvarez, however, were tame compared to the most unlovable of all the Lopez dance teams. This pair of prime battlers joined the band after Florence and Alvarez whirled away into the sunset at the close of one of our tours. They quickly demonstrated that when it came to fighting they were in a class by themselves.

She was a petite, curvaceous brunette with a king-sized temper that could explode in a vocabulary of truly remarkable vulgarity, followed by a deadly barrage of kicking, scratching, and biting. He was a large, handsome Latin type. He was also graceful, temperamental, gay, and madly infatuated with trombonist Mike Durso. Mike, the band's premier ladies' man, spent a goodly portion of his working hours dodging the Latin dancer's advances. These rejections only served to worsen the dancer's already sour disposition.

Unlike Florence and Alvarez, who confined their battles to the dressing room, this pair frequently carried their violence into the public sector. I recall one incident at the Piping Rock Casino in Saratoga Springs, New York, when he missed his timing on a complicated dance routine and she crashed to the floor. Instead of resuming the performance with as much dignity as

104

possible, the fiery-tempered dancer leaped to her feet and chased her partner off the stage, firing a broadside of curses at his fleeing heels.

Striving to cover up the embarrassing disruption, Lopez called for me to whistle. As I stood and flicked on my microphone the band hurriedly began to play "Indian Love Call," which had been scheduled as my next solo number. I might as well have tried to whistle at the Battle of the Little Big Horn. The guffaws from the audience, combined with the sounds of battle from backstage, quickly drowned my efforts.

Lopez stopped the music in disgust and ordered little Bobby Lytle, our featured male vocalist, to put a stop to the dressing-room warfare. As the scene was described to me later, the dance partners emerged from backstage holding our squirming singer between them, and tossed him into the audience, scattering tables, chairs, and customers like tenpins. Then they returned to their dressing room to resume hostilities.

In Manhattan, Los Angeles, Chicago, or other American cities, such antics might have generated shocked headlines. But Saratoga Springs in those days was a swinging resort dedicated to horse racing and other forms of gambling, a plush oasis where celebrities gathered to let their hair down. The temperamental explosions of entertainers such as our brawling dance team were viewed with amused tolerance as part of the Bohemian charm.

On another evening at the Piping Rock Bobby Lytle rushed up to me during one of our breaks with the news that his idol, Bing Crosby, was in the crowd. "I saw him out on the floor dancing with a gorgeous redhead." Bobby's breathless excitement took on a wistful note. "Gosh, I'd sure like to meet him!"

Bobby Lytle was several years younger than I, and somehow he seemed like a kid brother, constantly in need of guidance as he bumbled through life. He had a strange way of alternating between pugnacious self-confidence and a naive, wide-eyed worship of celebrities.

I usually had little patience with Bobby's hero-worshiping. After all, he was a celebrity in his own right, an established vocalist in one of the nation's top dance orchestras. But I had to admit that Bing Crosby was somebody worth getting excited about; by the mid-thirties the onetime crooner from Paul Whiteman's band was fast becoming a legend.

"Well, it shouldn't be too hard to meet him," I assured Bobby. "Just walk up and say howdy."

"I couldn't do that!"

"Why not? I hear he's a real friendly guy. Besides, he's a musician, a singer. He got his start in the bands, so I'm sure he won't tell you to get lost."

Bobby sighed. "I know you're probably right. But somehow I just can't get up the nerve. Besides, I don't have time to go looking for him in this crowd."

"No use getting all shook up about it," I said as we headed back toward the bandstand. "Maybe he'll drop by and say hello while he's out on the floor."

My words were prophetic. Later that evening, while the orchestra was busy with one of Lopez's favorite waltzes, "It's a Sin to Tell a Lie," the dreamy mood was shattered by a sudden commotion. It started with a burst of laughter out on the crowded floor, a mirthful outburst that intensified as a man's voice began to chant an old square-dance caller's refrain, "Swing your partner round and round . . ."

The voice was drowned by a renewed tide of laughter, and the music faded. "My God, look at Crosby. He's really flying!" Johnny Morris's startled exclamation echoed from the drum section. I strained to focus on whatever was going on out on the floor, but the lights were far too dim and the action too far away. It wasn't until later that I got a play-by-play account of that evening's unexpected performance.

Bing Crosby had whirled onto the floor dancing with a chair. The startled dancers moved aside, and before long Bing and his chair had the floor to themselves, cheered on by the enthusiastic crowd. When Lopez saw what was going on, he called for the orchestra to swing into "The Band Played On." This lively refrain apparently spurred Crosby to greater exertions, for Bing began to whirl his "lady" in widening circles that crept closer and closer to the bandstand. From my seat I could hear the cadence of dancing feet and a familiar crooning, "Casey would dance with the Strawberry Blonde, and the band played on. . . ."

The voice seemed closer, louder—and then a shadowy form spun into range. It loomed larger and larger and suddenly crashed into the end of the bandstand where I was seated. A split second later, bruised and dazed, I found myself on the floor in a tangle of arms and legs and chairs.

"I say, ol' buddy, I'm awfully sorry. Are you all right?" The voice close to my ear was slurred and richly scented with prime spirits.

Groggily I grabbed somebody's arm and tried to zero in on the human projectile that had ended up in my lap. It was The Groaner—Bing Crosby in person.

"Hey, man, are you all right? You're not hurt, are you?" Crosby's voice, suddenly sober, was heavy with concern.

Slowly I pushed myself to my feet, aided by Crosby and several of the orchestra members who had hurried to my side. I checked my arms and legs, my fingers and toes. "Everything seems to be in working order," I croaked as I examined my head and face. Slowly my fingers moved upward and encountered an emptiness. My dark glasses were missing—and so was my artificial eye!

"Don't anybody move!" I yelled.

"What's wrong?" Bobby Lytle put a sheltering arm around my shoulders. "Do you feel faint?"

"No!" I roared in alarm. "But I've lost my eye. It's someplace on the floor!"

"You lost your *what?*" Crosby's voice was tinged with dismay.

"My eye, dammit! Somebody's gonna step on it!"

Lopez had joined the milling throng and quickly set the record straight, explaining to Crosby that I was blind and that the collision had apparently dislodged my artificial eye. "We've got to try to find it before it gets stepped on," he said.

Suddenly Crosby, Lopez, and several other orchestra members and customers were on their hands and knees cautiously scouring the floor in search of my missing eye. My glasses turned up mangled beyond repair, but my artificial eye—manufactured from glass in those days—was ultimately retrieved miraculously undamaged.

When the furor finally subsided Crosby again apologized, ruefully explaining how he had been seized by a sudden inspiration to demonstrate his dancing artistry when his date declined his invitation to join him. "It was a stupid stunt," he said. "I'm sure glad you weren't hurt. Anything I can do for you, let me know."

At that moment I remembered our hero-worshiping vocalist. "Come to think of it, Bing, there's one favor I'd sure enough appreciate."

"You name it!"

I called for Bobby Lytle, and when our pint-size singer joined us I cashed in on Crosby's offer, introducing the Lopez vocalist to the former Whiteman vocalist.

Crosby chuckled as he shook hands with Lytle. "You mean to say this is the favor you want? How come you didn't just walk up and say hello?" he asked Bobby.

"Guess I was scared," Lytle replied. "Anyway, Fred said you might drop by the bandstand during the evening!"

Chapter 10

My job with the Lopez orchestra took me into a world peopled by a wide assortment of characters from show business, high society, journalism, and sports. For me it was a dizzying transition. One moment I was part of the nation's army of jobless. The next, I was in an unreal, glittering world I had never imagined.

My $50-a-week starting pay—and my subsequent raise to $75—was a handsome salary for a young bachelor with no responsibilities. And I soon discovered several significant fringe benefits, such as outside "moon-lighting" jobs, song-plugging, and recording. Best of all—or maybe worst of all—the fame and glamor that attended membership in a major dance orchestra created opportunities for seemingly endless rounds of merry-making, with party girls, free liquor, and free food. Being only human, I did my best to make up for lost time.

By the time the summer of 1934 began to scorch Manhattan I had become a full-fledged man-about-town. My Texas wardrobe had been replaced by a derby, Ivy League suits, spats, and a gold-knobbed cane. I used the cane not as an aid in getting about but to provide the ultimate mark of distinction for my new playboy image.

The new Fred Lowery quickly cultivated a taste for fine wining and dining and an appreciation of the quality bonded boozes. I even became a steady customer at the St. Regis florist shop, brightening my already gaudy wardrobe with boutonnieres and pampering my dates with corsages and, occasionally, bouquets of roses. Thank heaven, Gracie Johnston—and a lot of my other friends and relatives—didn't witness that transformation into a mindless hedonist and a pretentious boob. Looking back on my first year with Lopez, I realize it was only the sensible influence of drummer Johnny Morris that kept me from making a complete fool out of myself.

For some reason Johnny liked me despite my ridiculous airs. He patiently briefed me on the dos and don'ts of life in the Lopez organization. He instructed me in the finer points of dance music. He also introduced me to the special haunts of Manhattan's musicians and diverted me from some foolish indiscretions.

In those days each of the bands had retinues of loyal fans. For Vincent Lopez it was Clara Bell Walsh and her sizable flock of friends and freeloaders. The dowager of the Plaza had been a close friend of Lopez since the early twenties and, it was said, had been instrumental in his cafe society success. She had even helped bankroll the Casa Lopez, his midtown cabaret, during the Prohibition years.

When I joined Lopez many of the orchestra's engagements in Manhattan were still due to Clara Bell's influence. She knew the right people—the people who controlled the bookings at the city's swank hotels. She kept Lopez afloat in the social swim by arranging appearances at important charitable and social affairs. And at least once a week she brought a bevy of guests to the St. Regis Roof to dine and dance to our music.

These occasions often culminated in a night on the town after the show ended, when Lopez and a few of Clara Bell's favorite musicians would join the party for late supper and gossip at the 21 Club or one of her other favorites.

The "smart set"—the cast of Clara Bell Walsh's world—was an exotic mixture of the wealthy, the famous, and the just plain interesting. It was a crowd that included politicians, sports heroes, show girls, and stars of the stage, screen, and radio, as well as sons and daughters of high society, gossip columnists, and a scattering of well-heeled businessmen who somehow had survived and prospered in the midst of hard times.

You never knew who you might meet at any gathering of Clara Bell's friends. I remember one night after I had been with Lopez for a year or so Clara Bell announced that she thought a tour of Greenwich Village bistros would be fun. We all seconded her recommendation with high enthusiasm. As we hurried down from the Roof it became obvious there would be a problem moving our large group from uptown to downtown. Clara Bell summoned two cabs, and we all piled in.

I had just sat down when a last-minute partygoer pushed into the taxi and settled on my lap for the ride to the Village. Judging by her weight, my lapmate was petite, but she was also girlishly plump in the right places.

"Golly, I hope I'm not crushing you." Her soft voice caressed my ear and a spray of scented hair tickled my nose.

"The pleasure's all mine. My lap's always available for lovely ladies," I replied, silently cursing the defective vision that blacked out this enchanting creature.

Her laugh, like her voice, was soft and musical. "You're not only gallant, you're cute." She changed position, adjusting her precarious perch in a maneuver I found devilishly diverting.

"What's your name?"

"Fred . . . Fred Lowery," I said.

"Oh, you're Clara Bell's friend, the whistler. Such lovely, lovely music." A pause, another change of position, and then the bombshell. "I'm Mary Pickford!"

"Who?"

"Mary Pickford. But don't worry. I promise I won't bite you!"

Again the beautiful laughter as I sought desperately to find something smart and sophisticated to say. But all I could think of was that the world's most famous movie star was sitting on my lap.

"I can't believe it. I just can't believe it!" My man-about-town front crumbled.

"What can't you believe?"

"I can't believe this is really happening. I've got to be dreaming!"

"Oh, pooh! Don't be silly!" she said. Then after a second she added, "Listen, Fred, tonight, I want to have a good time. For a few hours I want to forget who I am. Just pretend I'm the girl next door and we're out on a date. Is it a deal?"

"I'll try," I answered. "But it sure isn't going to be easy pretending you're just another girl!"

Mary Pickford, who was then a vastly wealthy celebrity of forty-two, was sensitive about her age. I suspect she always looked upon her eternal–teen-ager screen image as the real Mary Pickford. She purposely put the wrong interpretation on my remark.

"That wasn't a very gallant thing to say, Fred." A wistful note in her voice seemed to reproach me. "I may not be a dewy-eyed maiden, but at least I feel like a girl inside."

"I didn't mean that you're too old to be a girl," I said. "It's just that you're so lovely—and so famous. Ever since I can remember, you've been a big star." I groaned, suddenly realizing what I was saying.

This time, however, Mary Pickford giggled. "Don't worry, Fred. I know what you're trying to say." The star of such silent screen epics as *Tess of the Storm Country* and *The Poor Little Rich Girl* switched back to her girlish mood. "Just go along with me and pretend I'm the girl next door!"

Although she had recently retired after starring in 194 movies during a legendary screen career dating back to 1909, Mary Pickford was still Hollywood's star of stars. She was also a shrewd show-business veteran and founder and boss of United Artists Studios. Beyond that she was America's

110

Sweetheart, the movie princess who married Hollywood's Prince Charming, the swashbuckling Douglas Fairbanks. They should have lived happily ever after in a beautiful palace called Pickfair.

Only a few months earlier, however, Fairbanks had shocked the nation by suddenly divorcing his movieland princess and hurrying off to England to marry Lady Ashley, the possessor of a bona fide royal pedigree. As her ex-husband cavorted around Europe with his new bride, Mary Pickford brooded alone at Pickfair until—as she told me during that Greenwich Village expedition—she decided to cheer herself up with a visit to her fun-loving friend Clara Bell Walsh.

During our party's first few stops, though, Mary Pickford was a mighty melancholy girl next door. After she explained why she happened to be in New York she seemed to abandon her determination to have a good time. Instead she held my hand, wept softly, and talked about Fairbanks. Her conversation wasn't bitter or self-pitying. It was just sad talk by a distressed woman striving desperately to figure out what had gone wrong with her dreams. It was the same familiar, timeless, sorrowing cry that haunts the lyrics of a thousand blues songs.

Suddenly Mary Pickford's mood changed. As we settled down in the third Village pub of the evening she again clasped my hand. But this time she didn't weep. She thanked me for listening to her troubles and reverted to her girl-next-door role. "No more blues tonight, Fred," she announced. "Let's have fun. Let's pretend we're a couple of kids doing the town after the prom."

Mary Pickford, I'm sure, had never been a girl on a date after the prom. She had gone on the stage when she was five to help support her widowed mother and two younger children, and in her entire life she had less than a year of formal schooling. But she obviously delighted in make believe, and I was happy to join in the game. What's more, I soon found myself almost believing in it. Like her longtime friend Clara Bell, she seemed to be a woman without pretensions, a woman who relished life and enjoyed people, a woman with the common touch. Her enthusiasm was contagious.

The uproarious night ended with the dawn at Clara Bell's Plaza suite, where I collapsed on a sofa and slept until well past noon, when it was time to head for another day's rehearsal. Mary Pickford and Clara Bell Walsh were still asleep somewhere in the big apartment when I left, and I never met America's Sweetheart again. I hadn't thought about that Village adventure in a long time, until a few years ago when I learned of Mary Pickford's death. It was impossible for me to associate the aged woman who had stubbornly clung to her enchanted Pickfair to the end of her life with the

111

vibrant actress who had recruited me as her date in a game of make believe so many years ago.

Although we played hard, life in the orchestra was not all fun and games. There were long daily rehearsals, with frequent seven-day work weeks and no overtime. No matter how hard we had partied the night before, we knew better than to be absent from work the next day.

Music dominated our lives. We lived for music. We talked music, practiced music, dreamed music. Even our late-night prowlings were often devoted to touring the night spots to hear other bands and mingle with their sidemen. In those days when the big bands were beginning to flourish, Manhattan's musicians formed a close-knit community. The boys in the bands were young and ambitious, and the promise of the American music scene provided endless conversation for our late-night get-togethers.

Lopez shared this kinship. And he was tolerant of drinking so long as it didn't affect our music-making. He even accepted marijuana as part of the life-style of many musicians, although he himself never tried it. But his tolerance had limits. He made it clear he would not tolerate alcohol or marijuana on days when his orchestra was scheduled for radio broadcasts.

Twice a week when we were in New York the Lopez orchestra presented live broadcasts of dance music from the St. Regis Roof, or whatever night spot we might be playing. In addition St. Joseph Aspirin sponsored Lopez in a weekly program over NBC. Lopez, with good reason, viewed these broadcasts as vital to the orchestra's success. Radio was an increasingly important facet of the business because it carried our music far beyond the dance floor.

"If you mess up during a dance, nobody pays much attention," Lopez said. "But if you mess up on a broadcast, it's heard by thousands and thousands of listeners and our reputation suffers. That's why if I catch anybody high on a broadcast day, he's fired!"

Members of the orchestra disagreed with a lot of Lopez's rules. But they never disputed his insistence on abstinence on broadcast days, for radio was as important to the individual musician as it was to the orchestra as a whole. In the days before radio, a musician could spend a lifetime on the bandstand without gaining recognition. But now a few noteworthy solo numbers could bring overnight fame. Wednesday was the day of our big broadcast, the hour-long network show that attracted huge audiences from coast to coast. So NBC rehearsals on Wednesday afternoons found us as sober and clean-living as a crowd at a temperance convention.

I had only been with Lopez a couple of weeks when I got my first featured role on the network program. It was a variety show with at least one celebrity a week in addition to the orchestra. On that particular Wednesday I was teamed in a skit with our guest star, Jack Dempsey, the former heavyweight boxing champion. The skit, in which I was supposed to teach the ex-champ how to whistle in exchange for lessons in fisticuffs, was nothing special. In fact, it was pretty ridiculous. But I didn't mind, since it would give me a chance to meet one of my heroes from the world of sports.

Knowing Dempsey only as a killer in the ring I expected him to be a rough-and-tough character. To my surprise he turned out to be a gentle-mannered, rather shy hulk of a man with an oddly high-pitched voice. Everything went smoothly at rehearsal. The man who had whipped some of the toughest fighters in the world didn't voice even a mild protest against the silly charade the scriptwriters had prepared.

But while Dempsey was a lamb at rehearsal, when I arrived backstage before the broadcast that night I found him pacing like a caged tiger. I asked what was bothering him, and his response revealed an unexpected side of the fighter's personality. "I'm scared, that's what's the matter!"

The mighty Jack Dempsey scared? Could it be that the mauler who had battled before the largest crowds in boxing history was suffering from stage fright? It didn't seem possible that a mere studio audience could bother him, and I told him so.

"Hell, it ain't the audience," Dempsey responded. "I'm used to crowds. I beat Carpentier in front of nearly 100,000 fans at Boyle's Thirty Acres. I fought Tunney twice before crowds way over 100,000!"

"So what's bugging you?"

"It's that microphone!"

"How come?" I asked. "It didn't seem to bother you during rehearsal this afternoon."

"That was different. That was just practice," he confessed. "But it terrifies me to think about talking through that mike to God knows how many people I can't see!"

In the end, though, Dempsey proved himself a champ in the studio, too. He stepped up the the mike with me and we emoted our way through the skit without a hitch, just like a couple of veteran actors. Of course, Jack's voice squeaked and quavered as if he might still be scared. But that seemed to be the way he always talked.

Summer was a time when the dance bands followed the migration of the more affluent citizenry away from the stifling heat of the city. During the summer of 1934 the Lopez organization was on the road playing dates on

113

Long Island, at Saratoga Springs, at the Meadowbrook across the Hudson in North Jersey, and down at the gigantic Steel Pier theater and ballroom in Atlantic City. I especially looked forward to our two-week booking at the Steel Pier, anticipating leisure time between performances to enjoy the sand and surf and the famous Boardwalk. But our Steel Pier schedule turned out to be all work and no play—fourteen consecutive days crammed with five daily stage performances plus nightly dance music in the huge ballroom.

It was an insane schedule, and there was only one thing that kept us going. That was the realization that after the Atlantic City booking ended we would have ten free days before beginning a scheduled cross-country tour. But that holiday also faded on our last day at the Steel Pier when Lopez announced he had just been advised of a one-week booking at a fancy nightclub near Buffalo. The announcement touched off a storm of angry protests which Lopez brushed aside with a quick bit of hardheaded reasoning. "The money's great . . . too big for us to pass up!"

"You mean there's a bonus in the deal?" Larry Tice, our bandstand lawyer, wanted to know.

Vincent Lopez sighed. We all knew that wasn't exactly what he had in mind. But he was trapped, and he knew it. "Okay," he agreed, "there'll be an extra week's pay for everybody."

There were no further thoughts of rebellion. That night, with scarcely a grumble, we packed our gear aboard a chartered bus and headed north for upstate New York and a shattering confrontation.

The nightclub on the outskirts of Buffalo was a posh establishment with lots of paneling, leather, velvet, crystal and indirect lighting. It had a liveried doorman, a burly maître d' who doubled as a bouncer, a hatcheck girl, a couple of scantily clad cigarette girls, and a battalion of tuxedoed waiters. It was run by a man named Schuman who took us on a tour of the club.

For such a large club the dance floor was small—an insignificant island in a sea of tables and chairs. Lopez promptly observed that he ran a dance orchestra and asked Schuman to expand the dance floor by getting rid of some tables.

"No way!" Schuman replied. "We ain't in business for dancing!"

We soon learned why. Schuman led us past a lounge and bar area and pushed open a pair of heavy double doors. We found ourselves in a huge, chandeliered back room equipped with a wide assortment of gambling devices. "This is our real business—this and selling booze," he explained.

There was nothing unusual about the setup. Many of the bigger clubs were fronts for elaborate gambling operations. In fact, we had already completed two casino bookings that summer. But Lopez was still puzzled by the postage-stamp dance floor. "How come you hire a big-time dance orchestra when you're only interested in the gambling trade?" he asked.

"We hire bands to bring people into the club. But we don't like to have the guests waste a lot of time dancing when they could be drinking or playing the tables. That's why we got a small dance floor," Schuman said.

Vincent Lopez showed no signs of being awed by Schuman. He couldn't do anything about enlarging the dance floor, but he set out to provide the customers with as much dance music as we could cram into the hours between 8 P.M. and 2 A.M. That was always the Lopez way. He came to play music, to give the customers their money's worth, and he seemed to resent every minute spent off the bandstand. When we were on tour our routine rarely varied—thirty minutes on the bandstand followed by a ten-minute intermission, after which Carlos Kent, our young "gofer" would step up to the mike and ring the chimes, summoning the musicians back to work.

When we completed our first half-hour dance session on opening night in Buffalo, the crowded floor emptied fast. Most of the dancers headed for the back room to try their luck. Ten minutes later the chimes rang out, the musicians returned, the old, familiar call of "Nola" sounded, and the customers surged out of the back room to resume their dancing. Twice the pattern was repeated. But when we returned to the bandstand after the third intermission we were confronted by a furious Schuman.

"What in the hell do you think you're doing?" he shouted. Lopez pretended amazed innocence. "What do you mean? It's pretty obvious we're playing dance music."

Schuman wasted no time sparring with our leader. He got right to the point. "What's the idea of these short intermissions?" he demanded. "We just get a good crowd at the tables when you guys start up again and we lose our customers."

"That's the way we always play, thirty minutes on and ten minutes off. There's nothing unusual about that."

"Well, that ain't the way it works here," Schuman hissed menacingly. "Here you play thirty minutes, take a break, and you don't come back until I tell you to. Understand?"

Lopez chose to ignore the threat. "Mr. Schuman," he replied stiffly, "when I'm on the bandstand I call the shots."

Schuman left without another word, and the Lopez orchestra returned to action at the same pace. As the night progressed with no further interference it appeared our leader had won his battle. But as the last intermission of the night drew to a close Schuman went into action. When Carlos walked up to the mike to ring the chimes for the final round of dancing Schuman leaped onto the bandstand and clobbered him with a roundhouse right that sent him sprawling across the dance floor, unconscious. Schuman then turned on Lopez. "Apparently you didn't get the message," he said. "Remember it tomorrow night!"

"There's not going to be any tomorrow night," Lopez raged. "We don't have to take this kind of abuse from anybody!"

But we were back on the bandstand the next night—all but Carlos Kent, who was hospitalized with a concussion and sundry bruises and abrasions. Lopez had reported the incident to the police, but they had refused to take any action. He had also received an early-morning phone call from someone who had strongly advised him to cooperate with Schuman. When Lopez voiced his determination to walk out on the club booking, the man on the phone told him that if he failed to complete the engagement the orchestra would encounter severe problems in obtaining future bookings.

"So what are we going to do?" Lou Bring asked.

"Like it or not, we don't have any choice," Lopez said. "We've got to play by their rules. We've got to finish the gig. These boys have too much muscle. They could hurt us bad if they wanted to."

So we completed our Buffalo booking playing by Schuman's rules and returned to Manhattan with no further casualties.

A few days later, on a gray September morning, I said my good-byes to Irvin Taubkin, the Jere Buckleys and Clara Bell Walsh, and joined the other orchestra members on a chartered bus for our coast-to-coast trip. The first leg of our journey was brief—a quick trip across the Hudson to the Robert Treat Hotel in Newark for a dinner-dance, followed by a series of Jersey appearances at Montclair, Morristown, Princeton, and Hackensack.

For me the only memorable date in Jersey was at a nightclub in Hackensack. I had completed my first solo numbers of the evening when one of the guests came up to where I was seated on the bandstand. I could tell he was a short, scrawny man with an oversized Roman nose. He patted my back in a fatherly fashion, introduced himself, and favored me with extravagant praise. His deep voice was tinged with an accent that hinted at immigrant roots. "I just wanna let you know that's the most terrific whistling I ever heard!"

I had no idea who he was, but I enjoyed his appreciation of my talent. In return for his praise I asked if there was any special number he'd like to hear, hoping he wouldn't cross me up by naming some unfamiliar operatic aria.

There was no need to worry. His musical tastes apparently didn't run to Puccini or Verdi. He pondered for a moment, then came up with one of the

116

popular tunes of the late twenties. "How about 'Ain't Misbehavin' . . . ya know that one?"

I did, and during my next solo session I whistled it, with a dedication to him. When I was finished, he hurried up to the bandstand with another guest. Again I was the recipient of lavish praise, and this man—apparently wanting the same bandstand recognition his friend had received—asked if I would whistle "Chinatown, My Chinatown." I assured my new admirer that I would favor him with that tune. Overwhelmed by my demonstration of good fellowship, my two fans each pressed a crisp bill into my hands and hurried off to rejoin their party.

During the next intermission as I was chatting with Lopez I pulled the bills from a jacket pocket where I had hurriedly stuffed them. He grabbed the bills and whistled in amazement. "Who's handing out this kind of tip?"

"What are you talking about?" I asked.

I heard Lopez crackling the money. "You mean to tell me you don't know what these greenbacks are?"

"Of course not! I'd look pretty silly trying to look at them on the bandstand!"

Lopez's voice was properly reverent. "These are C-notes . . . two hundred bucks!"

Lopez handed the bills back to me, and I hurriedly held them close to my eye. They were $100 bills! As I carefully tucked them into my wallet, Lopez again asked who had given them to me.

"Two real friendly fellows. The guys I dedicated a couple of tunes to."

Lopez was normally not a merry type, but he exploded with laughter. When his mirth finally subsided he managed to wheeze, "Do you have any idea who those two friendly fellows are?"

I admitted my ignorance.

"Those friendly fellows happen to be the mob's toughest triggermen. The way I hear it, they can't remember how many they've killed!"

In later years, as the full story of Mafia intrigue unfolded in various federal crime investigations, it was difficult to picture the two men I met that night in Hackensack as prime characters in the underworld's grisly saga of corruption, violence, and terror. What's that old saying about judging a book by its cover?

Our New Jersey appearances marked the beginning of a road tour that dragged on for months—from New York to Chicago to Los Angeles, then eastward again to Texas, to Florida, and finally back to Manhattan, with all manner of stops along the way. We had lengthy engagements in Los

Angeles, San Francisco, Dallas, and Miami Beach, but mainly it was an ordeal of one-night stands. I had received my initiation in touring with the Early Birds and Ligon Smith's band in Texas, Arkansas, and Oklahoma, and I was certain nothing could be more exhausting than that. But I learned that life on the road with a large orchestra was no easier, no more romantic than touring through the boondocks with a small-time musical show.

In those days there was no jet service, and if there had been we couldn't have afforded it any more than we could afford the comfort of train travel. The big bands, with their wide variety of talent, were costly operations that often teetered precariously on the edge of insolvency. Lopez's fee for one-night dates in those depression years seldom topped $600, out of which the booking agency pocketed 20 percent.

At that time some bands traveled in the musicians' cars—a tedious and frequently dangerous form of transportation in the days before super-highways. In the scramble for dates, bands frequently found themselves ending a performance after midnight in one town and faced with the problem of opening in another town 500 or more miles away within twenty-four hours. Maintaining that schedule called for all-night driving, often over unfamiliar roads. Inevitably there were accidents, with an alarming toll of dead or gravely injured musicians.

Lopez preferred chartered buses. He felt they were safer, and they enabled him to keep his musicians and their equipment together. Even more important, bus travel enabled us to sleep between towns while somebody else handled the driving. By sleeping on the bus we cut hotel stops to every two or three days—a significant personal saving, because Lopez paid for our transportation while we picked up the tab for our meals and rooms.

On tour we lived out of suitcases, ate at odd hours, performed in all manner of places from big-city theaters and ballrooms to college campuses and sleazy small-town clubs. Our routine rarely varied. We'd close out a job, crowd into the bus, and try to sleep as the clumsy vehicle jolted through the night along rough two- or three-lane highways. At daybreak we'd stop at the first sizable town to gas up the bus and bolt down a quick breakfast. Back on the road again, we passed the time dozing, gossiping, playing cards, quarreling, reading, or staring out the windows. Eventually we'd arrive at our destination, climb stiffly off the bus, unpack the equipment, grab a hurried dinner, shower and shave, change clothes, perform, and then start the same cycle all over again.

After one, two, or three days and nights of this frantic routine, our schedule would permit a stopover at a hotel. Then we would get our suits pressed and our shirts laundered. We would wash our underwear and socks and hang them in the bathroom or drape them on steam registers or on desks and chairs, hoping they'd dry overnight. We would soak out our aches in a hot tub and get a luxurious night's sleep on a bed that wasn't bouncing through the night at fifty miles an hour.

The inconveniences and physical discomforts of touring were mild compared to the less obvious stresses and strains. We discovered after a few weeks that there's nothing like a tour to produce a "togetherness" that gradually disintegrates into boredom and ultimately into hostility. We found ourselves shuddering at hearing and rehearing the same anecdotes, the same jokes and puns, the same prejudices, the same views on all manner of topics from baseball to sex, from politics to religion, from music to the weather. We became overly sensitive to what others said and brooded over things that really didn't matter. We rode an emotional roller coaster, high one day and down the next. Nagging annoyances ballooned into monumental hangups. Simple fatigue, the discomfort of a cold, the flare-up of an aching molar far from any dental help, the insistent throb of a hangover, the aggravation of faulty acoustics or an out-of-tune piano, worries about problems back home, all could become incredible psychological burdens.

Yet all the unpleasantness seemed to vanish once the orchestra began to play. Somehow the music revived our spirits and restored our inspiration. Somehow the music was bigger and more important than the problems we went through to reach the bandstand. Tomorrow, we realized, would revive the discontents, discomforts, anger, and doubts. Tomorrow would bring another town and another theater or dance hall or pavilion peopled with another faceless crowd. But each night as the band played we were united by music and intoxicated with its sound. We were joined in a common dedication to the beats and rhythms and melodies and harmonies that were the only significant realities in an otherwise tedious world.

Chapter 11

When I think about that long journey from Upper Darby to Hollywood, some amusing and amazing events are still clear in my memory.

There was a night in Pittsburgh . . .

We had just completed a booking at Bill Green's Supper Club when a young singer appeared and asked Lopez for an audition. Lopez listened to him and thought he was pretty good, but we already had a full contingent of vocalists, and it would have been necessary to make special arrangements with our booking agency, MCA, if we were going to add more. So he told the kid we couldn't use him.

The aspiring vocalist didn't give up easily. "Take me along, Mr. Lopez. I'll sing for nothing if you give me a chance to prove myself!"

Usually Lopez was patient with young musicians because of his own struggles to break into the business after he gave up study for the priesthood. But he was tired, and we were faced with a rainy bus trip into Ohio that night. "Sorry," he said. "We just don't have any openings."

"Not even if I work for nothing?"

"Not even if you pay me to let you sing! We just don't need another singer." Lopez walked away, putting an end to the conversation.

The youngster still lingered backstage as we packed. He was twenty years old and worked as a barber, but music had been his ambition ever since he'd started singing with small neighborhood bands around Pittsburgh when he was fifteen. "They call me the Singing Barber," he said.

To us he was just another of the star-struck kids we encountered along the road. We listened, kidded him about his bragging, and put him to work helping us carry instruments and luggage out to the waiting bus. We told him there were a lot more vocalists than jobs and that he'd be smart to stick to barbering.

Perry Como stood in the alley and sadly watched us board the bus. He was still there, huddled in the rain, as we pulled away.

In later years Lopez admitted he made a big mistake that night. Before the decade ended Perry Como had become the biggest attraction of the Ted Weems band and one of the hottest vocalists of the swing generation. Every time Lopez learned of a new Perry Como hit record, heard him on a big broadcast, or read about him being mobbed by adoring young fans, he would moan: "Just think, Perry Como is making a fortune, and I could have had him for nothing!"

There was a night in Columbus, Ohio . . .

I had been sharing hotel rooms on the tour with our band boy—a surly teen-aged lummox with an enormous appetite and a larcenous instinct that became evident when I began missing money from my wallet and change purse. It was never any large amount—just a steady drain of dollar bills, quarters, and dimes. Apparently Roger figured that a sightless man would never be sure just how much money he was carrying around, and would never miss small amounts of cash. But since my early days at Blind School I had been trained to take care of money, to recognize coins by their sizes, and to identify bills with my faint vision and keep them folded in different patterns for quick and accurate recognition. I had also been taught to maintain a careful daily record of where my money went.

When I first began missing money I shrugged it off, deciding I had probably been careless. But when the shortages continued I began to suspect Roger, and I reported my suspicions to Lopez. He was skeptical. "You can't be sure, Fred," he cautioned. "With your sight problem, I know you must have trouble keeping track of your money. You're probably spending more than you realize. You can't accuse the kid unless you have proof."

I realized it was futile to try to convince Lopez that I was capable of managing my own financial affairs. After months of close association, he still fretted about my walking around with money in my pockets. So I didn't argue. I merely got him to agree to assign me a new room-mate.

When we pulled into Columbus for a weekend "career" at a ballroom— on tour, we called any booking of two or more days a "career"—my new room-mate turned out to be a moody musician hired by Lopez during our stay in Pittsburgh. Nobody seemed to know much about Stanley. He was a competent instrumentalist, but a loner. He never had much to say and always seemed to be isolated in his own personal fog, even when he was on the bandstand.

"Maybe he's on the weed," I suggested to Johnny Morris on the bus one day when we got around to discussing Stanley's weird behavior.

Johnny rejected that speculation. "No way! He acts too dopey . . . no zip, no fire. You don't see guys on the weed walking around like zombies."

121

I had to agree. No one had seen Stanley touch any kind of cigarette, and when the bottles were passed around to ease the monotony on the bus he always declined. He definitely wasn't a boozer. That left one possibility. "Do you think we've got a junkie on our hands?" I asked. Hard drugs were something outside our experience.

Despite all the speculation we were never really sure Stanley was on hard stuff—until I ended up sharing a room with him in Columbus.

Sometime during the night I was awakened by a hair-raising crescendo of groaning, moaning, and whimpering. It wasn't a ghost. It was my new roomie.

"Wake up, Stan!" I yelled, believing he was having a nightmare. "Wake up, man. You're having a bad dream!"

"I'm . . . I'm not sleeping . . ." Stanley's response was punctuated by new outbursts of suffering.

Now I was thoroughly alarmed. I was certain my room-mate was stricken with some horrible malady. I fumbled for the telephone and managed to knock it off the nightstand.

"What . . . what in the hell . . . you doin'?" he muttered.

"I'm trying to find the blasted phone. I'll call the desk and get you a doctor."

Stanley's voice shrilled with panic. "No, Lowery . . . don't do that, man. I don't need a doctor!"

Still groping for the phone I tried to calm my hysterical room-mate. "You're sick, Stan. I've got to get a doctor. I can't help you!"

"Dammit, Lowery," Stanley shrieked, "I tell you I'm not sick. Keep the hell away from that phone."

"If you aren't sick, what in the devil's wrong with you?"

"I need a fix . . . that's what's wrong. You've got to get me a fix, Lowery. . . ." Stanley's babbling modulated into a new eruption of groaning. "Please, Lowery . . . for God's sake, help me!"

I was frantic. I didn't know what to do. I dressed and hurriedly fled from the room with Stanley's cries and curses speeding me on my way. I groped my way to the suite occupied by Lopez and pounded on the door.

After hearing my frightened tale Lopez summoned a doctor. I spent the rest of the night in the lobby dozing in one of the big lounge chairs while the doctor and an ambulance attendant from a nearby hospital struggled with Stanley. Finally he was sedated and whisked away to begin a long and painful cure. I had the room to myself for the remainder of our Columbus gig, and when the band continued on its way Lopez assigned Johnny Morris as my new room-mate.

"Don't pester me any more about rooms," Lopez said. "Just keep out of trouble and *let me get some sleep!*"

And there was an afternoon near Needles, California . . .

We had continued on an uneventful trail down through Kansas, Colorado, New Mexico, and Arizona. It was a warm fall afternoon when we finally crossed the bridge over the Colorado. Suddenly Lopez ordered the bus to stop at a roadside rest area on the outskirts of Needles. Ignoring the stares of a cluster of Dust Bowlers who had paused in their westward migration to rest, Lopez slowly climbed off the bus and knelt on the sand beside the pavement. Solemnly he bowed down and kissed the earth, then leaped to his feet shouting, "California, we are here!"

Lopez's unexpected antics touched off an uproarious celebration. We all flocked off the bus, planted kisses on the sun-baked sands, pounded one another on the back, and whooped and hollered like a bunch of movie Indians on the warpath. Some of the musicians brought out their instruments and soon "California, Here I Come!" rang out across the Mojave Desert. At last we had reached the promised land.

Our booking at the Beverly Wilshire Hotel was a welcome relief from the rigors of touring. The older, married members of the band were joined by their wives and children and set up housekeeping in furnished houses or apartments near the hotel. The rest of us doubled up in apartments or found lodgings in private homes.

Looking back, I have to think how lucky we were. In many parts of the nation there were still long lines of jobless workers outside factory gates. Homeless men and women still roamed the streets, sleeping in parks and begging on street corners. All this while we were visiting the movie studios, mingling with the stars who patronized the Beverly Wilshire, and being paid to do what we loved best.

The swing mania which was starting to rock the East Coast band scene hadn't yet reached the Far West. In Los Angeles the sweet sounds of the twenties and early thirties still prevailed. Jimmie Grier's band with its dreamy music and the singing of Larry Cotton and Pinky Tomlin was packing the famed Cocoanut Grove. So the Lopez brand of music, which was becoming old hat in Manhattan, was in the groove at the Beverly Wilshire.

Lopez sensed that our audiences were still in the mood for sugar coating and decided to feature me in a nostalgic finale each evening. Just before closing the lights would dim and one purplish spot would zero in on me at the mike as I whistled a medley of romantic oldies. This lovely closing, which

123

we called "The Moonlight Dance," continued to be a popular feature on our long tour back to the East Coast. But when we tried it on our return to New York it bombed.

Only one incident marred our month at the Beverly Wilshire.

I hadn't been the only one to question our band boy's honesty. During the tour other members of the orchestra had complained that money, watches, and other pawnable possessions were missing. They also suspected Roger. But Lopez was fond of the youngster he had hired in New York to handle the equipment and run errands during our tour—a menial job that paid only a few dollars a week plus meals and whatever tips could be scrounged from the musicians—and he refused to credit our suspicions. In fact, when we opened at the Beverly Wilshire he gave Roger the authority to charge purchases to the orchestra's account at the hotel and certain stores, a privilege that enabled Roger to handle a lot of Lopez's shopping chores.

Lopez showed up for rehearsal one day asking if anyone had seen Roger. No one had. The next day brought the same question and the same answer, and our leader began to fret. After four days it was apparent that Roger had taken a powder—and that wasn't all. Our band boy had charged some $2,000 to the orchestra's account at the hotel's various shops and at the bar. His liquor purchases, supposedly for thirsty musicians, were probably quickly redeemed for cash out on the street. He had charged another $1,500 in clothing purchases to the Lopez account at expensive Wilshire Boulevard shops. He absconded with Lopez's portable typewriter, his luggage, his wristwatch, and choice items from his wardrobe. Lopez at last notified the police, but it was too late. Roger ended up as the best-dressed, wealthiest former band boy in the nation and was never apprehended.

Late in November our job at the Beverly Wilshire ended, and we reluctantly packed for another cross-country tour. This time, however, MCA spared us the ordeal of starting out with a dreary succession of one-nighters. We even managed to escape the indignities of bus travel. Instead we boarded a Southern Pacific train at Union Station and headed eastward in style. Our destination: Dallas!

It was eleven months since I had left Dallas on a Greyhound bus bound for New York in search of fame and fortune. I remembered how I had been haunted by the fear of failure. Now I found myself returning home a hero— a member of a big-time dance orchestra and a featured soloist on nation-wide broadcasts.

Even so, I hadn't envisioned the welcome that was awaiting me. The train station at Dallas was crowded with well-wishers and bedecked with a banner proclaiming, "Welcome home, Freddie!" Lopez and my fellow musicians were startled by the turnout, and so was I. It seemed as if all the people from my past were there—members of the Lions Club, the Chamber of Commerce, the Salesmanship Club of Dallas, the "Early Birds" cast, the management of station WFAA, and a lot of other friends and fans who had helped me in my career. And, of course, there were Grandma White, Uncle Ed, some of my Skillern cousins, Peggy Richter, and my sisters, chaperoning Gracie Johnston, the fiancee from whom I had been parted for so long.

We were in Dallas for a three-week run at the Baker Hotel, and the city's newspapers and radio newscasters heralded the engagement as a great triumph for Fred Lowery, the hometown boy, giving the Lopez orchestra only brief mention. The maestro was unhappy with this publicity. He was not accustomed to being overshadowed by a member of his organization. And his dismay turned to anger when he saw the marquee above the entrance to the hotel. My friend Fenton Baker, proprietor of the city's finest hostelry, had elevated me to top billing. In huge letters the marquee proclaimed: FRED LOWERY RETURNS!!! And below, in smaller letters: *Starring with the Vincent Lopez Orchestra!*

When Lopez saw the marquee he stormed into the hotel and furiously ordered Baker to change it. "Fred Lowery's just one musician. Vincent Lopez gets top billing!"

Fenton Baker, a crusty Texan, wasn't awed by celebrities. He just laughed at our raging leader. "Maybe you get top billing in other places, but in Dallas it's Fred Lowery!" he replied.

Lopez persisted, however, and finally got his way, but he never forgave Baker. A few weeks later, during a network broadcast from the Chase Hotel in St. Louis, Lopez announced over the air that he had just learned that Fenton Baker was in a Dallas hospital. And he declared from coast to coast that he was dedicating the next song to Baker. The number—"I'll Be Glad When You're Dead, You Rascal You!"

In the excitement of returning home I scarcely noticed the feuding between Lopez and Baker. During the hours before and after our afternoon and evening performances at the hotel I was much too busy with guest appearances, newspaper and radio interviews, parties, visits with friends, and my renewed romance with Gracie.

My weekly salary had now mushroomed to $125, and we talked again about marriage. Although Gracie was still studying for her nurse's degree at Baylor, she was tempted to join me on tour. But, ever practical, she suggested we discuss our plans with Lopez.

125

It didn't seem like a very good idea to me since I was aware of our leader's antimarriage philosophy. "Your daddy's already said yes. I don't see any need to ask for Lopez's approval," I argued.

But Gracie pointed out that Lopez would have to agree to having an extra girl tag along with the orchestra. As usual, Gracie won the argument, and we talked to the boss.

Lopez was tactfully negative. He noted that touring was a rough, tiring life with little privacy for newlyweds. He further observed, in the fatherly manner he sometimes assumed, that Gracie was in her last year of her training. "Why don't you two lovebirds wait until we get back to New York and then think about marriage?" he suggested.

Gracie appreciated such practical reasoning, and so we agreed to wait. Of course Lopez knew that once Gracie and I were again separated we'd become involved in other pursuits and more willing to let marriage wait. Maybe he even thought we'd wait forever.

After Dallas, we had an engagement at the Chase Hotel in St. Louis. Then we got back on our chartered bus and headed south for a scheduled engagement at the Deauville Club in Miami.

With the fifth year of the depression limping toward its end, it was not the best of times. Florida's tourist season was off to a slow start, and even the fashionable Deauville was afflicted. At our first performance Lillian Roth sang "Brother, Can You Spare a Dime?"

Lillian had been a big-time musical comedy star on Broadway. She was a singer whose talent was exceeded only by the troubles that plagued her life—liquor, dope, unhappy romances, debts, and failing health. She had just embarked on a well-publicized comeback, and the Deauville hoped her fame coupled with the Lopez sound would put some life back in the club's slumping business.

For two weeks we played to almost empty houses. Business was so bad that members of the band had a nightly pool based on how many customers would straggle in. I recall winning the pool one night with a prediction of two couples. And they soon fled from the sad-eyed Lillian's melancholy melodies.

At the end of the second disastrous week Lillian vanished from the scene. Her replacement was another tragic figure—the legendary Helen Morgan. For years, Helen had been the toast of Manhattan both on stage and in supper clubs. Like Lillian, the tiny, dark-haired torch singer had a fatal weakness for alcohol. But unlike Lillian she was full of fire and showmanship. She also had a voice one critic described as "the cry of all the ruined women of the world."

126

Helen Morgan's fame dated back to the twenties when she starred in Ziegfeld's *Follies* and Jerome Kern's smash Broadway classic, *Show Boat.* Helen brought customers flocking to the Deauville. During the remainder of her stay at the club we played to packed houses.

Unfortunately, Helen was drinking more and more and riding an emotional roller coaster. Early in February she returned to New York. With her departure business at the Deauville dropped abruptly. After we spent two weeks playing to empty tables the club's management hired a cheap local orchestra and dispensed with our more costly services, even though our booking still had a month to run. That was when the Lopez orchestra, as reported in *Variety*, ended up "going to the dogs."

We clustered anxiously around Lopez as he phoned Jules Stein at MCA headquarters to report our plight and ask him to line up a job to tide us over until our scheduled resumption of one-nighters in mid-March.

Lopez listened to the voice at the other end of the line, then reported: "Stein says he's only got one spot open in the Miami area."

"What's that?" we chorused.

"One of the dog tracks over at Miami Beach is looking for a band to play between races!"

"It's better than nothing," Johnny Morris observed, no doubt thinking of his mortgaged house on Long Island and his wife and kids.

Lopez sighed in resignation. The man whose music had delighted high society for so many years spoke slowly into the phone. "Okay, Jules, we'll take it." And the following day we began the weirdest gig of all.

From a makeshift wooden bandstand in the middle of the racing oval we aired the sweet Lopez sounds between races from eight to eleven o'clock every night but Sunday. The race fans and the mechanical rabbit didn't pay any attention to us. Only the dogs seemed to appreciate our efforts. They always started howling when we began to play.

After a month of music to howl to, any change—even starvation—would have been welcome. For once we greeted the sight of our chartered bus with cheers. At that moment the trials of the open road and its one-nighter miseries seemed insignificant. But within the week we were once more cursing fate.

The remainder of our tour was pure drudgery, right up to our final road date, the customary late-summer booking at Piping Rock. But our spirits finally revived as we entered the city we had left twelve months before on our national tour. We shouted, tooted horns, pounded drums, whistled, sang, and generally acted like lunatics. It was, as Lopez observed, great to be back home.

Our new engagement was at the Astor Hotel, another of high society's sedate havens in the big city. Around town the younger set was swinging to the new sound, truckin' and shaggin' and jitterin'—shocking their elders with such outlandish dances as the Big Apple and the Suzy Q. At the Astor, however, the Lopez brand of sweet dance music was waltzed to by the same—and only slightly older—loyal followers, including Clara Bell Walsh and her cafe society set. In our off hours we renewed the merry rounds of partying and barhopping with them.

Bobby Lytle was one of our newcomers to the New York scene. Lopez had hired him during the tour after hearing him sing in a Midwest nightclub. In New York, Bobby and I shared a one-room efficiency apartment at the Belvedere Hotel, an aging off-Broadway haven for show-business types.

Although he had added Bobby Lytle to our roster, Lopez had not had an outstanding girl vocalist since the departure of Frances Hunt with her husband, pianist Lou Bring. The defection of the singer who had been one of the orchestra's stars for so long seemed to intensify his suspicions of the fair sex. It wasn't until the summer of 1937 that our band finally acquired another exceptional girl vocalist. In fact, we added two girl singers at one time, although one of them ended up chaperoning the other.

We were in Detroit playing at the Graystone Ballroom when a bouncy teen-aged blonde invaded rehearsal one afternoon. Lopez was in the midst of one of his periodic lectures when she sashayed up to the bandstand amid an outburst of appreciative whistles and wolf calls. Lopez was startled by this sudden manifestation. "What in the devil do you want?" he demanded.

"An audition," the pert young thing replied, apparently undaunted.

"Go away! Can't you see we're busy?"

The young lady ignored the maestro's command. "I'm not going to leave until you hear me sing," she announced.

Lopez sighed. "Miss Whoever-You-Are, we don't need another vocalist!"

But she refused to retreat. "Don't be a grouchy old fuddy-duddy," she answered. "You need a girl singer. Everybody knows that!"

We expected Lopez to erupt in one of his tantrums and personally give the girl the heave-ho. But for some strange reason he seemed to be amused. Perhaps he had a secret weakness for strong-willed women.

He gave the girl an audition, and the results were electrifying. Although her voice was lacking somewhat in depth and power, her personality had enough voltage to light all the neon ribbons on Broadway. She had a bouncing, swinging, impudently sexy style that quickly got everyone's attention.

128

"How'd you like it?" the girl asked when the music stopped. "How'd I do?"

"Not bad," Lopez admitted.

"Do I get the job?"

Lopez's voice was tinged with alarm. "Whoa! Hold it, kid! I didn't say anything about a job. I've got to think about that. What's your name?"

"Betty Jane Blair."

Lopez shook his head. "That's a dopey name!"

"What's wrong with it?"

"It's too schoolgirlish. It's just not sexy. Sounds like a girl who's never been kissed."

"Well, I've been singing at a few clubs around town under a different name," Betty Jane said.

"What's that?" Lopez asked.

"Betty Darling. Sounds kind of cute, don't you think?"

Lopez groaned. "It stinks! It's worse than Betty Jane Blair! We've got to do something about your name if we hire you," he warned.

That's the way he was about names—kind of squirrelly. Before and after my time with the orchestra Lopez was noted for his ability to develop young musicians. Among the many he trained through the years were bandleaders Artie Shaw and Xavier Cugat. And he was convinced that with the guidance of his astrological and numerological charts he could create names for his young stars guaranteed to attract public recognition. So he went to work renaming Betty Jane Blair. After pondering and consulting the stars and numbers, he summoned Betty Jane to another rehearsal. "How about Betty Hutton, America's Number One Jitterbug?" he asked.

Betty Jane didn't exactly swoon over his brainchild. She just shrugged and said, "It sounds like any other name, but if you like Betty Hutton it's okay by me. I don't care what you call me. I just want to know whether or not I get the job."

"You've got it if you want it," Lopez replied.

She wanted it all right, but there was one complication. Her mother wouldn't let her out of Detroit with a gang of male musicians unless she had a female companion. The companion she had in mind was Betty's older sister Marion, who also happened to be a singer.

Lopez reluctantly gave Marion an audition, and she had a far better voice than her sister. However, she didn't have Betty's high-voltage sex appeal, and Lopez informed their mother that he didn't need a second girl vocalist. But she stood firm. So Lopez finally agreed to hire Marion as a $25-per-week chaperone. Marion promptly adopted the Hutton name, but the change did little to further her musical ambitions. While Betty became an instant success Lopez continued to keep Marion in the background. Occasionally he'd let her join Betty in a duet, but most of the time she served only as a companion for her sister.

As the weeks passed it was evident that Marion was disenchanted with her "baby-sitting." In fact, a definite coolness developed between the girls, and there were rumors within the organization that Betty, jealously aware of her sister's superior voice, was pressuring Lopez to keep Marion off the bandstand.

It wasn't until September, when the band was playing at the Carlton Roof in Boston, that Lopez finally resolved the dilemma of too many Hutton sisters. Actually, it was Glenn Miller who helped him out of his predicament. Miller had traveled an uneven road since leaving his job as arranger for Lopez. After helping Ray Noble organize his first American band, Miller decided to form his own organization. He put together a band with some exceptional musicians, including the great clarinetist Irving Fazola, trumpeter Les Biegel, and tenor saxist Jerry Jerome. But, as usual, a new band was hard to launch, and Miller was forced to fold his group. A few months later, however, he was back in business forming a new band. Violinist Nick Pisani and I knew that Miller was looking for talent, and since we thought Marion Hutton was exceptional, we got word to him that she would probably be available. Miller showed up at the Carlton Roof one night, and Lopez gave Marion one of her rare opportunities to share the mike with sister Betty.

Glenn liked what he heard and he liked Marion when he met her. She got the job, and the rest is part of America's musical lore. Marion Hutton became the starring vocalist of one of the greatest of all the big bands. I always thought it was fitting that this Cinderella finally became a singing princess.

During this period I became a regular featured soloist with the Lopez orchestra. I began to get more exposure, more elaborate arrangements, and a greater publicity buildup. This starring role not only boosted my salary to $200 a week, but also helped make whistling a more familiar sound to the public.

When I broke in with Lopez in 1934 the only whistler on the scene was Elmo Tanner with the Ted Weems orchestra, and he was usually limited to background music and a few specialty numbers. Even the great "Heartaches" record he had cut with Weems in 1933 had been quickly forgotten. (In 1947 it was rediscovered and turned into an overnight hit by a North Carolina disc jockey. By that time, of course, Elmo Tanner had become a famous whistler.)

Once Lopez began to feature me as one of his headliners, whistling became a respectable part of the pop music of the times, enhancing Elmo's career as well as mine. More and more bands, copying Lopez and Weems, began to introduce whistling into their arrangements. Mostly, though, it was done by instrumentalists who doubled as whistlers. Throughout the big-band era Elmo and I were the only full-time professional whistlers. Not surprisingly the public frequently got us mixed up in their minds. Ted Weems once told me a funny story about a "mistaken identity" incident that occurred when his band was performing at the Aragon Ballroom in Chicago. Elmo, as usual, was perched on his bandstand chair with a guitar. There was a standing joke in the band business that Elmo's guitar had rubber-band strings, and everyone kidded him about his playing.

During one number a dancing couple paused at the bandstand. "Isn't that Fred Lowery, the blind whistler?" the lady asked Weems, pointing to Elmo Tanner.

"No, m'am," Weems replied. "Fred Lowery is with a different band. This is Elmo Tanner. Elmo never gets blind before midnight!"

I'm sure my fame as a whistler was primarily the result of my constant exposure on network radio. The astounding growth of radio had produced a vast audience for musicians. Seldom has a medium been so perfectly attuned to a particular art form. But as television impresarios discovered a generation later, it takes an awesome amount of programming to keep the airways filled with revenue-generating entertainment. The bosses of the NBC and CBS radio networks wanted live music for a major share of their programs. And the leaders of the nation's top bands were ready, willing, and able to give them what they wanted—at a price, of course.

By the mid-thirties radio was becoming the most important factor in the music business. Dates at hotels, ballrooms, nightclubs, theaters, and casinos—and the money a band could charge for these engagements—were all part of the harvest produced by national network exposure. The bigger a band's reputation on radio, the bigger the bookings and the pay. Life became a constant round of competition, with musicians concentrating on getting more and more radio exposure and the networks and sponsors battling over the big names.

Vincent Lopez inevitably got caught up in this struggle. In 1937 he suddenly dropped his long association with St. Joseph Aspirin in favor of a more lucrative deal with Nash Motors, and we moved to CBS where we acquired a young, wisecracking announcer named Bert Parks. Although it was a different network and sponsor, the format was basically the same— lots of music with a smattering of celebrity appearances and hurriedly contrived skits.

As radio grew, the record industry began to revive. Before the crash, record-making had been an important part of the music business. In 1927 sales of phonograph records in the United States totaled 130 million platters. But by 1932 sales had plummeted to less than 6 million, and only a few bands were still recording. Times got so tough that if a record had a sale of 10,000 copies it was considered a smash. But radio and the jukebox turned the tide, and in 1937 record sales again topped the 100 million mark. The Lopez orchestra was one of many that began to reap the extra income generated by records, although in those times they did not yield the huge bonanzas that enriched the lives of later musicians.

Recording techniques were primitive compared with today's sophisticated methods. We didn't even have the advantage of recording on a tape that could be spliced to edit out the rough spots. We cut the recordings directly on acetate or wax discs, and frequently we were jammed into a small recording studio for hours, doing a number over and over again until we got it right.

Lopez gave me a chance to cut my first featured solo number in 1937. That record, "Beautiful Lady in Blue," was on the Bluebird label, a subsidiary of RCA. It proved to be a modest success, and I soon cut other records, including two specialty platters with Johnny Morris, "Knock, Knock, Who's There?" and "The Laughing Boy Blues." In the latter number I didn't whistle a single note. I just provided occasional outbursts of maniacal laughter.

By this time I had become both a seasoned veteran of the bandstand and as dedicated a New Yorker as ever came out of the Piney Woods. Although the band was spending considerable time on tour, I now considered Manhattan my home. I suppose my transformation from a Texan into a New Yorker was due largely to Clara Bell Walsh's influence. Like me, she was a transplanted outlander who had long before bid farewell to her native Kentucky. She couldn't imagine anyone, especially her friends, wanting to live anywhere but New York.

Long after I joined Lopez the dowager of the Plaza continued to help my career. Just as she had assisted the Lopez band through the years she tried to make sure that whenever we were in New York I met the right people and made the personal appearances that would be the most beneficial. At times she went to extreme lengths to promote my talent. For instance, she introduced me to Joe McCarthy, manager of the world champion New York Yankees, and arranged for me to whistle the national anthem at the opening of a ball game at Yankee Stadium. I ended up getting that booking several times during a number of summers, both at Yankee Stadium and the Polo Grounds, home of the New York Giants.

Clara Bell's efforts to promote my career concentrated mainly on social and charitable events. Many of the appearances she arranged were unpaid benefits at which I always seemed to meet the same collection of the city's monied aristocracy. By introducing me to them she provided me with several extraordinary opportunities. Knowing I was Clara Bell's friend, the socialites sometimes called on me to entertain at their more special functions.

One of these occasions occurred when I was asked by one of Clara Bell's friends to perform at a posh white-tie-and-tails benefit at Radio City Music Hall to raise money for victims of a devastating Pennsylvania flood. I was the first whistler to appear on the Music Hall stage—an appearance which, prior to the program, several of New York's music critics deplored as a "travesty." After my performance, however, the same critics praised my talent and marveled at the range and complexity of my whistling.

At Clara Bell's benefits I frequently met Gene Buck, a founder and president of the American Society of Composers, Authors and Publishers (ASCAP). Buck was a longtime friend of Clara Bell Walsh and like Lopez and me was often called on to give a helping hand. Buck and I became good friends, a friendship that resulted in one of the greatest honors of my life.

In February of 1937, shortly before the Lopez band embarked on another tour, I received a telephone call from Gene. He wanted to know if I would be free for a special performance. His approach had a familiar ring.

"Good grief, Gene!" I groaned. "Are *you* giving benefits now?"

Buck chuckled. "Sort of, I guess. This involves a trip to Washington. Can you get away for a couple of days?"

"I suppose. But how come you've got to recruit talent here for an affair in Washington? Who's throwing the party?"

"A fellow by the name of Roosevelt!"

I had never dreamed of performing for the president. "You've got to be kidding," I said.

Buck explained that presidential advisor Harry Hopkins had asked him to assemble a group of celebrities for one of the Roosevelts' parties at the Willard Hotel. "It's nothing fancy," Buck assured me. "Just a get-together of friends and political associates. The Roosevelts like to have a few interesting people as special guests. You know—authors, musicians, poets, actors . . ."

"How come you want me? I'm just a whistler. Roosevelt won't know me from Adam!"

"Roosevelt likes whistling," Buck replied. "He's heard you on the radio, and he especially requested that you come!"

That was one command performance I didn't miss. I was one of a group of special guests that included Babe Ruth and songwriter Billy Hill. The dinner turned out to be a huge banquet in the hotel ballroom for key White House staffers, cabinet members, congressmen, Supreme Court justices, diplomats, and other VIPs. Despite the collection of dignitaries it *was* a lot like a family get-together.

I'm sure there was plenty of noteworthy table talk that evening. But I was most fascinated with the soft-voiced lady who came to talk with me after the president had made his grand entrance. The soft-voiced lady was Eleanor Roosevelt. Had I been sitting next to the Queen of England I'm sure I would have been totally tongue-tied. But Mrs. Roosevelt radiated a comfortable warmth. She seemed more like a friendly neighbor than the First Lady. She had a way of immediately putting a person at ease and making him feel she was truly interested in his life, his problems, and his aspirations.

We discussed the gypsy life of the big-band musicians, the art of whistling, education of the blind, and my recollections of hard times in the Piney Woods. She had toured that region during her travels through the nation's impoverished rural areas. It wasn't until later that my hostess got around to mentioning my role in the evening's entertainment. It had been arranged in advance that I would whistle several of Billy Hill's compositions with the composer accompanying me on the guitar. We had spent an entire afternoon in New York rehearsing. But the First Lady had a special request—a request she voiced a bit shyly, as if she felt she might be imposing on me. "Franklin has asked that you whistle a special number for him."

"I'll be happy to oblige if I can. What would be like to hear?" I crossed my fingers, hoping the president's request wouldn't be some exotic number that wasn't in my repertoire.

"He'd like very much to hear 'Home on the Range.' It's his favorite song!"

When I was introduced to FDR after whistling a medley of cowboy songs, including his favorite, the president shook my hand and observed, "That was a wonderful combination . . . whistling and western music. That's what I call genuine American music. It was a real treat hearing you perform in person."

By the late 1930s the popularity of the big-name bands of the twenties was plummeting. The swing generation had really arrived, and new bands were leading the Hit Parade. Even Paul Whiteman, the 280-pound King of Jazz, was fading from the scene, still clinging to music that had begun to seem terribly old-fashioned.

Like Whiteman, Vincent Lopez refused to change. The orchestra suffered through a constant turnover of arrangers as talented young musicians became discouraged with his stubborn resistance. Our bookings in Manhattan, which had once been Lopez territory, were becoming briefer. Even Clara Bell Walsh's influence was on the decline, for the city's social set was starting to swing to the new rhythms. While Benny Goodman, Sammy Kaye, Woody Herman, Tommy Dorsey, and other new big bands were packing clubs all around the city, Lopez was spending more and more time on the road.

When our engagement at the Ambassador Hotel ended in the spring of 1938, we boarded another bus and headed out of Manhattan. It was my last tour with the Lopez orchestra—another dreary succession of one-nighters that took us deep into the Midwest and finally back to Saratoga Springs for our annual appearance at the Piping Rock. There Lopez announced a big engagement in New York, news that sparked an eruption of cheers from the bandstand. Not only were we heading home; we were going back in style to a highly prized date at Billy Rose's famed Casa Manana, the swank Broadway supper club that had become the new "in" place for cafe society.

We had previously been exposed to Billy Rose's showmanship during a two-week engagement at Rose's Aquacade, a gigantic ballroom in Cleveland that extended over the waters of Lake Erie. It featured a movable stage and bandstand, all manner of trick lighting, and other dramatic effects that enhanced the music. We had encountered only one problem at the Aquacade. Our booking had been in late September, and we soon discovered that performing over the icy waters of Lake Erie in the autumn was a job best suited to Eskimos. But despite the cold we had enjoyed being a part of a Billy Rose production. It had meant large crowds, great publicity, and plenty of radio time. When we heard the news at Piping Rock we realized that a lengthy engagement at the Casa Manana could produce even greater benefits, without Lake Erie's freezing nights.

But there were things we didn't know. The Casa Manana booking was a big break for Lopez, but for me and other featured soloists it proved to be a disaster. We quickly learned that Lopez had been hired primarily to accompany Billy Rose's own big-name performers. With the exception of Betty Hutton our soloists were pushed into the background. During our twice-nightly shows from 7:30 to 9:30 P.M. and 12:30 to 2:30 A.M. I had little to do but sit on the bandstand and whistle a few background choruses in specialty numbers.

Even these brief performances apparently disturbed Billy Rose. After the first week of our engagement Rose confronted Lopez and our business manager Mannie Hecklin and demanded that I be fired. "It makes me sick seeing a freak up on the bandstand," Rose said in his customary blunt manner. "He's bad for business. Nobody at the Casa Manana wants to sit here paying big money to guzzle booze and watch a blind man tootling on the stage. Get rid of him!"

Lopez brought me the news at the close of rehearsal one afternoon. Recounting his conversation with Rose, he said, "I was so mad I could have killed him!" Then he broke down and wept in outrage and frustration. "But I didn't kill him. I didn't even tell him to go to hell. I had to sit there and take it, Fred. I didn't have any choice. You know that's true. We need this New York job. If we lose it the band could be finished!"

"In other words, I'm out?" The full realization of Lopez's words was beginning to register.

"I'm afraid so, Fred. I have no other choice. . . ."

There was much more conversation. Lopez and I went out and tried to drown our troubles before he had to return for the first show of the night at the Casa Manana. But the liquor couldn't ease the pain or the hard knot of fear in my belly. When Lopez left I sat alone at the bar brooding about my fate. I was still there at midnight when Bobby Lytle showed up and helped me back to the hotel.

The Texas School for the Blind Orchestra, under the direction of Henry Leiberman (center), ca. 1926. I'm at the far right, on soprano sax.

Courtesy of Andrew Broome

137

New York banker Jere Buckley helped launch my career.
Courtesy of Doris Buckley

Vincent Lopez and his Orchestra at the Drake Hotel in Chicago, 1937. I'm
sitting behind the piano. Among my friends in the orchestra are Bob Lytle
(front row left, next to vocalist Lois Still), violinist Nick Pisani, second
pianist Gil Bowers, bass Thurman Teague, drummer Johnny Morris, and
saxophonist Bob Snell (right).   *Courtesy of Bob Lytle*

Bon voyage party aboard the *Queen Mary* for Charley of Charley's Tavern.
Next to me, holding his hat, is my lifelong friend Stafford Chiles.

Horace Heidt and his Musical Knights at the Biltmore Hotel, 1939. Front row (left to right): F.L., Ruth Davis, Larry Cotton, Horace, the Four LeAhn Sisters. Second row: Frankie Carle, Bob Knight, Bobby Hackett, Henry Russell. Violins: the Drane Sisters. Sax: George Dessinger, Loys Johnson, Bob Riedel, Jerry Kasper. Trombone: Wayne Webb. Trumpets: Ralph Wingert, Frank Strasek. Drums: Bernie Mattinson. Top row: Eddie McKimmey, Art Carney, Red Farrington, Bob McCoy.

Courtesy of Art Thorsen

With Jimmy Stewart during a break in shooting *Pot o' Gold.*

My sister Minnie Lee and niece Carol Ann visited the movie set a few days before Carol Ann's accident. *Photo by Virginia Bergquist*

With Gracie atop the Empire State Building, February 1941.

142

Fred M. Lowery's first Christmas, 1941.

With Horace Heidt on the "Pot o' Gold" radio show.

Courtesy of Dorothy Rae

Bing Crosby threw the script away for our Kraft Music Hall broadcast.

With Mel Ott in the New York Giants' dugout. *Courtesy of Ken Smith*

Dizzy Dean was a great storyteller, on and off the air.

This item appeared in Ripley's syndicated column while I was staying at the Eastgate Hotel in Chicago in 1944.

My first singing partner was the lovely Dorothy Rae.

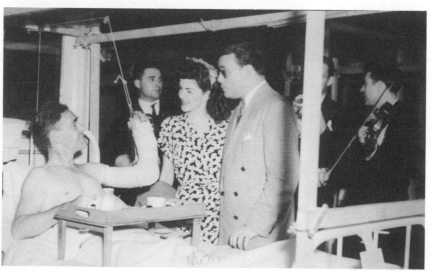

Dorothy and I perform at the Walter Reed Hospital on "Victory Over Japan" Day.

During a 2-hour broadcast at Bob Schaad's Record Shop in Evansville, Indiana, we sold 5,000 copies of "Indian Love Call." The local cab company delivered the records.   *Photo by Jack Kanel*

During the forties and fifties people turned out by the thousands for record promotions like this one in Boston.

Surrounded by members of my fan club, the Whistling Josephines, in
Miami, Florida.   *Courtesy of Fred Lowery Fan Club*

Loew's State was the first New York theater Dorothy and I played as a team
in 1945.

"The quality of his whistling is like that of a finely tuned musical instrument."
                                                        N.Y. Daily Mirror

---

At the Hippodrome in Baltimore we needed an emcee, so I suggested a young comedian named Joey Bishop. It was his first big date.

Courtesy of Dorothy Rae

"Act has considerable appeal and scores big."   Variety

Loew's Capitol, Washington, D.C., 1945.

"Fred Lowery is sure-fire for any type audience."   Variety

National Theater, Richmond, Virginia, 1946.

"Top billing goes to Fred Lowery. If you haven't met this melodious gentleman from Texas, you've a musical treat in store."   Richmond News Leader

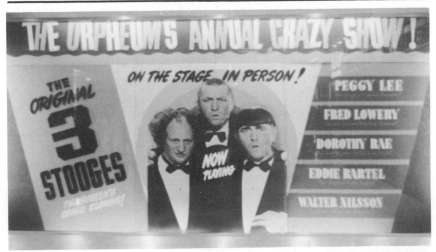

Orpheum Theater, Los Angeles, 1947   *Courtesy of Dorothy Rae*

Olympia Theater, Miami, Florida, 1947.   *Courtesy of Dorothy Rae*

"Fred Lowery ran away with the show."   Billboard

Headlining this week at Olympia Theater is Fred Lowery, whose whistling technique is nationally known through his phonograph records. He scored a tremendous hit here last year and repeats that performance. He's an exuberant fellow, and must have music in his heart. We noticed him beating out every note while his beautiful partner, Dorothy Rae, was doing her solo singing bit. Together they'll stir your heart with 'Whistling Joe.' Alone, Fred will bring goose pimples to the back of your neck with his Gershwin tribute."   Miami Herald

Fred Lowery, sound marvel, is back with his array of prodigious whistling. It's fascinating and phenomenal. He reaches the tones of the violin's E string and spins out the silver thread of melody with perfection."   Miami Daily News

---

I called Claire Stewart "my little Texas Bluebonnet."

My last singing partner, Catharine Toomay, had a beautiful, highly trained
voice.   *Courtesy of Catharine Toomay McMullen*

With Gracie and Fred at LaRue's. Supper Club in Indianapolis, 1956.

Tootling with one of my most loyal fans, Mrs. Bing (Brownie) Grunwald of Omaha, Nebraska.

My friend Art Linkletter and me in 1957. Art was in Indianapolis headlining the Indiana State Fair, and he appeared on my WISH radio talk show.

Photo by Fred M. Lowery

With Gracie at our home in Jacksonville.   *Photo by Merv Dawson*

Whistling with sixth-grader Chris Bush at 10th Street East Elementary School in Anderson, Indiana.   *Photo by Frank H. Fisse*

Delightful and delighted audience at 10th Street East Elementary School.
Photo by Frank H. Fisse

The Lowery clan on an outing at Loves Lookout Park, Jacksonville. From left: Julie, John, Fred M. Jr., Grace, Fred, Astrid, Fred M.

Photo by Fred M. Lowery

I've always enjoyed talking to young people and sharing my thoughts and experiences with them. Gracie and I hosted this get-together in the backyard of our Jacksonville, Texas, home in August 1982.

Photo by Fred M. Lowery

159

Whistling in the park.

Photo by Fred M. Lowery

Chapter 12

Arthur Godfrey summed it up for me years ago. I had finished a guest appearance on his network show, and we were relaxing after the tension of the broadcast. The talk drifted around to the vagaries of life.

In a reminiscent mood, Godfrey recalled his early struggles. "When I was out of work, broke, and hungry, no one ever offered to buy me a meal," he said. "But when I reached the top and could afford to eat in the ritziest restaurants, everybody wanted to pick up my tab."

Godfrey's observation was on target. The whole world flocks around a winner, but nobody likes a loser. After Vincent Lopez bowed to the demands of Billy Rose and fired me, I might as well have been an unknown. The word got around that I was a Billy Rose reject, and suddenly people of influence in show business began turning away when I came near.

Money—or the lack of it—was not the most critical problem that confronted me. During my four years with Lopez I had managed to save a few hundred dollars, giving me some cushion against insolvency. And Jere Buckley, Clara Bell Walsh, and a few other friends had offered me loans. What I really needed was a job and some hope of a future. During those final months of 1938 my life was shadowed by frightening questions: What does an out-of-work whistler do? Am I a has-been in the world of music before my twenty-ninth birthday? Where do I go from here?

Clara Bell Walsh wasn't "in" with the swing generation, but she was still concerned about my career and managed to line up an occasional paying performance for me at a charitable or social affair. She also tried to convince Vincent Lopez that he should rehire me. But Lopez was afraid to defy Billy Rose. However, he did give me a role in a Warner Brothers film short featuring the Lopez orchestra. And he battled the union when it tried to bar me from the set because I was delinquent in my dues.

"What in the hell are you talking about?" Lopez exclaimed when a union representative showed up at the film studio in Brooklyn and demanded that I be ejected.

"Lowery's behind in his dues. He can't work this job," the union's enforcer replied.

"Sure he's behind in his dues. He's been out of work. How's he supposed to pay union dues when he's not working?"

"Doesn't make any difference. No dues, no job!"

"By God," Lopez said, "if you guys force Lowery off this job I'm going to tell the newspapers what a crummy outfit you are, keeping a man who's out of work—and a blind man at that—from earning a few bucks."

The threat of bad publicity sent the union representative scurrying to the nearest telephone. He returned a few minutes later to announce that the front office had reconsidered and that I could do the movie if I agreed to have Warner Brothers deduct the delinquent dues from my pay.

I agreed, and the cameras rolled on what is now a long-forgotten bit of film trivia. It earned me $100 minus the union dues, but it didn't open any doors to a new job.

There was a brief flicker of hope when Fred Waring invited me to audition with his band. He seemed enthusiastic and said he'd get back to me in a couple of days to discuss a contract. But after more than a week of nerve-wracking waiting by the telephone, Waring called to tell me the deal was off.

"I'm sorry, Fred, but I can't figure out how to use your talent," he said. "I tried to think of something different than Lopez did with your whistling, but I couldn't come up with an answer. Sorry, pal."

Waring's turndown was a bitter blow, a disappointment that intensified my depression. Day after day I made the rounds, trying to keep in touch with the many contacts I had made during my years with Lopez. Everywhere I turned I got words of sympathy, vague promises, even a few offers of loans, but no jobs. My career as an entertainer seemed doomed.

I wasn't alone. Bobby Lytle had also been fired by Lopez because, with Billy Rose employing big-name vocalists at the Casa Manana, he had become excess baggage on the payroll. And we had plenty of company in our fruitless job hunting. The Belvedere Hotel where Bobby and I shared an efficiency apartment was a haven for a small army of unemployed entertainers.

Today, the midtown Manhattan of my Lopez years is only a memory, replaced by porn movies, muggers, fences, prostitutes, and drug pushers. The Belvedere vanished from the scene years ago. Even back in 1938 it was way past its prime, with cracking plaster, worn carpets, mildewed lobby, creaking elevators, and noisy plumbing. But it was home.

Once the other indigent residents of the Belvedere learned that Bobby Lytle and I were jobless, they started giving us helpful tips. They were especially dismayed to discover that, though unemployed, we were continuing to pay our weekly rent.

"That ain't kosher!" advised Billy, an elderly juggling veteran of the Keith Circuit. "There's more important things to spend money on. The only paying guests in this joint are those with jobs. And that ain't very many!"

I quickly set out to puncture my new friend's logic. "If we don't pay the rent we'll be kicked out!"

Billy snickered. "Don't you believe it! Nobody gets kicked out of the Belvedere these days. And you can always make it up when you get work."

Given this assurance, Bobby and I decided to join the rent evaders in order to take some of the strain off our dwindling savings. But our friend was prematurely optimistic. About a week later the Belvedere brought in a new credit manager, appropriately named Mr. Hawk, who promptly initiated an all-out war on delinquent tenants.

Bombarded by dunning notices and tough "pay up or get out" edicts, we devised all manner of subterfuges to avoid the relentless Hawk on his rent-collecting rounds. At first it seemed like a game, but finally we realized the new credit manager really meant to enforce his demands. It was Mike, an unemployed trombonist, who came up with a solution to our problem.

During a romantic interlude with a Belvedere coffee-shop waitress Mike picked up a fascinating bit of hotel gossip. It seemed Mr. Hawk had one big weakness. He was a drinker who went on binges that lasted weeks at a time. This bit of intelligence led to a council of war in Mike's room. "Maybe if we can get Hawk to take a few drinks he'll go off and leave us alone for awhile," the musician suggested.

"Maybe so, but where are we gonna get the kind of booze Hawk likes?" our juggler friend asked. "The way I hear it, he sure ain't gonna be tempted by the cheap wine or gin most of us drink around here."

"Why don't we all chip in and buy a jug of good stuff . . . something that's sure to tempt him?" someone else suggested.

Everyone agreed, so we took up a collection and sent Bobby Lytle to a cut-rate store on Ninth Avenue to buy a quart of their best bourbon. After displaying the prized bottle amid a hospitable array of glasses and ice cubes on a table in Mike's room, we telephoned the desk and invited Hawk to join us for a discussion of our delinquent rents. He hotfooted it up to the room. As soon as he got settled in the most comfortable chair Mike suggested, "How about a drink before we get down to business?"

As Mike and Bobby Lytle later described the scene to me, Hawk thirstily eyed the big bottle. "Really, I shouldn't. I'm still on duty," he said, striving to maintain a businesslike attitude in the face of temptation.

163

"Hell, one sociable drink never hurt anybody," Mike coaxed. "Come on, man, relax for a few minutes."

Hawk abruptly surrendered his good intentions. "Well, maybe just one quick drink."

Two hours and a full quart later Hawk had forgotten about the unpaid bills. At last, seeing that the bottle was empty, he struggled to his feet, mumbled his thank-yous, and lurched across the room into a closet.

Bobby Lytle retrieved Hawk, steered him out into the corridor, and headed him toward the elevator. We later learned that he disembarked from the elevator and staggered across the lobby into the night. He never returned—not even to pick up his belongings or his last paycheck.

The tough Mr. Hawk was replaced by a far less aggressive credit manager named Randy Jenkins. Although we expected to indulge in our game of wits with him, it was soon apparent that no artful dodging was necessary. Randy Jenkins launched only halfhearted rent-collection campaigns.

Most of my compatriots were skilled evaders of harassed credit managers, but I had more difficulty because of my sight problem. I was frequently cornered by Randy and soon became familiar with his technique. He didn't bully or threaten. He begged. "Can't you at least pay a couple of bucks on account?" he'd whine, a plea which could always be countered by a demonstration of empty pockets.

One day after my customary response I asked Randy why he didn't just evict us.

He sighed. "If I kicked all you guys out I'd just get another bunch of jobless deadbeats. I figure that by being patient and giving everybody a break, when you guys find work you'll be grateful and pay at least part of what you owe." It was a smart philosophy. A lot of us delinquent guests did pay the hotel when we finally landed jobs.

The Belvedere's jobless residents were constantly concerned about financing such important items as food, cigarettes, and the grooming aids necessary for maintaining a respectable appearance for job hunting. To accomplish this we became a kind of commune, sharing our problems, our fun, and whatever food and drink we could scrounge. We even set up a "bank" to which we contributed a few bucks whenever we could—and from which we could draw small loans to tide us over whenever we were totally broke.

A couple of the more exotic types gave up job hunting and engaged in panhandling for a livelihood. They managed to collect a few dollars a day, and they usually put a share into the communal pot.

An unemployed carnival contortionist named Eddie built a double-

164

decker contraption substantial enough to camouflage his legs from the knees down. With his legs folded under the deck of the platform he scooted about midtown New York, apparently legless, gathering contributions in a battered World War I helmet decorated with the patriotic plea: *Help a crippled soldier!*

Maisie, another Belvederian, was a tiny girl in her twenties, a skinny, three-foot-plus veteran of the Singer's Midget Troupe. Dressed in patched clothes and sporting pigtails and a woeful look, she went from door to door posing as an impoverished child seeking funds to pay for medical help for her dying mother or food for her orphaned brothers and sisters or whatever other tear-jerking fantasy she chose to create.

Eddie and Maisie were the Belvedere's regular "beggars," but from time to time other jobless entertainers put their talents to work on the streets of New York in an effort to survive. They usually abandoned these careers quickly, for the hours were long, the work degrading, and the take seldom more than a dollar or two. There was one exception that I recall. A middle-aged couple with years of minor acting roles behind them decided to try their luck. Like Eddie and Maisie they developed a scenario complete with costumes. Dressing up as a priest and nun, they took to the streets to solicit nickel and dime contributions to their personal "church charities." They never made much money, but they truly enjoyed the game, feeling it gave them a chance to practice their thespian skills.

Of course a sharp-witted entrepreneur of the streets like Eddie was convinced I was a natural for panhandling. He repeatedly urged me to join the beggar's parade with a tin cup and white cane. He could never understand why I indignantly turned him down.

"You're wastin' time lookin' for a job, Lowery," Eddie berated me on more than one occasion. "Fakers like me make out pretty good, but it makes me sick to think what you could do out on the street. You're the real thing! You could make a fortune sitting on Broadway with a tin cup and whistling them pretty tunes!

Two other fascinating characters came to stay at the Belvedere during that period. One was an over-the-hill vaudeville and radio comedian. The other was a polar explorer named David Irwin whom I met at one of Clara Bell Walsh's parties. He was one of Manhattan's adopted heroes—a twenty-eight-year-old "retired" adventurer who was living off the royalties of his best-selling book, *Alone Across the Top of the World*, while savoring the unaccustomed luxuries of civilization.

Irwin was, at the very least, eccentric. No one in his right mind would have set out for the North Pole single-handed with only a secondhand dog sled and a team of cast-off huskies for company. And only a very lucky man would have returned from such a slapdash expedition. Irwin had crossed more than 2,000 miles of Arctic wastelands, the longest polar trek ever undertaken by a man alone.

I secretly envied the life of action and adventure Irwin had led. He was the same age as I, but he had braved a primitive and exciting world I could never hope to enter. Despite my envy, though, I was fascinated by the man and his unpredictable temperament, and we soon formed a friendship that endured until his death many years later.

Irwin was as intrigued by my life as I was by his, and probably for the same reason. I lived in a dim and murky world he could never conceive of or enter. However, he could sympathize with and relate to physical handicaps because as a youth in the Midwest he had been sickly, plagued by a series of serious illnesses that doctors said would doom him to life as a semi-invalid. He refused to accept that diagnosis. As a frail sixteen-year-old he ran away from home and signed aboard an oceangoing freighter as cabin boy, determined to become whole or die in the attempt. His health improved, his muscles hardened, and he became an able-bodied seaman. In his spare time at sea he educated himself by reading all manner of books. One of these books, *Across Arctic America* by polar explorer Knud Rasmussen, stirred young Irwin's imagination. He decided that this bleak, unknown land represented man's ultimate challenge.

David Irwin, of course, was faced with a major problem in addressing that challenge. Polar expeditions were costly enterprises involving vast amounts of supplies, equipment, and manpower and were usually financed by governments, foundations, or universities. Irwin had access to none of these sources. As for personal assets, he was always broke a few days after his ship hit port. But that didn't stop him. He spent a year in Alaska as a trapper, learning the ways of the wilderness. Then in the autumn of 1932, with $250 in savings to finance his solo expedition, he headed for the remote Arctic lands of Canada's Northwest Territories.

At the tiny settlement of Barter Island Irwin bought a used sled, a team of six undernourished dogs, and provisions for six months. In January 1933, ignoring the warnings of the Eskimo hunters and trappers, he set out across the snow-swept ice fields on an exploration he hoped would take him to the North Pole.

Two years later, in January 1935, Irwin returned to Barter Island with an Eskimo hunting party that had found him wandering lost, delirious, and starving in the uninhabited Barren Lands of King William Island. A 129-man exploration party headed by Britain's Sir John Franklin had perished there in 1848. During those two years Irwin had managed to get within a few miles of the magnetic pole. But in the summer of 1934 thawing ice in the Barrow Straits had forced him to retreat.

For six months, from June to December, Irwin saw no other human. He wandered aimlessly, trapped by summer's thawing ice and later by the early storms of autumn. Somehow he survived on raw fish and dog meat. He ate his sled dogs one by one as they collapsed and could go no further. He finally stumbled onto King William Island, where he was found by the Eskimo hunters.

"I was about ready to give up, ready to collapse and wait for death, when they found me," Irwin told me. "I'd already reconciled myself to the fact that I'd never return to the civilized world."

Word of his rescue finally reached America, and the *New York Times* dispatched a reporter to interview him. The story of Irwin's solitary conquest of the Arctic made him a hero by the time he returned to the civilization he had once despaired of seeing again.

Despite his sudden fame Irwin remained a basically simple, independent man who found the demands of notoriety irksome. He liked the luxuries he had missed for so long, but he wanted to enjoy them in his own way. He relished the hero's role but wearied of the crowds of strangers who sought him out.

In David Irwin I once again found a friend when I needed one most. A week or so after I met the young adventurer, Bobby Lytle had to return to his home in Ohio because of an illness in his family. The departure of Lytle, who had been both my companion and my eyes, left me alone in the apartment at the Belvedere.

"I've been looking for a new place to roost—someplace where I can get away from all the hullabaloo," Irwin said when he learned of Lytle's departure. "We seem to hit it off pretty well. Why don't I move in with you and help with the expenses?"

"That would be great," I said. "But the Belvedere isn't very fancy. You might not like it."

Irwin assured me he'd spent most of his life in a lot worse places than the Belvedere and that he just wanted to start living with real, down-to-earth people again. So he moved in, and it was soon apparent that he was as kooky as everybody else in the hotel.

Irwin was an exercise freak. He didn't limit his exercising to ordinary calisthenics, although he did delight in starting each morning with one hundred push-ups in front of an open window—a practice which during those November and December days turned our tiny apartment into a replica of his beloved Arctic. His favorite conditioner was even more grueling. He scorned the use of elevators. Instead, when coming home or leaving, he raced full speed up or down the stairway that stretched from the lobby to our ninth-floor apartment — a mad dash punctuated by a series of blood-curdling whoops which, he claimed, helped maintain his lung power.

During his first night in the apartment I discovered that my new roommate had an even stranger compulsion. I was awakened by the noise of someone bumping into a chair. "Who's that?" I shouted.

"It's just me. David." Irwin's voice, usually strong and self-assured, was subdued, almost apologetic.

"What's wrong, Dave? Aren't you feeling well?"

"I'm okay," he mumbled. "Just woke up hungry. I was raiding the icebox. But it seems to be empty."

"I guess it is. Bobby always did the shopping and cooking. I've been eating in the coffee shop since he left."

That's when Irwin confessed his secret vice. "Ever since I almost starved up there I wake up in the middle of the night feeling like I'm starving. And I can't get back to sleep until I eat something. I know it's stupid, but I can't help it."

That night David appeased his hunger with a couple of candy bars I had stored in one of my dresser drawers. After that we always made sure there was food in the apartment's tiny refrigerator to take care of his nightly hunger pangs.

Irwin's hunger was nearly equaled by his thirst. He avoided the harder vintages, but had an amazing capacity for beer. For atmosphere he carefully avoided the city's celebrity meccas and was forever seeking out and enjoying the fellowship of Manhattan's back-street neighborhood saloons. It was in one of these that we collected a new companion. Irwin attempted to strike up a conversation with a stranger who had taken a seat beside us at the bar and ordered a stein of beer. But he got only noncommittal grunts from our fellow beer-lover. The stranger finally slammed his stein on the bar. "Give me a refill, Pete!"

The bartender, obviously acquainted with the man, quickly fetched the refill and observed, "Kinda thirsty, aintcha, Sassafras?"

"Sassafras . . . Sassafras," David remarked with his typical candor. "Surely that can't be your right name!"

"It's good enough for me, mister. Any objections?" Our companion seemed irked by Irwin's nosiness. Judging by his *basso profundo*, now tinged with hostility, he was not a man to be trifled with, and I began to wonder if Irwin might end up as the face on the barroom floor. But I was curious too, for the name had stirred something in my memory.

"Say, friend, are you by any chance Charley Sands out of Abilene . . . the guy who played Sassafras on the radio?" I was glad Irwin was sitting between us in case my question riled the stranger even more.

"How come you know so much? Who in the hell are you?"

"I met you at the Rainbow Grill a few years ago at one of the Texas Society's shindigs. My name's Fred Lowery, out of the Piney Woods and Dallas."

"Yeah, I remember. You're Lowery, the whistler." The stranger's earlier hostility thawed abruptly. He admitted that he was indeed Charley Sands. "But everybody calls me Sassafras, or Sass for short," he added. And he proceeded to recount a sad but familiar tale.

Back in the early thirties when NBC's "Amos 'n Andy" became radio's first big comedy hit, rival CBS decided to put a similar show on the air. A new blackface comedy team featuring a couple of veteran vaudeville comics was formed and given starring roles in a show titled "Honeyboy and Sassafras." The show was an immediate success, and Charley Sands and his longtime vaudeville partner Jim Slocum became high-paid radio celebrities. However, fame only dropped in for a visit and not to stay.

At the peak of their popularity Honeyboy died, and Sassafras learned that there's no future in being the surviving member of a comedy team. The show was canceled, and Charley Sands was out of a job. Except for an occasional bit part Charley, typed by his Sassafras role, found all doors closed to him. By late 1938 he was drifting on the fringes of show business, living off dwindling savings from his few years at the top, and waiting in vain for his luck to change.

Our chance encounter in the Eighth Avenue bar would probably have ended there except for a belligerent tippler who stormed in from the street roaring that he was the "mayor of Eighth Avenue." Nobody challenged the newcomer's claim—which seemed to infuriate him even more. "I said I'm the mayor of Eighth Avenue," he bellowed. "Anyone here man enough to say it ain't so?"

Again, silence. The enraged "mayor" decided to launch his own war. He threw a punch that whistled past Sassafras's ear and landed on the side of David Irwin's head, knocking David into me. We both crashed to the floor, and our assailant pounced on us. But Sassafras picked up a barstool and clubbed the stranger over the head. He then dragged the "mayor of Eighth Avenue" out onto the sidewalk. Returning to the bar, he ordered a round of beers and announced, "Boys, you've got a new mayor!"

That incident cemented our friendship. When we learned that Sassafras was drifting from one flophouse to another, we brought him to the Belvedere to share both our small apartment and our explorations of Manhattan.

Apparently his bad luck didn't rub off, because it was Sassafras who chanced on a news item that ultimately revived my career. We were sitting in the apartment one December afternoon waiting for Dave to return from a visit to his publisher. To pass the time Sass was skimming through *Variety*, reading me choice bits of celebrity gossip.

"Hey, this ought to interest you," he suddenly exclaimed.

"What's that?"

"It says here that the Horace Heidt band is coming to town for a gig at the Biltmore. It says Heidt has had a big shake-up . . . that Alvino Rey and the King Sisters have quit and that he's going to be looking for new talent when he gets to New York."

That last bit of information caught my attention. Several years before, while the Lopez orchestra was in Hollywood, Heidt had phoned me with a job offer. Even then Horace Heidt and his Brigadiers—a name later changed to the Musical Knights—was one of the nation's biggest dance bands. It was a "show band" that had gained considerable popularity even though it was scorned by many musicians and critics as being short on talent and long on gimmicks. Nevertheless I had been flattered by the offer, although I had turned it down because I was happy with Lopez.

When I told Sass about that earlier job offer, he was as elated as if the network had suddenly decided to revive his old show. "You've got it made," he said. "Get in touch with Heidt as soon as he hits town. If he wanted to hire you a couple of years ago, he'll probably want you even more now, seeing as how he's hunting for talent."

I wasn't so enthusiastic. "I don't know about that. Heidt has probably never forgiven me for turning down his job offer in L.A. These bandleaders are strange cats. You can't figure how they're going to react."

"Don't be a jerk!" Sass said. "What have you got to lose?"

Even though I was feeling sorry for myself I couldn't argue with that logic. As soon as the Heidt band arrived in New York I telephoned the Biltmore. Horace was out, but I talked with his secretary, Helen Wingert. She recognized my name and said she was sure Horace would be interested in giving me an audition.

"We'll be in touch with you," she said. It was a familiar refrain that, as I knew too well, usually added up to a polite brush-off.

"Maybe she means it," Sass said. But there wasn't much hope in his voice. He'd also heard that song before.

"Not a chance!" I replied glumly. "I'll never hear from Heidt. No use kidding myself!"

Despite my pessimism I spent two days in the apartment close to the phone. The call didn't come. A few days earlier Johnny Dilliard, one of my friends from the Lopez orchestra, had invited me to a holiday party at his Long Island home. I decided to give up my telephone vigil and join the fun.

Johnny met me at the Jackson Heights station and drove me to his home where a bunch of musicians and their wives and girl friends already had the party well under way. It was a splendid party—an evening marked by good food, a lot of toasting, and fun-filled recollections of the good old days with Lopez. Just before 9 P.M. the phone rang.

David Irwin was on the other end of the line informing me that Horace Heidt had just called and wanted me to contact him immediately at the Biltmore. Minutes later I had Horace Heidt on the phone. The ensuing conversation undoubtedly reflected my woozy state. After all, we had consumed a considerable amount of holiday spirits.

"Can you be here by eleven?" Heidt asked.

"Eleven in the morning?"

"Hell, no! Eleven tonight!"

"Gosh, isn't that kind of late for an audition?"

"Who said anything about an audition? That's our first broadcast from the Biltmore."

"But Helen Wingert said something about an audition . . ."

"I don't care what Helen said. I've heard you perform. I know what you can do, and I want you here for this broadcast." He paused. "You don't sound so hot. Think you can make it?"

"Mr. Heidt," I said, "I'll be there if I have to sprout wings!"

Hearing the sounds of laughter in the background, Heidt said, "Sounds like you're already flying." And he hung up.

The news of my good fortune was greeted with cheers by my partying friends, and they had a fresh round of holiday cheer to celebrate my return to the big-band scene. Then Johnny Dilliard addressed the problem of getting me to the Biltmore in time for the broadcast.

"Just drive me to the station," I said. "I'll make it okay."

Johnny quickly vetoed that idea. "You aren't in any condition to make the trip back to Manhattan by yourself. God knows where you'd end up."

"I've got to make it," I protested. "I can't afford to miss this chance."

"Don't worry, you'll make it," Johnny assured me. "I'll drive you into the city myself."

"Fred needs more than a lift," Johnny's wife observed. She wouldn't let us leave until she had filled a thermos jug with black coffee. And she insisted on accompanying us, feeding me cup after cup of the steaming brew while Johnny chauffeured us back to Manhattan, followed by three cars loaded with merrymaking guests who decided to move the party into the city.

By the time we pulled up in front of the Belvedere I was feeling a little more clear-headed. Dave Irwin and Sassafras had laid out my tux and tie and polished my black dress shoes. They rushed me through my grooming and got me back out to the Dilliard's car in record time. I strolled into the Biltmore's Terrace with my entourage a half hour before broadcast time, ready to go to work.

Horace Heidt wasted no time on formalities. He didn't even bother to discuss the question of salary. The band was taking a break before the broadcast, and Heidt had one of his sidemen escort the Dilliards, Dave Irwin, and Sassafras to a table while he tried to determine if I was ready to perform.

"Are you sure you're okay?" he asked as he led me over to meet pianist Lou Bush.

"I'm feeling okay," I assured him. "But I wish I had time to rehearse . . . time to work up at least a couple of arrangements instead of starting cold."

As we sat down at a table with Lou Bush, Heidt admitted he was taking a risk asking me to go on the air without a rehearsal and with a strange band behind me. But he explained that he needed at least one new personality for his first New York broadcast to counteract the publicity generated by the defection of Alvino Rey and the King Sisters.

"You're our first new performer since we arrived in New York," he said. "You're a big-band star with a national reputation. I feel it's important for you to take part in this broadcast even if it's just for one or two numbers."

I agreed, but I again cautioned him that I couldn't guarantee a polished performance on such short notice.

"Don't worry, Fred. You're a pro. I'm sure you'll be fine. Just talk it over with Lou and settle on a couple of numbers you're familiar with. That'll be enough for tonight."

I had listened to broadcasts by the Heidt band frequently and thought I was familiar with its style. After a brief conference we decided on two favorites with relatively simple arrangements—"Heartaches" and "Indian Love Call."

Lopez had always refrained from mentioning my disability in public. But when Horace Heidt introduced me on the air for my first number it was evident that this master showman looked upon my blindness as a new and uniquely merchandisable feature of his band. "Tonight we're delighted to introduce the newest star of our band . . . that nationally famous musical wizard, the man with a million golden melodies, Fred Lowery, the blind whistler," Heidt announced with his customary flair for flowery verbiage.

Vocalist Larry Cotton led me to the microphone and the band began to play. As a performer, I immediately discovered there was a vast difference between the Lopez and Heidt styles. This was not the smooth, melodic flow to which I was accustomed. It was a vastly more intricate sound featuring Heidt's triple tongueing trumpeteers. And the melody was constantly embroidered with all manner of sliding and glissing, not to mention the twanging of a steel guitar. Somehow I managed to adjust and bluff my way through "Heartaches" without committing a "clam," the expression we used at the time for a sour note or missed beat. A short while later we got through "Indian Love Call" without a mishap; my curtain raiser with Horace Heidt was a success.

After the broadcast Heidt congratulated me and finally got around to talking business. Although he had introduced me as the band's newest star, I hadn't received—or accepted—a salary offer. And it was soon apparent that when it came to money Horace wasn't talking at "star" level. I had been making $200 a week with Lopez, but Heidt offered me only $50 a week to start. Despite my professional status I was back at the beginner's scale I had received when I was hired by Lopez in 1934.

"It's just a starting salary until we're sure everything will work out okay," Heidt hastened to assure me. "If it does, there'll be a raise plus good money on the side from recordings with Columbia."

I didn't protest. At that point I would have accepted a lot less. Of course I didn't admit that to my new boss; I merely accepted his offer, thus being officially signed on by Heidt an hour *after* he had announced my hiring on the network show.

With the delayed formalities settled, Heidt asked me if I could show up at the Biltmore for a special rehearsal the next afternoon, Christmas Eve.

"I'd like to work up a few arrangements . . . enough so you can be on the bandstand tomorrow night." Horace seemed almost apologetic. "I know it's kind of sudden, getting hired right before Christmas. Maybe you've got something planned for the holidays and need a couple of days off. If you do, let me know. I'll understand."

I hastily assured him I had no plans for the holidays—and that I'd be happy to show up for the rehearsal. "Besides," I thought, "Santa Claus has come around early this year. This job is the best Christmas present I've ever had."

Chapter 13

For obvious reasons I never experienced one childhood delight of my generation—the wonderment of a kaleidoscope. I remember being overwhelmed by a sense of loss whenever I heard anyone describe the fragile beauty they could witness by peering into the kaleidoscope, watching hundreds of bits of colored glass form a shimmering pattern that quickly disintegrated to be replaced by another and another and another. Horace Heidt was as great an enigma to me as that toy I never knew.

Evidently most of the music critics of his era were as baffled by this complex man as I was. Generally, they caricatured him, portraying him as a buffoon, a brawling leader of a vaudeville band—a band that once featured a dog as a star performer. Most swing-generation musicians were scornful of Heidt too, looking upon him as an untalented, humorless, money-hungry opportunist who contributed only sour notes to the music of his time. I suspect that much of his contemporaries' scorn was generated by professional jealousy—because Heidt, a nonmusician, organized, promoted, and led one of the largest and most successful dance bands of the 1930s and 1940s.

Heidt possessed little if any musical talent. When he sang he sounded like a bullfrog with laryngitis, and he was never able to master an instrument, not even the harmonica. But he was smart enough to recognize his shortcomings. He never tried to fake musical ability and never pushed himself into the spotlight at the expense of his band. Instead, he capitalized on the abilities he did possess—showmanship and a flair for discovering and promoting new talent. Combining showmanship and talented people, he created dance-band extravaganzas that charmed the public, if not the critics.

As for personality, Horace Heidt was often tense and abrasive. He was a big, athletic man with a quick temper and a penchant for fisticuffs. And early in his career he was too much concerned with making a buck and too little concerned with making beautiful music. But there were other sides to his kaleidoscopic personality. In his relationships with members of his organization Heidt could be a warm, understanding friend. And he not only assembled a large group of talented, high-voltage egos but also managed to keep them reasonably free of the inner feuds and frictions that plagued so many of the big bands.

Heidt unquestionably was a sharp businessman. Making a profit was his main objective. But it was his money-making talent—and his willingness to give his people a piece of the action—that kept the Musical Knights prospering when other talented bands faltered and failed.

Much of the criticism of Heidt was rooted in the bizarre reputation of his early bands, in which music was only a backdrop for all manner of vaudeville acts. But after a disastrous New York engagement in the early thirties Heidt set about building a band loaded with musical talent. Even though he continued to surround his musicians with all manner of supplementary entertainment, from acrobatic dancers to jugglers, from impressionists to radio's first giveaway show, the Musical Knights eventually became a top-quality band. But the critics retained their prejudice, reluctant to recognize Heidt's metamorphosis from vaudevillian to music-maker.

I realize that to some I may appear to be naively ignoring Heidt's faults. That is not really so, for like others closely associated with him during the big-band era I alternately admired and cursed, loved and hated him. He was a man who could change rapidly from icy aloofness to compassionate friendship, from awkward shyness to fiery rage. Even before I met Horace Heidt for the first time I had heard fascinating stories about him. He was a popular target for gossip among musicians. And it wasn't long before I personally encountered his unpredictable nature.

At my first rehearsal the nice guy of the previous night was in a vile mood. He raged at Art Thorsen, the band's manager, over some business matters. He criticized Helen Wingert for some real or imagined miscarriage of her secretarial duties. And he stormed at his sidemen for all manner of musical gaffes. Finally he got around to me.

During a lull, Heidt approached the piano where I was discussing an arrangement with Lou Bush. "Fred, I've been thinking about last night's performance," he announced brusquely. "Your whistling was fine, but it seemed kind of plain . . . too high-pitched. Seems to me we ought to jazz up your style a bit, give it some oomph."

Although I was a newcomer midway in my initial rehearsál after a trying jobless interlude, I found it difficult to hold my temper in check. I was not accustomed to criticism of my whistling techniques. But I managed to

175

restrain an intemperate response and asked him what he had in mind.

"Well, I feel you should get in a lower key . . . not so many high notes. And you ought to liven up your whistling. You know, fancy up the melody with some trills, sort of like a nightingale!"

I was nonplussed. After just one performance Heidt not only was trying to teach me how to whistle but was urging me to use a hackneyed technique I despised. I decided I had to establish my position even if it cost me my job.

"I'm afraid that's not possible, Mr. Heidt. Whistling is just a lot higher than the human voice, and I can whistle at least three notes higher than the highest note on the piano. A lot of my most beautiful effects are in the high ranges. And I never use bird-chirping."

"What if I order you to change your style?" Heidt asked.

It was a challenge I couldn't ignore. "Mr. Heidt," I said, "it's your band, and you can tell me what to wear, where to travel, what time to report for work, and what numbers to perform, but you can't tell me how to whistle. I've got to do it my way, and either you like it or you don't."

I waited for the axe to fall. Instead, Heidt erupted in a burst of laughter. "By God, you're a nervy character!" he exclaimed. "I like a man with enough spunk to say no!" And he punctuated his unexpected approval with a friendly slap on the back as he hurried off to resume the rehearsal.

Other band members, of course, had witnessed the exchange. Later that afternoon, as we straggled away from rehearsal, Art Thorsen and Ralph Wingert—one of Heidt's trumpeters and the husband of Helen Wingert—invited me to join them for cocktails in the Biltmore bar. Thorsen, the band manager and a former tuba player, had been with the band since its early days in the 1920s. Wingert was also a Heidt veteran. They were the band's elders who watched over the younger musicians, attempted to keep them out of trouble, and tried, not always successfully, to oil any squeaky relationships that developed.

Thorsen edged carefully into the main subject of our tête-à-tête, the not-so-gentle art of getting along with Horace Heidt. "You played it smart with Horace," he said. "He likes people who stand up to him."

"Yeah, but don't think Horace has given in," Wingert cautioned. "He'll keep trying to change your style, testing you to see if you'll give in. Sometimes he'll treat it as a big joke when you say no, like he did today, and sometimes he'll get sore and won't talk to you for days or weeks."

"That's right," Thorsen agreed. "Horace is a very strange guy. Unpredictable. But don't let his moods get you. Deep down, he's a real great guy, a stand-up guy who treats his people right."

"No doubt about it," Wingert said. "We've got a real great organization,

176

and we don't want you to get the wrong impression. We've had some rough times the last few months. A lot of changes. People being fired, people quitting, losing our network sponsor, looking for new talent. It's no wonder Horace is kind of edgy."

It was obvious that they were working hard to paint the best possible picture for me. I was flattered, for I realized they wouldn't be taking such pains unless Heidt wanted me to become a permanent member of the band. So I settled back with my drink, a willing listener.

"You've got to understand that Heidt's not like Lopez or Goodman or the Dorseys," the band manager explained. "He's not a musician . . . can't carry a tune in a bucket. He's an ex-athlete who decided to form a band, and sometimes he has trouble understanding musicians, especially when he feels they're poking fun at his lack of musical knowledge."

Thorsen recalled Heidt's beginnings. He had been an all-American guard on the University of California football team when he suffered a broken back during the 1922 Rose Bowl game. During his long recovery he decided for some perverse reason that he wanted to organize a band. His father, a California businessman, tried to dissuade him, arguing that he knew nothing about music. But Horace couldn't be swayed from his ambition to break into show business.

When Heidt recovered he began to assemble the band he had dreamed of. It wasn't a plain, everyday dance band, not even a jazz group. It was what was known in those days as a "show band" or vaudeville band—a large collection of musicians and vocalists who produced all sorts of novelty ragtime sounds. Heidt utilized a bizarre assortment of instruments, ranging from the customary piano, drums, brass, reeds, and strings to such exotic contraptions as cowbells, kazoos, marimbas, tambourines, ukuleles, and even a silver cocktail shaker loaded with rattling dice. As an added dimension the band featured dance teams, acrobats, magicians, comedy acts, and a German shepherd named Lobo who played "The Bells of St. Marys" on a set of musical bells.

"Lobo was really something," Thorsen said. "The mutt was owned by one of our sax players, a guy named Howard Woolsey, who happened to be the brother of Horace's first wife, Florence. One day Horace remembered a vaudeville act he'd seen as a kid, an act where a dog played the bells, and he and Woolsey decided to train Lobo as a 'musician.' "

As Thorsen remembered, it took about a year—and considerable cursing and cuffing—to train Lobo to pick up the bells in the proper sequence and shake them. Apparently the dog produced a fairly recognizable "St. Marys."

"Finally we included the dog act in our program, and Lobo was an overnight sensation," Thorsen said. "As a matter of fact the mutt wasn't bad. Had about as much musical talent as the rest of the band in those days. Funny, though. On stage, Lobo obeyed every command by Heidt. You'd think they were real buddies. But off the stage Lobo hated Heidt . . . tried to bite him every time he came near. I guess the dog held a grudge against Horace for all the smacks it got."

The bell-ringing pooch helped bring a measure of local renown to the Heidt band on the vaudeville circuit during the 1920s. But it wasn't until a tour of Europe in 1930 that the band gained international notoriety. Thorsen chuckled as he recalled the unintentional role he had played in bringing sudden fame to Heidt.

"We were playing at one of the fancy casinos in Monte Carlo, and we were having a ball on the bandstand and off. One evening at dinner I stuffed a couple of hard rolls in my pocket. When we got on the bandstand and Horace was going through some fancy gyrations with the baton I threw one of the rolls at him. It missed Horace and beaned the King of Sweden, who was dancing cheek to cheek with a gorgeous doll."

Thorsen roared at the memory of the king's retaliation. "He didn't know who tossed the roll, but bouncing a biscuit off his royal noggin couldn't go unpunished. So he asked the gendarmes to toss Horace in jail. Horace wasn't a bit happy, and he floored a couple of the cops before they finally dragged him off to jail."

But they let him out next morning, Thorsen said, and while photographers snapped pictures and reporters shouted silly questions, the King of Sweden shook hands with the bandleader and even apologized for the inconvenience he had suffered. A flood of stories and photographs appeared in newspapers and magazines around the world. Horace Heidt and his band were celebrities when they returned to the States. They had barely stepped off the boat at New York when they were handed a contract for a national tour, starting at the prestigious Rockefeller Center.

"We really laid an egg," Thorsen recalled. "We were so bad the Rockefeller people canceled our show after a week. When Horace claimed they were breaking the contract, they pointed to an 'act of God' clause. The $30,000 loss resulting from our appearance certainly qualified as a disaster, they said. Horace didn't argue. He knew when he was licked."

After that, Heidt got an engagement at a theater in Brooklyn. The band bombed there too, and Heidt and his musicians, dancers, jugglers, and bell-ringing dog retreated to the West Coast, their national tour ended before they had crossed a single state line.

"I guess that experience shook Horace up and made him realize that if he

178

was ever going to have anything but a lousy vaudeville band he'd have to make some drastic changes," Thorsen said.

He started getting rid of a lot of the band's carnival acts, including Lobo, and went hunting for some genuine talent. He hired musicians like Ernie Passoja on the trombone and Frank DeVol, who played lead sax and wrote arrangements. There were other important additions like vocalist Larry Cotton, the King Sisters, and Alvino Rey, the master of the electric guitar and one of the finest jazz musicians in the country.

"They were all great, but Alvino was probably the most important addition," Thorsen said. "He was an Irishman who hated Latin and Hawaiian music, even though he had adopted a Latin stage name because he thought it was more romantic. But he could really play that guitar. He gave our band a new sound that went over big."

Despite the critics, Horace Heidt was emerging as the leader of one of the most popular of the big bands. The band still overindulged in theatrics, but it also had considerable talent. Then, as Thorsen put it, "everything went sour."

"One night while the King Sisters were in the middle of one of their numbers Alyce got too bouncy and knocked over a mike," he said. "It struck a woman who was dancing near the bandstand. Knocked her down and caused a nasty commotion. Heidt was furious. He fired Alyce on the spot, claimed she was juiced up. That made the other King Sisters sore, and they quit right there on the bandstand. Before the night was over Horace had gotten into two fights, and five more members of the band—good friends of the sisters—walked off the job, including Alvino Rey, who was sweet on Louise."

Thorsen then brought me up to date on the recent crisis within the Heidt organization. Rey had formed his own studio band at station KHJ in Los Angeles and hired other musicians away from Heidt.

"Losing so many of our best people left the band in a shambles with an important date in New York coming up," Thorsen said. "It's been tough. We're looking everywhere for new talent, but because of our troubles musicians are leery of us. That's why Horace is in such a rotten mood these days. He's got problems."

I was the first of the "new talent" to climb aboard the Heidt bandwagon. Others joined me in the ensuing months. But actually, even before they arrived, Heidt's "talent drain" was not nearly as severe as Art Thorsen and Ralph Wingert had claimed. Performers like Alvino Rey and the King Sisters weren't easy to replace, but Heidt had a large reservoir of talent to draw on in the emergency.

At the time I joined the band Heidt's sidemen included Bob Riedel, Bill Tieber, Loys Johnson, and Jerry Kasper in the sax section; Wingert, Warren Lewis, and Frank Strasek, the famed triple trumpeteers; Jimmy Skiles and Wayne Webb on trombone; Lou Bush at the piano; Eddie McKimmey on the bass; Bernie Mattinson on drums; and Jack Kovach, who replaced Alvino Rey on the electric guitar before the band left California.

It was an impressive array of musicians, but they were just one segment of the band. There was an equally talented lineup of vocalists including tenor Larry Cotton, hired away from Jimmie Grier's band; Lysbeth Hughes, who also played the harp; Red Farrington; Bob McCoy; Charlie Goodman; and Jerry Bowne. There was also a young singer-comedian-impressionist named Art Carney, out of Mt. Vernon, N.Y. This platoon of vocal entertainers not only presented a wide selection of pop, classical, and novelty numbers, but also provided talent for various specialty groups. In my memory no other swing-generation band had such an array of voices. It was a musical smorgasbord designed to satisfy every taste.

It was quickly evident to me that even with the defections Horace Heidt had plenty of musical talent. But, typical of the man, he was constantly trying to acquire more, just as he was always searching for new investments. He couldn't resist the urge to pick up a new act any more than he could turn down a good business deal.

Usually Heidt's judgment of talent was as sharp as his instinct for money-making. Sometimes, though, he got more than he bargained for. Perhaps the most notable case was when he hired a musician and genuinely flaky comedian named Doodles Weaver, who later became well known for his vocal antics with Spike Jones.

Doodles, the wayward son of a wealthy California family, first gained notoriety when he was a student at Stanford University. A crowd of distinguished citizens had gathered on the Palo Alto campus for the unveiling of a large statue of Stanford's most illustrious alumnus, President Herbert Hoover. When the curtains concealing the statue were pulled aside the crowd gasped at the spectacle of Doodles Weaver, naked except for a straw hat, nestled in Hoover's marble arms.

That was just one of his countless pranks, including the time his parents returned from a European vacation to discover that Doodles had painted their Beverly Hills mansion black and decorated it with neon signs. Such antics should have discouraged Heidt. But he felt that Doodles's comic talents would add zest to the band's routines.

With Doodles around, life was never dull. But his job with Heidt came to a sudden end one night at the Cocoanut Grove when, in the midst of a comedy routine, Doodles leaped off the bandstand and led most of the customers in a giant conga line out onto Wilshire Boulevard and into a rival nightclub where, as a "gracious" host, he signed Horace's name to a gigantic tab.

But Doodles Weaver was an exception. During my years with the band Heidt's roundup of new talent included trumpeter Bobby Hackett; clarinetist Irving Fazola; trombonist Warren Covington; a handsome young singer named Gordon MacRae; Bill Finegan, the arranger for Glenn Miller's band; and Henry Russell, an organist-vocalist-composer who had been director of music for station KNX in Los Angeles. But the biggest prize was Frankie Carle, a pianist who skyrocketed from obscurity to fame early in 1939 after composing "Sunrise Serenade," a hauntingly beautiful number that rose to No. 1 on the Hit Parade within a few weeks.

Horace Heidt apparently recognized Carle's genius before fame caught up with him. We were on a weekend gig in Boston when Heidt heard "Sunrise Serenade" for the first time on a radio broadcast.The local disc jockey predicted, "This new number is going to be a biggie!" After hearing the record, Heidt agreed. He launched a search for the composer and found Frankie Carle playing the piano with a combo at the Seven Gables, a suburban Boston nightclub.

With the band's longtime pianist Lou Bush anxious to return to his family on the West Coast, Frankie Carle was able to take over at the piano immediately. And it was soon apparent that this was no run-of-the-mill thumper of the keyboard. Aside from his talents as a composer and performer, Frankie was handsome and had a warm personality. Moreover he was a showman who adapted perfectly to the flamboyant Heidt style. He could do all manner of tricks, like playing the piano with his hands behind his back, a gimmick that always enchanted the customers.

Gimmicks delighted Horace Heidt, too. He was constantly devising new ways to promote his musicians. Heidt's introductions were never simple. It was Frankie Carle, the world's greatest pianist . . . Larry Cotton, the king of tenors . . . Bobby Hackett, the man with the golden trumpet . . . Henry Russell, our musical genius. Right from the start he headlined me as "The Blind Whistler," a billing that I deeply resented.

"Hell, Fred, there's nothing to be ashamed of," Heidt exclaimed when I protested. "As a matter of fact, you've got an awful lot to be proud of, the way you've accomplished so much in spite of your handicap."

"That's the point," I argued. "I don't look on myself as handicapped, and

I don't want other people to. I'm not ashamed of being blind. It's just that I don't want it to become a big deal. I just want to be treated like everybody else."

Heidt couldn't be swayed. He insisted on focusing public attention on my disability. Not only was I "The Blind Whistler" on billboards and marquees, but he also made sure my blindness was emphasized as much as possible on the bandstand. After introducing me, Heidt would have Larry Cotton make a great show of leading me across the bandstand to the mike. He also retrieved me after I finished my numbers, with the spotlight zeroed in on us continually.

Unlike most people in show business Heidt was convinced that a talented blind person was a highly merchandisable commodity. Privately, though, he was constantly concerned about my sightlessness. He couldn't believe I could manage even the simplest functions of life off the bandstand without assistance. He fretted constantly about the dangers involved in my traveling alone about the city, even on the short walk from the Belvedere to the Biltmore.

When I explained that I knew every building and every crack in the sidewalk by heart, he wasn't convinced. My assurances that my feeble sight enabled me to see at least a faint outline of the world around me didn't impress him either. He was certain that if I didn't get hit by a car I would be an easy mark for hoodlums.

"Good grief, Fred," Heidt snapped one day when I tried to defend my capabilities as a pedestrian, "a person with 20-20 eyesight isn't safe on the streets of this city. So don't you tell me that you're okay."

Heidt's worries about my safety were eased when Bobby Lytle returned to New York from the Midwest. David Irwin and Sassafras had moved on— David to Pennsylvania and Sassafras to parts unknown. When I remarked one day that Bobby had rejoined me in the apartment at the Belvedere, Heidt offered him a job as band boy. Lytle balked at the offer, reminding Horace that he had been a vocalist with Lopez for two years. But he finally accepted the humble job after Heidt made a vague promise of a singing spot if an opening should occur. Bobby realized that in a band overpopulated with vocalists this was a dim prospect, but he decided that any big-band job was better than no job at all.

Heidt quickly made it known that Lytle's main duty was to serve as my companion and guide whenever I ventured off the bandstand. Bobby laughed when he got that assignment. "That's right up my alley," he told Heidt. "During my time with Lopez I was Fred's seeing-eye dog. Lopez relied on me to keep him out of trouble."

"Why don't you tell it like it really was?" I joked. "You may have been my seeing-eye, but I spent most of my time getting *you* out of trouble."

Heidt was intrigued by the talk about seeing-eye dogs. His instinct for publicity told him there were potential headlines in that area. "Isn't there a school over in Jersey that trains dogs to help the blind?" he asked one day.

I assured him there was such a school. The Seeing-Eye Institute at Morristown had become famous in recent years for its work in training dogs to guide the blind.

"How come you've never gone there to get a dog?" Heidt asked.

I pointed out that I had been taught to take care of myself at the School for the Blind before the development of techniques for training dogs to serve the sightless. "Somehow I've always felt that having to depend on a dog to lead me through life would just make people pity me. And that's something I don't want," I said.

Heidt immediately disputed my reasoning. "There's no reason to pity a guy because he's using a dog to help him get around safely. Aren't dogs supposed to be man's best friend?"

"I don't even know if I could get a dog," I argued. "I've heard that the Institute is mighty choosy about who they give one of their dogs to."

"Who said anything about wanting them to *give* you a dog?" Heidt said. "We'll go out there and arrange to buy one."

I tried to dissuade him, but as usual when Heidt was seized by a sudden inspiration it was impossible to budge him. He insisted on personally driving me across the Hudson, out past Newark and the Oranges to Morristown. Before we set out Heidt alerted the New York press. The combination of a big-band personality and the fascinating Seeing-Eye Institute was something the newspapers couldn't resist. As we began our journey we were followed by a small caravan of reporters and photographers assigned to cover the latest Heidt story.

Heidt was an impulsive man who seldom bothered with formalities, a man who plunged through life on a single-minded course that rarely adjusted to the daily lives, customs, plans, problems, or feelings of those who crossed his path. We arrived unannounced at the Seeing-Eye Institute where he blithely informed the startled director that he wanted to purchase a guide dog—"the best pooch you've got."

Dr. Morris Frank, the blind founder and director of the Seeing-Eye Institute, was obviously unimpressed by Heidt's celebrity status, and he was definitely not amused by Heidt's flip approach. In icy tones Dr. Frank informed Heidt that the Institute did not sell its dogs to sighted persons. "We train our dogs exclusively for sale to the blind," he said.

Heidt hastily explained that he didn't want the dog for himself, but for me. Dr. Frank, who had been blinded in a boxing match when he was sixteen, quickly vetoed that also. "I'm afraid it's not possible for you or anyone else to buy a guide dog for a blind person," he said. "We require a blind person to earn the money for the purchase of a dog rather than receive one as a gift or an act of charity."

"That doesn't make any sense," Heidt argued.

"It most certainly does," Dr. Frank replied. "We devote considerable time, money, and love to the training of our guide dogs. We want to be sure they are used properly and not abused or neglected. We believe that if a client has to earn the money himself he will be far more inclined to take good care of the dog."

"Maybe so," Heidt conceded. "But there's still no problem. Fred's one of my top musicians. He's making good money. He can buy the dog."

"Quite possibly Mr. Lowery could qualify," Dr. Frank admitted. "Even so, he must make a formal application. Our dogs are sold to sightless persons who we feel are most in need of help. We have a long list of applicants, and they're all screened very carefully. It's a long process. Even after they're approved they must undergo special training here with their dogs."

By now Horace was beginning to realize that his inspiration for a quick bit of publicity was turning into a long-term project. But with our escort of newsmen looking on he couldn't very well retreat. So he asked the director to start the process that could lead to my purchase of a dog, a decision to which I reluctantly agreed.

However, when Dr. Frank learned that I had some vision in one eye, he balked again. "We only provide dogs for the totally blind," he said. "There's no question that Mr. Lowery is legally blind—almost totally blind, perhaps. But even with the slight vision he possesses he's likely to confuse the dog."

Heidt interrupted impatiently. "I don't follow you. With just one-percent sight, how can you say that Fred doesn't need a dog?"

Dr. Frank explained that to perform properly in the role for which it was trained a guide dog had to have the complete, unquestioning trust of its master. This was possible only if the master was totally blind and totally dependent on the dog for getting around the sighted world safely. A person with even the faintest sight would subconsciously rely on what little he could see rather than trust the dog. And ultimately he would end up leading the dog rather than being led.

"This destroys the role for which the dog is trained and leaves the animal confused, nothing more than a simple pet," the director concluded.

Horace still refused to be convinced. He insisted that I needed help, that without a guide dog to lead me through the big cities in which the band performed my life was in constant danger. Finally Dr. Frank wearily announced that he would demonstrate to Heidt—and to me and the newsmen—why it was not feasible for a partially sighted person to use a guide dog.

He summoned one of his sighted assistants and asked him to conduct the demonstration. It was a clever test designed to determine whether I would "blindly" follow a guide into a dangerous predicament or act independently to protect myself. Dr. Frank's assistant, outfitted with an oversized harness, played the role of the dog. I was handed a leather handle attached to the harness and we began strolling down the sidewalk outside the Institute, followed by a noisy gaggle of reporters and photographers.

Everything went smoothly at first. When my seeing-eye stopped at an intersection, I stopped. When he turned a corner, I turned too, right on his heels. After a few minutes he abruptly took a shortcut across an open field. Again I followed, firmly clutching the handle.

Then my leader, evidently distracted by our noisy press escort, wandered off course. Suddenly I heard a startled shout and felt the harness being ripped from my hand. I automatically reacted to the unseen danger by leaping forward. I landed in a clump of weeds at the far side of the ditch my guide had stumbled into. The incident drew curses from my fallen seeing-eye guide and guffaws from the members of the press.

"Looks like it's my assistant who needs a guide dog," Dr. Frank remarked when we returned to his office to report the results of the aborted test. For once Horace Heidt had nothing to say. By now, all he wanted was to drop the entire matter. We returned to Manhattan without a dog, and the seeing-eye subject was never mentioned again.

A seeing-eye dog was the last thing I needed to enjoy life in Manhattan, since I had the constant care and guidance of Bobby Lytle and Art Carney, the band's hilarious young vocalist and impressionist. With them I once more began making the familiar social rounds. We visited with old friends from the Lopez band and the Belvedere. And we joined in the traditional parties and nightclub-hopping safaris arranged by Clara Bell Walsh, who had added the Heidt band to her itinerary. There were also new friends, members of the Heidt band and a fun-loving couple named Bud and Ruth Russell.

Bud Russell was not smitten with show-business dreams; he was devoted to flying. But he was also devoted to his lovely wife, and her ambition was to become a songwriter. About the time I joined the Heidt band, Bud and

Ruth—or Ooie, as she was called because of her frequent excited exclamations over life's wonders—left their two young children with grandparents in Maine and headed for Manhattan to launch Ooie's career.

Bud took a job as private pilot for a New Jersey industrialist, chauffeuring the tycoon around the country in his company plane. Between flights he helped Ooie in her efforts to sell her songs. In those days it was almost impossible for unknowns to get an audience on Tin Pan Alley, so Ooie sought to interest the leaders and arrangers of the big bands, concentrating much of her effort on Horace Heidt.

Maybe for that reason Bud and Ooie became a part of the Fred Lowery–Art Carney–Bobby Lytle Manhattan Madness Society. We introduced Ooie to the treacherous world of music publishing in the Brill Building on Broadway, one of the toughest of all entertainment fortresses. Competing with an army of established songwriters, Ooie waged a futile battle to get her music published, but the repeated rejections didn't dampen her fun-loving nature. She and Bud joined us in exploring the city's night life for several months, until the pressure of the Heidt band's schedule drastically curtailed our socializing. They even moved into the Belvedere for a time.

I recall one particularly memorable event involving Ooie. Bud Russell was out of town flying his boss on some sort of business mission, and Ooie had joined Art, Bobby, and me at Muller's, a wonderful German restaurant adjoining the side entrance to the old Madison Square Garden.

Mr. Muller was a genial Old World host who was famed for his food, his beer, and the muzzled German shepherd, Fritz, that served as his bouncer. On command from his master Fritz would bound from his station by the cash register and descend on an unruly customer with a series of ferocious growls guaranteed to put the unwelcome patron to flight.

Since we were regulars at the restaurant Mr. Muller had seated us at our favorite quiet booth near the back of the dining room. This time, however, it was soon evident that we were not alone. A party was in progress in a booth directly behind our table, and one of the merrymakers was not only deep in his cups but loudly obscene.

It was extremely embarrassing because in those days, even in show business, ladies were traditionally shielded from profanity and obscenity. Telling even mildly off-color jokes in mixed company was frowned on. The language in the adjoining booth was not just off-color. It was real gutter talk.

At first we sat in silence, trying to ignore the recital and hoping the joker would run out of material. Finally, after the unseen comedian launched into still another lurid tale, I stood up and peered over the back of the booth, hoping he would take the hint. But the voice thundered on.

186

"I can't see who you are," I shouted in the general direction of the voice. "But whoever it is that's using that filthy language, I'm going to punch him in the nose if he doesn't shut up!"

The dirty joke halted abruptly. "Who in the hell d'ya think you are?" the joker's booming voice wanted to know, adding a few more virulent words for emphasis.

"Yeah," one of his companions echoed, "why the hell should we shut up?"

"Because," I yelled angrily, "there's a lady at our table, and there's no reason why she has to hear your filthy stories."

With that pronouncement I sat down again, awaiting the call to battle. But it never came. The booth behind us was strangely silent. Minutes later the once-boisterous party broke up. As the celebrants filed past our booth one of them paused and spoke.

"I just wanna apologize for my language. I didn't realize a lady was present." It was the joker again, but this time his voice was humble and a bit embarrassed. A giant shadowy figure loomed over me. Before I could say anything a huge hand slapped me on the back.

As I gasped for breath the joker spoke up again. "I gotta hand it to you, fella. You sure got nerve." And his laughter boomed through the room as he hurried on to catch up with his friends.

"Who in the world was that?" Ooie asked breathlessly.

"Damned if I know," Lytle said. "But he's about the biggest thing I've ever seen outside a gorilla cage."

Carney agreed. "You're sure lucky he didn't ask you to step outside, Fred."

Mr. Muller came hurrying up to our table. "Mr. Lowery," he said, "do you know who that was . . . the man you threatened to punch in the nose?"

"No, I don't, and I don't care. All I know is that he's a dirty loudmouth, and I'd still like to bust him."

"Mr. Lowery, don't say things like that!" Muller spoke in an anxious whisper as if he feared the departed joker might overhear our conversation. "That was Jess Willard, the former heavyweight champion of the world. Jack Dempsey's the only man who ever beat him!"

"What did you say?" I managed to ask.

"I said that man you threatened was Jess Willard. And if he'd lost his temper I couldn't have helped you. Even my Fritz is afraid of Mr. Willard!"

Howls of laughter rang around my head. My companions thought the incident was hilarious, but all I could think of was what Jess Willard could have done to me if he'd taken a mind to.

Eventually Ooie and Bud Russell returned to New England to raise their family. Ooie never realized her dream of becoming a successful songwriter, although in later years I published two of her musical creations—"Easy Goin'," which I also recorded in a Decca album, *Walking Along Kicking the Leaves*, and "Robin the Reporter," included in another album, *Family Christmas*.

Ooie had talent, but the lucky breaks always seemed to elude her. She and Bud nevertheless made significant contributions to show business through their children and grandchildren. Their son Bing became a distinguished movie and television actor. And Bing's son, Kurt Russell, has followed in his dad's footsteps and is well known for his parts in Disney movies, his portrayal of Elvis Presley in the movie *Elvis*, and many other roles. Other grandchildren include free-lance motion picture producer Larry Franco and John Stewart Philbrick, a director of the weekly TV drama "Hill Street Blues."

I kept in touch with Bud and Ooie through the years. After Gracie and I were married we saw them on vacations. And during our years living in Manhattan our son Scooter spent summers in Maine with the Russell family, learning to camp, hike, hunt, and fish—things I couldn't teach him.

Whenever we get together Ooie invariably reminds me of that night in Muller's when I threatened one of the most fearsome heavyweight champions of all time.

And each time, after giggling at the memory, she consoles me: "Well, at least he was big enough so you could have seen what you were swinging at!"

Chapter 14

What was Art Carney really like? He was a talented impressionist . . . and he was crazy. He could do an FDR impression second to none, and he could get you involved in a practical joke that could land you in jail. Like the time he decided we should fake a robbery.

It was one of those rare days off for the band, a beautiful October day. Art and I had made the rounds looking for friends, but we found no one at our usual haunts. So we stopped for a beer at a side-street saloon. As a matter of fact, we had had several libations during the afternoon.

"We've got to do something to wake up this town," Carney said as the bartender fetched us two icy steins.

"Like what?"

"What would you say is the worst thing that can happen to a blind man?" Carney asked.

"That's easy," I wisecracked. "A blind date!"

Art Carney was always impatient with any puns but his own. "Be serious, Fred," he snapped. "I don't need any dumb jokes!"

"Well," I said, "the thing I always worry about is getting mugged or held up. A lot of blind folks I know have that same fear."

"That's it . . . a great idea!" Carney exclaimed. And he proceeded to outline an outlandish scenario—a make-believe mugging in midtown Manhattan.

"What is this supposed to prove?" I asked.

"We've been walking our legs off all day, and nobody's paid any attention to us. Let's stage this mugging and see if anyone will come to your rescue. Or will they just keep walking, pretending nothing's happening?"

When he put it that way his idea seemed like a noble social experiment rather than a harebrained stunt. So I agreed to join him as costar in the vignette. The setting: the busy corner of Forty-second Street and Fifth Avenue. The time: 5 P.M. rush hour. The cast: Art Carney as the world's

189

meanest heist artist and Fred Lowery as the blind victim. The audience: New York's multitude of faceless, nameless pedestrians.

We arrived at the preplanned intersection outside the giant marble mountain that houses the New York Public Library and got set for action. I stood near the corner while Carney pushed through the crowd of homebound commuters, jabbed a finger in my back, and shouted, "This is a stickup!"

"Help!" I yelled. "Somebody help me! I'm being robbed!"

Nobody stopped. I could sense the throng of pedestrians pushing away from us as they hurried on.

Suddenly Art threw an arm around my throat and clawed at my jacket with his free hand, pulling my wallet from an inside pocket. I struggled to free myself, sounding a renewed cry for help. "I'm blind . . . I can't see! Won't somebody please help me?"

Abruptly help arrived, in the form of two husky New York cops. One of them wrestled Carney to the sidewalk. The other grabbed my arm and demanded to know what the trouble was.

Before I could reply, Carney shouted frantically, "It's nothing . . . nothing at all, officer. We were just fooling around!"

"Fooling around, eh?" his captor grunted, pulling my wallet out of Art's grasp. "Then what have you got to say about this?"

During the next few minutes Art and I tried to explain our foolish stunt, but the more we talked the more ridiculous we sounded. The policemen weren't impressed, not even when we identified ourselves as members of Horace Heidt's band.

"Sounds phony to me," one officer muttered before he hurried to a nearby call box to summon a paddy wagon. "You guys either belong in jail or the funny farm. I don't know which. I'll let 'em decide down at headquarters."

And so we wrapped up a perfect autumn day in Manhattan with a free ride to the station house. It had obviously been a busy day for New York's finest. The station was packed, and we waited anxiously for nearly two hours before we were led upstairs for questioning.

"Sounds like a lot of baloney to me," the interrogating detective observed after hearing our version of the heist. "Why would a couple of guys from a big-time band pull a stupid stunt like this? If you're blind, how come you don't have a white cane? How do I know you're not just another con artist hiding behind dark glasses?"

I took off my glasses, did a little manipulating, and handed the detective my artifical eye. "Want me to take an eye test?" I asked.

190

The detective hastily ordered me to restore my glass eye and sighed wearily. "I guess there's nothing to do but lock you up until we can get to the bottom of this mess."

The prospect of spending the night in a jail cell put an abrupt end to our hopes of keeping our escapade a secret. "Officer," I suggested, "if you don't believe us, why don't you phone Horace Heidt? He's staying at the Biltmore. He can straighten everything out."

Finally the detective made the call. We could hear the crackling of Horace's voice all the way from the other side of the desk. When the conversation ended the detective slammed down the receiver. "Man, that's one mad bandleader! Maybe I oughta lock you guys up for your own protection." He paused, as if contemplating such an act of mercy, then voiced second thoughts. "But I guess I'll just let you face the music!"

"Very funny . . . verrrrry funny!" Carney said as the detective led us off to await our boss's wrath.

We didn't have long to wait. About half an hour later the door burst open and Horace Heidt entered.

"Yeah, that's them . . . Carney and Lowery," he said grimly, apparently making the identification for the police before negotiating our release. "You oughta lock 'em up and throw away the key!"

"Is that what you want?" a voice from behind Heidt asked.

"It's what I'd like, not what I want," Heidt replied. "Let's go upstairs and see the captain."

Before long an officer opened the door again and announced "Okay, you guys can leave."

"No charges?" Carney asked.

"Nope."

"You mean to say we can just walk out of here?"

"Yep."

We scurried quickly out of the lockup, pausing only to collect our impounded possessions at the front desk. There was no sign of Heidt, but our relief evaporated when we emerged from the building. Horace was waiting for us beside a taxi. Being a man of action, Carney didn't try to avoid the confrontation. Instead he hurried forward with an outstretched hand, voicing his thanks to Heidt for coming to our rescue. But Horace pushed Art away. "I've got a bellyful of you juvenile jerks," he roared. "Dumb stunts like this I don't need. You're both fired. Get out of my life!" With that pronouncement our leader climbed into the cab and disappeared into the night.

As we stood at the curb waiting for another cab to show up, I mourned my sudden return to the ranks of the unemployed. But Art refused to be dismayed. "Quit stewing about your job," he said. "Horace may be sore, but he's not nuts!"

"What's that supposed to mean? You heard the man. I heard him. He said we're fired! *Kaput!* Finished!"

Carney sniffed disdainfully. "Maybe that's what he said tonight. But wait until Horace remembers that he had to dip into his own pocket to get us out of jail. Horace isn't about to give us the boot when we owe him money."

Art was right. Horace was on the telephone the next morning inviting me to accompany him to the opening game of the World Series at Yankee Stadium that afternoon. "A friend gave me four tickets," he explained, avoiding any mention of the previous evening's unpleasantries.

"I thought you fired Art and me last night," I said.

"Forget it, Fred . . . forget it!" he exclaimed. "I just lost my temper when that cop called and asked me to come downtown and identify you guys." Horace's booming voice subsided to a near-whisper as he confided, "Just between us, Fred, that cop couldn't have picked a worse time to call. I was having cocktails with the most gorgeous redhead you've ever seen!" Our leader, a handsome hulk of a man, had quite a reputation as a ladies' man. "Frankly, I was mad as hell. But later I realized it was stupid for me to fire you."

"How about Art? Does he know?"

"Sure. I've already talked to him. Asked him if he wanted to go to the game, but he had other plans."

So overnight I went from being fired to attending my first World Series game with the boss, Ralph Wingert, and Red Farrington.

At the ball game that day Heidt, Wingert, and Red served as commentators, keeping me informed about what was going on. As the innings passed, Cincinnati's Paul Derringer, the National League's finest pitcher in those days, was holding the mighty Yankees to a 1–1 tie—a sad situation which our leader continually bemoaned. In the last of the ninth the Yankee loyalists finally got something to cheer about. The excitement was more than I'd bargained for.

The sharp crack of King Kong Keller's bat walloping a Derringer pitch touched off a mighty roar. Keller's triple catapulted Heidt into a frenzy. Screaming his approval along with some 60,000 other fans, Heidt dragged me to my feet and began bouncing me up and down like a rubber ball. My hat flew off and so did my dark glasses.

Red Farrington grabbed Horace. "Good God!" Red shouted. "What's got into you, Horace? Calm down before you hurt Fred."

Heidt apologized and explained that sometimes he got so excited he didn't know what he was doing. I wasn't so sure. I wondered if he wasn't administering a bit of delayed punishment for the previous night's escapade. One thing was for sure. I wasn't going to give him another chance.

It didn't take long for a new opportunity to arise. After Joe DiMaggio was intentionally walked, Bill Dickey came to the plate. Dickey took a strike, then singled to drive in the winning run, and bedlam erupted once more. This time I was prepared. As soon as I heard the crack of the bat and the howl of the crowd I leaped to my feet and grabbed Horace in a bear hug, joining with him in a delirious shout of jubilation while keeping a determined hold on his brawny arms.

Later, as we headed back downtown in a cab, a puzzled Heidt asked, "How come, if you can't see, you were on your feet grabbing me and hollering almost as soon as Dickey hit the ball? How did you know it was a base hit and not just an out to end the inning?"

I wasn't about to tell him the truth. So I fabricated a glib reply, hinting that my reaction had been the result of some mystical insight. "Sometimes I seem to get a feeling about what's going on around me," I explained, never thinking that Heidt would take my response seriously. "It's happened before . . . sort of a mental picture of what's happening. That's about the only way I can explain it."

To my surprise my tongue in cheek reply seemed to intrigue Heidt. In fact it inspired another of the legends he delighted in weaving around the band and its members. The theme of this particular Heidt fantasy was that I possessed some sort of supernatural "inner sight" that enabled me to see, or sense, what was taking place around me. It was this "inner sight," Heidt insisted, that enabled me to move about in the city without a white cane, a guide dog, or other outside help. In a way it was flattering to have such an exotic reputation, to be portrayed as a man with a strange power, but at times it was downright annoying.

Art Carney, for example, was forever testing my "inner sight." During our years with the Heidt band we were room-mates on the road. I can't recall a single time when checking into a strange hotel room at night that Art didn't expect me to plunge into the darkened room ahead of him to locate the light switch. "So help me," Art would tell others in the band, "Fred walks in and finds the switch with no trouble at all. No groping, no stumbling, no falling over chairs. I kid you not, ol' Fred's like a cat the way he can see in the dark."

At first I tried to reason with Art, assuring him that I couldn't "see" in the

193

dark any more than I could "see" in the light. Less, in fact, because when there was light I could at least use the slight bit of vision I possessed to discern the vague shape of things around me. But I couldn't convince him. "How come you can walk into a dark room and find the switch?" he'd ask.

I'd try to explain that being blind most of my life I'd had a lot of experience locating light switches and other objects in strange rooms. I'd also tell him that most hotel rooms are designed about the same, with light switches, beds, chairs, dressers, and lamps in the same general location. "Besides," I'd add, "you can't see me in the dark, fumbling around trying to find the switch." Carney just ignored my logical explanations and continued to tout my "inner sight."

Except for the pounding I took at the World Series neither Art nor I experienced any repercussions from the "firing." But Horace's change of heart didn't extend to his pocketbook. For the next month or so, deductions were taken from our paychecks until the $200 that Heidt claimed he paid the police captain to hush up our foolish stunt was recovered.

Paying back Heidt was no hardship for either of us. In fact, times were suddenly so good for the band that we scarcely noticed the deductions.

It was a delirious time for Horace Heidt's Musical Knights. We and the other big bands were playing live dates at theaters everywhere. Our afternoon and evening shows didn't draw mobs of bobby-soxers as vast as the thousands who lined up for hours outside the Paramount in Manhattan to listen to Benny Goodman, but we consistently attracted packed houses. Because of the variety of our show we usually had a more mature audience than Goodman and some of the other groovier bands. But we, too, drew large numbers of young swains in pegged pants and saggy sweaters and their slick chicks in saddle shoes, culottes, or swirling skirts with "reat-pleats." And the ecstatic youngsters shouted and screamed and jived in the aisles to the rhythm of our music whenever we ventured into upbeat numbers like "Jeepers Creepers" and "Beer Barrel Polka."

However, the delirium of the stage shows was mild compared to the frenzied jam sessions or swing carnivals that promoters around the country staged in stadiums and amusement parks. Although nothing like the rock concerts of the Woodstock generation, these swing extravaganzas sometimes disintegrated into frightening demonstrations of mob hysteria.

Once during a stay in New York we joined with more than twenty other bands in staging a swingfest at Randalls Island. About 30,000 young fans jammed around the huge bandstand, howling and stamping to the beat of the music and battling each other to get as close as possible to their musical heroes. Finally several hundred police and firemen were summoned to protect us from our admirers and escort us safely back to Manhattan. That was the one and only swing carnival in which the Heidt band participated—a decision made by Horace that none of us protested. We discovered that when it came to adoration there could be too much of a good thing.

My four years with Vincent Lopez had brought me a taste of fame. But when my name blossomed in lights on the marquee of the Strand Theater on Broadway the Lopez years seemed only a prelude to a far grander future.

I had become a celebrity with Heidt almost overnight. My rise to a featured role with the band was not due to any sudden gift of talent or glamour. I was still the same whistler with the same skills and the same personality. With Lopez I had also had featured roles, but there was a big difference. Lopez only grudgingly shared the spotlight with his musicians. Heidt promoted us as important and separate personalities, blanketing us with an aura of uniqueness that inevitably brought personal fame. This personality building wasn't confined to the bandstands of hotels and nightclubs. Heidt extended it to the radio networks, and, in the process, made me and other members of his band celebrities on a national scale.

My rise to a featured role with Heidt also produced bigger and bigger paychecks. In a six-month period my base pay with the band soared from $50 a week to $250 or more, depending on our schedule. Despite my new prosperity, however, I now had little time for the fun-filled life-style of my Lopez days. For a few months after joining the Heidt band, when our work was limited to the Biltmore Hotel engagement, I had done a lot of partying. But Heidt ultimately kept the band so busy that we seldom had time for anything but work.

When the Heidt band had arrived in New York in 1938 it had been demoralized by defections and firings and the loss of the profitable Alemite radio sponsorship, but by late spring of 1939 Heidt had captured a prized top billing for us at the Strand and a major national radio sponsorship—Tums. Even then our leader wasn't satisfied. He lined up a series of recording dates, giving us a share of the profits, and was forever coming up with weekend club bookings and ballroom gigs for us around New York and as far away as Boston, New Haven, Philadelphia, and Baltimore.

Unlike the Lopez organization, where everybody pretty much went his own way after the night's work was finished, the Heidt band tended to be a "family," and we usually joined together for whatever free-time fun we could muster. But there was a lot of just plain hard work. Behind every melody that floated across the dance floor was endless rehearsing that the

195

public was never aware of. A new song, a new arrangement, a new routine meant long hours of memorizing, of working together to refine the music our fans would ultimately hear. Rehearsing for dance programs was often long and tedious and filled with unmusical dissension. But those sessions were mild compared to the stormy rehearsals during which we prepared for our hour-long network shows.

The big broadcast rehearsing seemed to intensify Heidt's normally high level of contrariness. In the process of striving to jazz up the program with elaborate special effects designed to lure listeners from other shows, Horace was forever dreaming up fanciful numbers that stretched the artistry of the band and the guest stars to the limit. These rehearsals seemed to emphasize the erratic moods and mercurial temperament that lay behind the bland, unemotional face he usually presented to the public. Heidt raged through the daylong prebroadcast practice hours like a belligerent bull suspiciously challenging everything that confronted him. In the process, as he ran the gamut from blazing salvos of vituperation to agonized demonstrations of hair-pulling frustration, Horace managed to bring his musicians, guest celebrities, and the network producer to near-insanity. Oddly, though, Heidt's outrageous behavior—like Rudy Vallee's—seemed to be a catalyst that sparked smooth, sharply timed, and sometimes superb performances.

I recall one Tuesday NBC broadcast for Tums. We began straggling into the studio before 8 A.M. for the beginning of rehearsal, all of us cranky and tired from only a few hours' sleep after our 1 A.M. supper show at the Biltmore. Heidt arrived in his usual black mood, primed for the weekly battle with Paul Dudley, the NBC producer of the Heidt show.

After the customary berating of tardy arrivals and the inevitable shouting match between Heidt and Dudley over placement of the various sections of the band, we began rehearsing a new number. Our arranger, Buzz Adlam, smitten with an unaccustomed hankering for culture, had revived and jazzed up a classic by Johann Sebastian Bach. We managed to run through it twice before Heidt erupted. "What in the hell kind of stupid music is that?" he roared.

"It's just a jazz arrangement of one of Bach's fugues," Buzz explained. "I thought it would be kind of a nice change of pace."

"Dammit, Buzz," Horace complained, "why do I have to keep telling you to quit fooling around with weird music by songwriters nobody ever heard of?"

Accompanied by a ripple of snickers from the band, Buzz inquired incredulously, "Are you talking about Bach?"

196

"You're damned tootin' I am," Heidt snapped. "You get hold of this guy and tell him we don't want any more of his lousy arrangements!"

The uproar over Bach had scarcely subsided when I had a similar confrontation with Horace. I had been working with Frankie Carle and the band on an arrangement of "The Bell Song" from the opera *Lakmé*. It had taken me six weeks of hard work to learn to whistle the difficult soprano aria, and I especially wanted to do it that night because I had heard through friends that Peggy Richter was ill back in Austin. I sent word that she should listen to that night's show.

We had an excellent run-through of the number, and I was more than pleased with the results. When we finished, Horace turned to me and said, "Six minutes! It's way too long, Fred. We'll have to shorten it."

I couldn't believe my ears. "This is one of the classics, not some silly pop tune you can butcher without any harm," I argued.

"I appreciate your feelings, Fred. But we've only got so many minutes on the air, and we've got to pack a lot into that time. Our sponsor wants variety, and that's what I want, because he's picking up the tab. So, like it or not, we've got to cut back on long numbers like this."

"We've already cut it, Horace," I pleaded. "You just can't condense it any more without destroying it."

Horace looked at me meaningfully. "Fred," he said, "if the angel Gabriel agreed to play a trumpet solo on my show he'd have to keep it under three minutes!"

I knew that if I didn't shut up, Horace might cut the number out of the show altogether. So Frankie and I hastily fashioned a shorter arrangement of one of opera's more complex arias. At last I returned to the bandstand with a three-minute version, only to be sent back for yet another cut.

When we went on the air coast to coast that night, "The Bell Song" had been slashed to two and a half minutes. It is doubtful if Delibes would have recognized this stepchild of his genius. But at least it gave the Horace Heidt Show a brief and unaccustomed touch of culture, sandwiched between "I Won't Dance" and "Nice Work If You Can Get It."

There was a bittersweet aftermath to my performance. As we were preparing to leave the studio I was summoned to a telephone. A woman's voice, faint and trembling, sounded from the other end of the line. "Fred . . . Fred Lowery? This is Peggy Richter."

"Peggy!" I said. "How are you?"

"I heard you whistle 'The Bell Song,' " she said. "You know it was always one of my favorites. As soon as the program ended, I got on the phone to tell you how thrilled I was. Your whistling was simply magnificent."

We chatted for perhaps five minutes, the sort of jumbled, self-conscious conversation that so often results when two long-parted friends try to bridge the years. I could sense that Peggy was tiring.

"I've been having some miseries," she admitted. "I'm going in the hospital tomorrow to let the doctors fuss over me. But I just couldn't resist talking with you, letting you know how much I loved your music. . . ."

For hours that night I lay awake reliving the memories that Peggy's phone call had revived—memories of the woman whose faith in my talent was in large measure responsible for my success. Somehow, I was haunted by a feeling that Peggy had really called to say good-bye. Two weeks later I received a letter from Gracie telling me that Peggy had died. My sorrow was eased only by the realization that at least she had had the chance to hear me perform one of her favorite arias on the air before our final parting.

Horace's aggressive display of authority at rehearsals was the opposite of his behavior on the bandstand at hotels or nightclubs. In public he frequently took a backseat, turning over the bandleader's post to Buzz Adlam or whatever other arranger was in favor at the time and joining friends or business associates at their tables. It was always difficult for me to associate this rather withdrawn man who avoided much of the public limelight with the tyrant of our behind-the-scenes endeavors. But even Heidt's broadcast antics couldn't compare with his frenzy in the recording studio. For some reason known only to himself, he approached every record-cutting session with the conviction that he had to exert iron-tight control over everything and everyone.

Horace sat in the control room, surrounded by all manner of mysterious electronic gadgets operated by a newly emerging breed of sound technicians. He shouted an endless stream of orders and irate criticisms into the microphone that connected the studio bandstand with the glass-enclosed booth. He argued with technicians over recording processes. He rushed out, sometimes in the middle of a number, to change the positioning of instrumentalists or vocalists. He took individual band members aside to deliver pep talks, denounce mistakes, or insist on changes in style— particularly when the brass section or a vocalist, or even his wayward whistler, strayed into the high notes that he despised. In short, he was a disruptive force in a record-cutting procedure that was becoming more and more complex under the industry's broadening technology.

I imagine that part of Heidt's problem was nervousness. Of all the mediums of dissemination employed by bands, recording was by far the most nerve-wracking. By the late thirties it was becoming a technical, precision craft that could generate all manner of tensions. There was the

198

pressure of trying to produce a finished record in a three-hour session crammed in between other engagements. There was the pressure of knowing that we were creating a permanent musical document, something that very well might exist long after we'd played our last gig. A sour note or a mediocre performance at a dance or even on a network broadcast faded quickly, but a mediocre record was a lasting thing, a damning piece of evidence that a band might be losing its touch. And there was the pressure of trying to keep pace with the public's often upredictable tastes in music. Even the best record could flop if it failed to tickle the fickle fancy of the record-buying, jukebox-playing big band fans.

By 1939 the revival of the record industry had mushroomed far beyond expectations. More and more the record sales of individual bands were being used by radio sponsors and the big hotels, nightclubs, and casinos as a popularity gauge in putting together their entertainment packages. A few of the bands, most notably the once-dominant Paul Whiteman organization, refused for a long time to join in the recording mania. They insisted that records—and particularly the jukebox variety—amounted to "giving away" their music. But most bandleaders, including Heidt, quickly realized the enormous earning potential of the record market.

Whether we were in New York or Los Angeles or on the road, the Heidt band almost always held at least one Columbia recording session a week. It was a lucrative sideline for musicians—a $41.75 fee for a three-hour session. It was an even bigger bonanza for those with featured roles who got a share of a record's royalties. It was this extra income, plus the knowledge that future bookings depended on the quality of our work and its popular appeal, that kept us striving for perfection and helped us tolerate Heidt's outlandish behavior in the studio.

I had been with the band less than a month when Heidt gave me my first featured role on a record. It was a duet arrangement of "Whistling in the Wildwood," blending my whistling with Larry Cotton's singing. The record did well, and I began to get more featured roles, all of which brought in modest royalties. However, it wasn't until my second year with the band that Columbia agreed to let me cut my first solo record—an experiment to test public reaction to a whistling number with no lyrics.

It happened at the close of a record-cutting session in Chicago where we were playing a summer engagement at the Edgewater Beach Hotel. The band had completed four sides, and we were getting ready to leave the studio when Heidt told Henry Russell, Jack Kovach, and me to stay for another recording.

Surprised, we asked what Heidt had in mind. He told us that Columbia

199

had given the go ahead for me to make a solo recording of "Indian Love Call," my favorite number, accompanied by Russell on the organ and Kovach on the electric guitar. For once Heidt didn't interfere. In fact he headed for the hotel, leaving the three of us and the studio's technical crew to cut the record. Using our regular bandstand arrangement, we recorded "Love Call" without a hitch, then concentrated on the platter's flip side— another old favorite, "I Love You Truly," with Russell singing the chorus. The entire session took less than one hour.

About a month later, while we were playing an engagement at the Circle Theater in Indianapolis, I heard the record for the first time. It was, I decided, a pleasantly professional rendition of a lovely melody, but nothing to get excited about. Too old-fashioned for today's audience, I told myself.

Early sales after Columbia put "Love Call" on the market seemed to justify my pessimism. My whistling record was apparently going nowhere. Then one of those lucky breaks occurred. A jukebox operator in Cleveland discovered that his supply of an old recording of "Indian Love Call," a duet by Nelson Eddy and Jeanette MacDonald, was exhausted. When he went to a Cleveland wholesale house to replenish his stock he learned that the Eddy-MacDonald record had been discontinued. "But we've got a new Columbia record with some guy whistling," the clerk said.

The jukebox operator bought ten records of my version and placed them in some of his better downtown locations. Within a week he discovered that my record was getting heavy play. He ordered twenty-five more, and the word got around. Within a month, jukebox operators throughout the Midwest were clamoring for the record, and in another few weeks orders for "Love Call" were piling up across the country.

At that time we were still on tour, so I didn't learn of the record's success until Bobby Weis, the band's promotion manager, rushed into my dressing room one day with a week-old copy of *Variety*.

"Hey, Fred, you've got a hit. *Variety*'s got your record in the Top Ten!"

"What record are you talking about?" I asked. I couldn't imagine what he was referring to.

" 'Indian Love Call'—the platter you cut back in Chicago," Weis said.

"You've got to be kidding!" I exclaimed.

But "Love Call" was indeed one of the ten hottest records in the country. Long before we arrived in Manhattan my whistled version of "Love Call" was playing on jukeboxes everywhere we stopped. By some quirk of fate I'd scored with a hit on my first major solo recording, a record that eventually sold more than two million copies.

Chapter 15

Of all the places where I performed with Vincent Lopez and Horace Heidt, the St. Regis Roof and the Bowman Room of the Biltmore in New York and the Ambassador Hotel's Cocoanut Grove in Los Angeles were the most elegant and memorable. These three were more than posh, expensive supper clubs and ballrooms in fashionable hotels. They were elaborate showcases, in many ways like the flamboyant Hollywood film sets of the period's musical extravaganzas.

Even had it been less splendiferous, the St. Regis Roof would have been an unforgettable part of my life, for it was there that I began my career with Lopez. It was a truly prestigious starting point. The Roof was a mirrored, paneled, chandeliered haven for high society's wining, dining, and dancing. The Biltmore's Bowman Room also had an elegantly unique feel seldom found in contemporary hotels. It was a festive room featuring an exotic decor highlighted by twelve gilded cages suspended from ornate wall brackets. Each cage housed a golden canary that burst into song whenever I whistled.

The Cocoanut Grove was opulently and boldly theatrical. The ballroom's centerpiece, which even my dim eyesight could discern, was a mammoth mural—a South Pacific scene complete with a lustrous full moon, sandy beaches, and churning surf. Real palm trees were scattered about the room in giant planter tubs, and special lighting effects could transform the vast ceiling into a dark blue night sky filled with stars and planets and wispy clouds. Art Carney said the Cocoanut Grove stirred visions of tropical orgies, and he was sure it would be banned in Boston.

The Heidt band arrived in Los Angeles for a six-week engagement at the Grove in late autumn of 1939 following a successful cross-country tour of major theaters, a tour in which we traveled in style and comfort by train rather than the crowded, plodding buses of my Lopez tours. When we arrived an assistant manager of the Ambassador Hotel handed Heidt a lengthy list of house rules governing the conduct of entertainers. Most of

201

them were commonsense regulations, but one immediately drew Heidt's wrath: Members of the band were not to mingle with the guests during intermissions. They were to retire quietly to an upstairs room reserved for musicians and await the call to return to the bandstand.

Horace Heidt could be a tyrant at times, belligerent and infuriatingly obtuse, but he was loyal to his people. Nothing could trigger his indignation quicker than outsiders trying to belittle his musicians or push them around. This time—even though an important engagement was involved—was no exception. "You can take that order and stick it!" he told the assistant manager. "My people are ladies and gentlemen. What's more, they're stars in their own field. They're musical artists, tops in their profession, and I'm not going to let you or anybody else treat them like flunkies!"

The assistant manager refused to retreat in the face of Heidt's anger. The rule, he insisted, would stand.

"Then we won't be on the bandstand tonight!" Heidt proclaimed.

Confronted with this unexpected rebellion, the assistant manager hastily summoned his boss. The hotel manager listened to both sides of the argument, and when he realized that any other choice would leave the Cocoanut Grove without music he decreed that during the Heidt band's engagement the visitation ban would be dropped. Despite our sometimes wild antics the subject of barring us from mingling with the guests was never mentioned again during this or subsequent engagements at the hotel.

For Larry Cotton, a longtime performer at the Cocoanut Grove during his years as vocalist with Jimmie Grier's orchestra, the gig at the fabled Wilshire Boulevard night spot was old hat. But for the rest of us it was something special, because the Grove was *the* prestige booking on the West Coast.

When I had performed with the Lopez band at the Beverly Wilshire Hotel a few years earlier I had encountered a number of Hollywood celebrities. But during the Lopez engagement Hollywood was struggling to survive the depression. Now the studios were entering their glory years. It was a time of big-budget, blockbuster movies featuring superstars who commanded astronomical salaries. And the Cocoanut Grove was one of the prime stops for movie royalty and their retinues as they made their merry rounds.

Even though we had all met many celebrities, we found ourselves awed by the screen stars. We were smitten with "hero-mania," just like any bunch of movie fans gawking at the beautiful people arriving for a premiere. Socializing with these living legends, combined with the make-believe South Seas atmosphere, gave a sense of unreality to our working hours at the Cocoanut Grove. It really seemed almost unbelievable—a fact Art Carney

202

and I had emphasized for us by an incident on the way to work one day.

At the time, Art and I were sharing a room in the Hollywood home of my sister Anna Mae and her husband Bob Skaggs. We also shared a battered Ford Model A roadster Bob loaned us for commuting to and from the Cocoanut Grove and prowling about the city in our free time. One day the old tin lizzie broke down on Wilshire Boulevard on our way to work. We had spent all our cash the night before, and we didn't even have enough on us for trolley fare.

Clad in our gaudy band uniforms—maroon jackets, black trousers with satin stripes, and gleaming patent-leather shoes—we started hitchhiking. Finally a rickety sedan pulled up, and its elderly driver and his wife invited us to "hop in." It wasn't exactly what we had hoped for. But a ride was a ride, so we climbed aboard.

The couple immediately wanted to know why we were gadding about in such outlandish trappings. I expected Carney to respond with one of the wildly improbable tales that he loved to spin. Instead, with unaccustomed respect for the facts, Art explained that we were members of the Horace Heidt band, that we dressed in our band uniforms each afternoon before leaving for work, and that our car had stalled on the way to the Cocoanut Grove where we were scheduled to set up for the evening's music within half an hour.

"My goodness, it must be exciting playing in a famous band at the Cocoanut Grove!" The driver's wife seemed duly impressed. However, her husband quickly let us know he wasn't so gullible.

"Sounds like a lotta baloney to me," he muttered over his shoulder. "What in tarnation would a couple of big-band stars be doing hitching a ride to work?"

His wife abruptly changed her tune in the face of this logic. She gasped as the enormity of Carney's fibbing dawned on her. "You boys shouldn't tell such lies!"

Poor Art! For once he was playing it straight, and his reward was to be called a liar. But Art didn't give up easily. He tried to assure the couple that we were indeed two of Horace Heidt's Musical Knights, and he came up with some anecdotes to prove it.

"Just last night," he said, "Clark Gable and Vivien Leigh and Leslie Howard and Olivia de Havilland were at the Grove, and they invited us to join them at their table during one of the intermissions."

Again Carney was telling the truth. The four superstars of *Gone With the Wind*, then being touted as "the greatest movie ever made," had been at the Grove the previous evening. While there, they had invited Horace Heidt,

Larry Cotton, Carney, and me to join them for a round of drinks. It had been a brief encounter devoted mainly to listening to Gable complaining about the hardships and inconveniences of film-promoting.

"You boys shouldn't tell such stories," the wife sniffed. "Imagine, trying to make us believe you really met Clark Gable and all those other famous stars!" Her skeptical husband grunted in agreement. And Carney, at last convinced that truth doesn't pay, lapsed into a sulking silence until the car pulled up in front of the Ambassador.

As we opened the car door, the driver responded to our half-hearted thanks by asking our names, perhaps figuring he could enter us in the year's biggest liars contest. Again Carney stuck stubbornly to the facts, identifying us as Art Carney and Fred Lowery the whistler.

"Nonsense, sonny," the driver snapped. "I've heard Fred Lowery on the radio dozens of times. You can't tell me he's the sort that goes around begging rides." The old boy allowed as how we were just a couple of busboys or dishwashers pretending to be somebody important. With that pronouncement the couple rattled away in their old sedan.

Today I sometimes wonder if that old couple wasn't right—if we didn't just make it up. The setting and the people we encountered seem more like bits of half-remembered dreams and fantasies than fact. Errol Flynn cavorting about the dance floor with his latest conquest. Rugged Duke Wayne celebrating his first big hit, *Stagecoach,* with champagne and all the trimmings. Dick Powell reminiscing about his rise to screen fame from vaudeville stages in the hinterlands. And Ronald Reagan . . .

One night a voice from the edge of the dance floor asked Heidt to have me whistle a number. I obliged, and later I asked Horace who had made the request. Heidt wasn't sure, but Larry Cotton knew him. He said it was a young actor named Ronald Reagan—a former radio announcer who had been featured in *Brother Rat* and *Dark Victory*. Larry said he was being heralded as a future star. At the time, though, everybody was more interested in his date, a lovely young actress named Jane Wyman, whom he had met and started romancing during the filming of *Brother Rat*.

The liveliest of the Grove's customers were two zestfully precocious teen-agers, Mickey Rooney and Judy Garland. During the past year they had costarred in *Love Finds Andy Hardy,* and at the time Judy was filming the *Wizard of Oz*. Despite their hectic studio schedules, Rooney and Garland dated regularly at the Grove, merrily disregarding the drinking-age law. Their table was always crowded with friends and hangers-on, and out on the floor they put on exuberant displays of jitterbugging.

I first met Mickey and Judy during the early days of our engagement at the

Grove. Just before a break one evening the two youngsters practically had the dance floor to themselves, entrancing everyone with the frantic gyrations of the latest dance craze. We were playing "The Music Goes Round and Round," a new novelty hit in which I whistled a recurring phrase. When the number ended they scampered up to the bandstand and led Horace and me back to the crowd around their table.

Judy Garland was about seventeen at that time, a spirited, talented young woman who seemed possessed with a feverish desire to experience every sensation life could offer. At that particular moment dancing was her passion.

Judy later told me that I attracted her interest at the Grove because she had never met a blind musician and wondered if it was possible for a sightless person to dance. In any event, she led me to her table and shooed one of her other guests out of the adjoining chair so I could sit next to her. She wanted to know if I enjoyed dancing. When I confessed that I had never once ventured out on a public dance floor even though I had spent much of my life helping make music for dancers, Judy was appalled. Was it my blindness? Was dancing an art the sightless couldn't master?

Judy listened as I recaled the time the School for the Blind decided that the students should be taught to dance. Unfortunately there was one problem—the school's long-established policy of separating the boys and girls. That problem was solved by a decision that the boys would dance with boys and the girls with girls. Every Saturday night for perhaps six months the teachers herded us into the school gym, boys at one end, girls at the other, and the school orchestra in the center of the floor.

"I dreaded those classes," I said. "Every time I had to waltz around the floor with another boy I felt like a sissy. By the time the school finally gave up and canceled the classes most of us had learned to hate dancing."

Judy found it difficult to comprehend such a sex-separated society. Why did the school feel it was necessary to keep the boys and girls apart? "Blind people must have the same emotions, the same feelings as anybody else," she protested. "Why shouldn't they be allowed to date, to fall in love?"

I assured Judy that although there were a number of things in which the sightless could not participate, love was not one of them. "It's one thing you don't need eyes for," I said. "And that's what worried the folks in charge of the Blind School. They meant well, I guess. They were always trying to protect us."

"I never heard of anything so foolish," Judy said.

I agreed that the policy had been foolish. Not only had it managed to make me hate dancing, but it had also created doubts about my ability to be

205

a successful husband and father. And that naturally brought me around to the subject of Gracie Johnston. "Traveling with the bands, there have been a lot of girls in my life," I said. "But there's only one that I've really wanted to marry, and that's Gracie. Yet every time I think of marriage, I'm still terrified."

Judy Garland patted my hand. There wasn't anything she could do to help me get over my fear of marriage, she said. But maybe she could help me overcome another fear. "I'm going to teach you how to dance," she announced.

"You're going to do what?" Horace Heidt said. My boss, I suddenly realized, had been tuned in on the whole conversation.

"I'm going to teach Fred how to dance," Judy repeated.

"That's out of the question!" Heidt thought it would be dangerous for me to be swinging around a crowded dance floor.

"Don't be a party-pooper, Horace," Judy replied. "You know I wouldn't do anything to hurt Fred."

Before Heidt could respond I jumped into the debate. "Don't you worry about me," I told him. "If Judy wants to teach me to dance, or jump out of an airplane, or fly to the moon, nobody's going to interfere. All I can say is Fred Astaire better look out!"

Horace didn't argue. In fact he let me take the rest of the evening off so Judy could introduce me to the gentle art of dancing, accompanied by the rhythm of the Musical Knights.

Judy Garland kept me out on the floor for several hours. But even she finally admitted that on the dance floor I was a klutz—a hopeless case. Still, I wasn't dismayed. For the first time in my life I had really enjoyed dancing.

After a few weeks at the Grove, a new excitement entered our lives. More and more during intermissions we began to hurry out of the ballroom and up the stairway to the musicians' private hideaway on the second floor. It was ironic in a way, because that was where the management had wanted us to spend our intermissions in the first place. It wasn't that we were bored with socializing. We had merely chanced upon a new diversion.

It began rather casually one evening when Art Carney and Buzz Adlam started rolling dice in the upstairs room. In the beginning it was a friendly nickel-and-dime game, but it soon expanded to bigger stakes as more of the musicians joined in. Before long, word of the crap game spread to Ambassador employees and even to some of the hotel guests. Soon we had the biggest game in town. By that time Art Carney had retired from active participation, having lost at least a month's pay during the first few nights. But he remained an interested spectator. In fact he set himself up as the unofficial, and unpaid, boss of the house, perching intently on the edge of a chair above the kneeling dice-tossers as he exhorted new suckers into the fray. Art seemed to take a perverse pleasure in watching others blow their bankrolls and morosely join him on the sidelines.

Heidt, as always, was engrossed in his own table-hopping and socializing—and in showing off his new wife, Adeline—so he didn't catch on to the band's extracurricular activities for several nights. Finally he noticed only a sparse scattering of his "redcoats" at the tables during intermission. A quick bit of sleuthing disclosed the reason.

Heidt watched this intermission migration for about a week, assuming it was just one of the band's passing fancies. But when the game showed no signs of abating he opened the next afternoon's rehearsal with a lecture.

"For the last few nights," he said, "I haven't seen any of you, not even the girls, mixing with the customers during intermission. Every night it's been the same story. Everyone racing upstairs as soon as they leave the bandstand. It's getting ridiculous—it looks like the British charging up Bunker Hill! Just what is going on? Has everybody gone nuts?"

"We're just relaxing . . . getting away for a breather. That's all." Carney sounded as innocent as a choirboy.

Heidt promptly demolished that alibi. "Relaxing, hell! I know you guys have a big dice game going. The word's getting around the whole hotel. Probably the whole damned town knows!"

Carney tried to assure him that it was just a friendly game, but Heidt refused to buy that line. His spies obviously had supplied him with a detailed report. "There's nothing friendly about that game," he observed. "The way I hear it you've even got Lowery hooked. And when you get a blind man rolling dice in a cutthroat money game it's about as *un*friendly as you can get!"

Art Carney had been my closest companion for months—my "seeing-eye" since Bobby Lytle quit his job as Heidt's band boy and left New York. So Heidt's accusation stung Carney. "Nobody's been cheating Fred. Matter of fact, he's been one of the big winners." His voice flared to a high pitch of indignation. "Isn't that so, Fred?"

I admitted that was the case. With Larry Cotton providing half the bankroll, and with me supplying the luck of the Irish, I had been rolling dice for several nights and had won more than $300, which Larry and I had split. "It was just blind luck," I told Heidt modestly.

"Maybe so," he grumbled. "But I don't like it. I'm going to put an end to this game before the cops raid it!"

Horace's manifesto touched off a flurry of protests, an outburst he countered by boasting that he certainly didn't have to order the game closed. He personally was going to put an end to the game by breaking it. "I'm going to show you guys how to roll those bones," he said.

Heidt led the way up the stairs during that evening's first intermission. He joined the circle of gamblers crouching on the carpet in one corner of the room where the wall served as a carom board.

Carney ceremoniously handed the dice to Heidt as the evening's first roller. When Horace made a great show of examining them Carney assured him they weren't loaded. Then, in his best satirical style, he announced the beginning of the game of the century. "Get your scorecards here, folks!" he cried. "You can't recognize the players without a scorecard!"

About twenty minutes later our distraught boss retreated hastily from the room, leaving behind about $500 he had lost in an unbroken string of bad luck. That was the grand finale of our private casino. When we returned to the room at the start of the night's second intermission we found one of the hotel's detectives posted at the door.

"Sorry, boys, but the game's finished," he announced. "Mr. Heidt asked me to tell you that from now on this room's off limits."

With our crap game closed we once again began hobnobbing with the guests during intermissions. Safe as it seemed, this socializing was not without its own hazards and pitfalls, since it sometimes led to the consumption of more than enough alcoholic beverages over the course of an evening.

I recall one festive night when, in the midst of a coast-to-coast NBC broadcast, Bobby Hackett rose unsteadily from his chair to perform one of the trumpet breaks for which he was famous. Hackett was teetering a bit, but he swung flamboyantly into his solo. Inspired by the evening's refreshments, he dipped and swayed, shuffled and whirled in time with the beat, inching dangerously close to the edge of the bandstand. Then, as he neared a magnificent closing crescendo, Hackett spun off the bandstand and crashed into one of the Grove's prized indoor palm trees.

Hackett's solo ended with a wail from his trumpet followed by alarmed shouts and screams as he and the palm tree scattered nearby tables and guests like tenpins. It was a chaotic climax for our broadcast—but one which our audience fortunately believed was a carefully staged comedy stunt. Louella Parsons described it in her Hollywood gossip column the next day as "an hilarious collision involving a potted palm and a potted trumpet player—an outrageously funny slapstick skit . . ."

As a matter of fact, even the Grove's dour manager thought Bobby Hackett's plunge off the bandstand—and the subsequent frantic efforts of four of our huskier sidemen to untangle Hackett from palm fronds and tables and carry him back to his chair—was just another of the rowdy comedy routines in which we sometimes indulged. Heidt wisely did not attempt to set the record straight. But, no doubt with his fingers crossed, he did promise to restrain the band's sometimes manic skits in the future.

Our run at the Cocoanut Grove ended with a New Year's Eve ball at which the band joyously joined guests in whooping it up for the bright new decade of the 1940s. The bandstand was engulfed by balloons, streamers, and confetti as I whistled in the new year with a midnight rendition of "Auld Lang Syne." Then we trooped off the bandstand to mingle with the crowd on the dance floor, hugging and kissing the ladies, shaking hands and pounding the tuxedoed backs of the gents, screaming good wishes to the world—an off-with-the-old, on-with-the-new celebration carried across the land by the NBC network.

It wasn't an ordinary New Year's party. It was a very special time, a time that demanded delirious nonsense. The drab, dreary decade of the thirties had ended at last. The bright, hopeful forties had dawned, and not even the shadows of war could dim our enthusiasm.

With none of the usual one-night, cross-country gigs to worry about, we now had time for a leisurely jaunt eastward to New York. Taking advantage of the holiday interlude, Larry Cotton and I made a side trip to Tulsa. For Larry it meant a reunion with his parents and brothers and sisters who lived in a nearby town. For me it was the first opportunity in nearly two years to get together with my long-distance fiancee.

Gracie had graduated from nursing school, worked briefly as head nurse in the operating room at Newburn Memorial Hospital in Jacksonville, and then moved to Tulsa as the nurse in charge of a doctor's office. She had written me faithfully, long letters of encouragement and love, assuring me of her devotion and concern. In return she received only an occasional note from me, dictated self-consciously to Art Carney or other friends who were willing to help me. Somehow I never could bring myself to pass along words of love through a second party. I could only say what was in my heart on those rare occasions when Gracie and I managed to be together.

It began as a joyous reunion, but then Gracie and I started talking about our long-delayed marriage plans.

"Times are getting better," I told her. "I've got a great job. I'm making fantastic money . . . more than I ever dreamed of. I've become a big-band star. And I've got a boss who's all for marriage, a guy who actually encourages his musicians to get married and take their wives on the road."

Gracie was understandably pleased by the news that Horace Heidt had a family band. But she wanted one final assurance that I had shaken all my doubts and fears. "Tell me the truth, Fred," she said. "Are you positively sure? It's what I've dreamed about for so long, to share your life. But I have to be convinced that you're not just trying to please me."

I should have swept Gracie up and rushed her off to the preacher. But I had to get hung up again in all my old doubts and fears about tying someone to me and my blindness and about the possible responsibilities of parenthood. What's worse, I talked about it.

Gracie's voice was soft and loving, but her words were firm and unyielding. "I can't chase away your fears, Fred. I can't make you forget your doubts. There's only one person in the world who can do that. And that's you. Until that happens all I can do is assure you that I really do love you, that I really want to share your life, both the good and the bad, and that I truly will wait for you. But you have to be sure."

Why couldn't I have kept my big mouth shut, I reflected bitterly as I left Tulsa with Larry Cotton, bound for New York. I was a sadly mixed-up man. I could, it seemed, enter into casual relationships with no qualms, no regrets. But I couldn't manage to marry the one girl I loved. With a casual date I rarely thought about my lack of sight. With Gracie, however, I could never forget it.

But it was more complex than that. I was afraid of asking Gracie to become a part of my restrictive world, and I was afraid also that she, with her mothering instincts, was willing to sacrifice her own ambitions and talents in trying to shelter me from harm. Gracie, on the other hand, wasn't afraid of any of those things; she was afraid of the fears in me. But she had been the one who brought the subject up. I had just been foolish in admitting to those fears again, or at least in talking about them.

By the time we reached New York my mood was as bad as the eastern winter weather. The euphoria generated by the fun-filled weeks at the Cocoanut Grove had faded. The high hopes for the beginning of the new decade had been tarnished by the frustrating conclusion of my visit to Tulsa.

It wasn't one of those periodic onsets of the blues that strike without reason or warning and vanish just as quickly. It went far deeper than that. Professionally, I was enjoying a success beyond the wildest dreams of my Dallas days. Despite my blindness I had been much more fortunate than most people. But it had begun to dawn on me during the trip that I had tried to make my professional accomplishments and a fast life-style compensate for my blindness and for the emptiness of my personal life.

That's why I had gone to Tulsa. Because I knew, somewhere in the core of my being, that Gracie was the answer to the riddle. She was the one person

210

who could make my life complete. If only I had thought things through beforehand, maybe I could have sidestepped her question about my doubts. But those fears had been implanted in me at an early age. The limitations of blindness, the pitfalls that threatened the sightless, had been the subjects of too many sermons during my formative years. There would always be times, I knew, when I would wonder whether it was right for me to ask those I loved most to become part of my world.

I might have wallowed in self-pity indefinitely, but once I rejoined the band in Manhattan I didn't have time to continue brooding. The pressures and excitement of new Horace Heidt projects quickly pushed my personal problems into the background. Someday I would have to confront them again, but now there wasn't time. The merry-go-round was speeding up, and there were new brass rings to reach for.

Chapter 16

Horace's latest brainchild was a novel idea called the "Pot o' Gold." It was, to my knowledge, network radio's first coast-to-coast giveaway program—a show with a $1,000-a-week jackpot. The idea for the show evolved from a nonsensical quiz feature, Answers by the Dancers, which Heidt had been using on his Tuesday night "Treasure Chest" show. From time to time during these broadcasts Heidt would circulate among the dancers, asking them silly musical questions and chatting briefly. He thought the quiz added an appealing personal touch and change of pace to our dance programs.

The broadcast version of Answers by the Dancers had a short life. One evening a bellicose dancer, apparently resenting being disturbed by foolish questioning, denounced Horace and our band over the network in extremely vulgar language. The network's reaction was immediate, because in those days radio executives were exceedingly timid about anything controversial. So Heidt was ordered to refrain from any further chitchat with dancers during live broadcasts.

However, when we obtained the Tums sponsorship Horace decided to make a modified version of Answers by the Dancers a part of our weekly program. There were no dancers in the NBC studio, so a script of questions and answers was written each week, and members of the band read the responses while others shuffled their feet on the bandstand to create the sound of dancing.

Tums' management and the company's ad agency weren't happy with the canned version of Answers by the Dancers, and they asked Heidt to come up with a more unique gimmick. Always eager to please the people who were picking up the tab, Horace tried out and discarded all sorts of cockeyed ideas before turning up with "Pot o' Gold." It seemed at first too complex a format for radio. But it worked, and in the process it turned out to be the band's biggest jackpot.

"Pot o' Gold" was a prodigious and ingenious audience generator. First, there was the prize. A thousand dollars at that time was a veritable gold mine—more than enough to buy a brand-new car, a fur coat, or even a modest bungalow. It was a sum designed to keep just about every American eagerly glued to his or her radio set during the Musical Knights' Thursday-evening Tums broadcast. Second, there was the important element of suspense built into the program. To be sure, the odds against winning were enormous. But nobody could be sure they weren't going to be the lucky winner until the last moments of the show. And third, there were no strings attached to the prize—no special rules, no questions to answer, no products to buy. The only requirement was that the lucky person personally answer Heidt's phone call.

Today such a show would never be aired. It involved no so-called element of skill or knowledge. It was quite simply a game of chance, an illegal lottery. Eventually the federal government cracked down on such giveaways, a crackdown that resulted in the evolution of the more elaborate quiz-type giveaways. But that took several years—ample time for "Pot o' Gold" to flourish and for Horace Heidt to prosper.

Here's how the "Pot o' Gold" program worked. Each week the Bell Telephone Company assembled fifty special minisized telephone books. Each book contained fifty pages of randomly selected telephone listings from various sections of the country. Each page in turn contained fifty telephone listings, all of them residential numbers. Some of the books contained listings from just one large city, like New York, Chicago, or San Francisco. Others had listings from several cities, towns, or rural areas.

These books were packed in a locked steel container under strict supervision. They were delivered by armored truck to the NBC studio on the afternoon of our Thursday broadcast. The steel chest was placed on a table near the bandstand with an armed guard standing by until the program was over.

This is how a typical "Pot o' Gold" program unfolded:

Before the eight o'clock broadcast a large carnival-type wheel of fortune bearing the numbers 1 through 50 is set up in front of the bandstand. After the opening announcements, Horace's greetings, and the band's first medley, Larry Cotton steps over to the wheel, portable microphone in hand, and delivers the "Pot o' Gold" ballyhoo. He explains how the game works, assures the secrecy of the chosen phone numbers, and urges everyone out there in Radioland not to stray from their sets or their telephones. Larry is a splendid singer, but on "Pot o' Gold" he displays an equally fine talent as a huckster. "You nice folks out there in Peoria, in Phoenix, in Pottstown, or wherever you are, wait for your phone to ring tonight. It could be the biggest moment in your life! It could be Horace Heidt calling to tell you that you're the lucky guy or gal!"

With that fervent exhortation completed Larry steps up and gives the wheel of fortune a mighty spin. Round and round the wheel clacks, with Larry holding the mike close to the action so the sound will echo across the land. At last the wheel stops at a number—perhaps the number 38. That first spin, of course, is just the opening teaser, for that number only indicates which of the fifty phone books is to be used that night.

With the phone-book selection completed, the Musical Knights play a few tunes interspersed with an Art Carney skit and a couple of commercials extolling the virtues of Tums, and then Larry Cotton goes into part two of his act. Again he approaches the wheel, again he voices an eloquent spiel designed to keep the audience tuned in, again he gives it a whirl. Round and round the wheel flashes, finally stopping on another number—maybe the number 27. Is that the winner? Don't be naive—not in the middle of the show! This number merely determines the number of the page in the already designated book from which the final spin of the wheel will determine the lucky person.

More suspenseful waiting. Another commercial, a couple of songs to soothe the jangled nerves of our listeners, a comedy routine, another commercial, and then as a prelude to the night's big moment Heidt introduces "the world's most famous whistler." Larry as usual leads me to the mike with the brass section blaring a noisy fanfare. As I whistle I wonder how many of my listeners are wishing I'd cut it short and get the heck off the air. I can picture families across America huddling tensely beside their radios waiting impatiently for the lingering notes of "Indian Love Call" to subside so Larry Cotton can get on with the important stuff.

"At last," Larry intones a few moments later, "this is the big moment you've all been waiting for! It's time for the last spin of the wheel of fortune . . . time for Lady Luck to smile on someone out there in our great, wonderful audience!"

Once again Larry spins the wheel. Clackety, clackety, clackety—it whirls about in an ever-slowing, heart-tugging circle and finally comes to a stop. "The lucky number tonight is 17!" Larry cries. "Stand by, America. 'Pot o' Gold' is going to be calling in just a few minutes!"

The armed guard unlocks the metal treasure chest, selects the previously determined book 38 and hands it to two certified accountants, representing NBC and the phone company. These trusted dignitaries solemnly turn to the previously determined page 27. While this is going on, the microphone

214

transmits a rustling of pages produced by the ever-creative sound-effects crew riffling the thick sheets of a wallpaper sample book.

With the fateful page located, the two accountants carefully zero in on the seventeenth telephone listing. One of them writes the name, address, and phone number on a piece of paper and hands it to the other to verify. These procedures are dramatically described to our radio audience by Larry Cotton, much in the the manner of a play-by-play announcer at a sports event. With the preliminaries carried to completion against a backdrop of soft music, the sheet of paper bearing the evening's most vital statistic is handed to Larry.

"Here is tonight's lucky winner of the Pot o' Gold!" one of the accountants announces in a splendid baritone. "Please deliver it to Mr. Heidt."

Larry hands the message to Horace, who is seated at a nearby table with a telephone and microphone at hand. He glances at the paper, then announces to the waiting world: "Friends, tonight's lucky winner of the Pot o' Gold is Clara Hemelgamp of 510 Pottery Lane, Bean Blossom, Georgia! I will now place a long-distance telephone call to Clara Hemelgamp. Remember, there are no questions to be answered, no requirements other than that it must be Clara Hemelgamp who answers the phone. If she is home, if she answers this call, she will win $1,000!"

Heidt picks up the phone and places the call through the long-distance operator with the conversation picked up for our broadcast. There is a muffled, far-off sound of a phone ringing. Once, twice, and then a woman's delirious voice shrilling, "Mr. Heidt . . . Mr. Heidt . . . it's me, Clara Hemelgamp!" We had another winner.

Sometimes, of course, there would be no answer when Horace phoned the lucky number. When that happened a check for $100 was mailed to the not-so-lucky person who neglected to stay home for the "Pot o' Gold" program. The remaining $900 was then added to the next week's pot. During the early days of the program before its fame had spread, we encountered a series of "no answers," and the pot swelled to more than $10,000, creating a wave of publicity that helped make "Pot o' Gold" a household word. After that, we rarely went more than a week or two without a winner.

Within four months of our first "Pot o' Gold" broadcast it was the hottest show on radio. Today, with the proliferation of elaborate television giveaway shows in which astounding sums of money and costly merchandise are handed out, it is perhaps difficult to imagine the national hysteria generated by "Pot o' Gold." But it did exist, and learned men advanced various complex explanations for the phenomenon. I think the explanation was very simple. Horace Heidt had plugged into mankind's eternal dream of "something for nothing." It was a surefire formula for success, as evidenced by all the later giveaways it spawned.

By the spring of 1940 all manner of wild reactions to "Pot o' Gold" were being reported in the nation's press. Phone calls, for example, declined dramatically every Thursday night during the broadcast. No one wanted his or her line busy when the magic moment arrived. In one eastern state an irate housewife sued for divorce, claiming her husband refused to get off the phone as the prize-awarding time approached.

Soon motion-picture theaters were deserted on Thursday nights. One enterprising movie operator in the Midwest began staging Thursday night "Pot o' Gold" parties in his establishment. In addition to offering free popcorn, he stopped the feature film for half an hour, channeled the Horace Heidt broadcast into the theater's sound system, and guaranteed that if anyone in the audience should be called by Horace the theater would pay the prize money. Not to be outdone, a competing movie mogul announced he would double the prize money if anyone in his Thursday night audience should miss the "Pot o' Gold" phone call.

Amid all the publicity *Variety* published one of its anonymous trade reports predicting that a motion picture, based on "Pot o' Gold" and featuring the Heidt band, was in the works. When we excitedly confronted Horace with the story he professed to be as much in the dark as we were. But a few weeks later, as our long run at the Biltmore neared an end, he announced that we really were going to be in the movies. Jimmy Roosevelt, son of President Franklin D. Roosevelt, had just concluded a deal with MGM to produce the film. Shooting of the movie was to start in November during another long engagement at the Cocoanut Grove.

The news that we were about to make a movie revived our spirits after a hectic stay in New York. Our crammed schedule had included the Biltmore's six-nights-a-week shows, the Tums program and other network appearances, a return engagement at the Strand, record-cutting sessions, and occasional short weekend gigs at nightclubs and theaters. Further, we faced another tiresome cross-country tour that would take us to the Grove after engagements in Pittsburgh, Milwaukee, Chicago, Kansas City, and Denver. Luckily we would have no one-night stands to contend with; our dates on this road trip ranged from one to three weeks in each city, and they would be enlivened by "Pot o' Gold" broadcasts from the theaters or hotels

216

where we were appearing—an enticement guaranteeing packed houses and lavish publicity.

Our weeklong engagement at a downtown Pittsburgh theater saw a new member added to the Horace Heidt band, an addition that infuriated Art Carney. The trouble began when a short, scarecrow-thin character showed up at the theater one afternoon. He introduced himself as Ollie O'Toole and said he was working at a local radio station as a disc jockey. O'Toole informed Heidt that he not only had a great voice but was also the best impersonator in the business.

Art Carney, among the band members listening as the stranger made his pitch to Heidt, reacted indignantly, but Heidt paid no heed to Carney's sideline sniping. He listened politely as O'Toole extolled his talents. Then, much to our astonishment, he agreed to give him an audition. Like all the bands we were constantly besieged by would-be performers pleading for tryouts, but Heidt almost always rejected these unknowns without a hearing, feeling it was a waste of time.

O'Toole sang a couple of Irish ballads in a pleasing voice. Then he adorned his upper lip with a paste-on mustache, brushed his hair down over one eye, and delivered a splendid impersonation of a raving, incoherent Adolf Hitler. Heidt was obviously impressed. He hired O'Toole on the spot and told him to report for the evening show.

Carney was furious. The rest of us, even though we recognized that O'Toole was talented, were curious. Why had Horace so unexpectedly relaxed his policy against auditioning unknowns? After much speculation we decided that our boss was either in a benevolent mood brought on by the lucrative movie deal or, more likely, saw a chance to torment Carney by hiring another impersonator.

At the time the flip, outspoken Carney and the stubborn, humorless Heidt were involved in one of their frequent disputes. One seldom could pin down the reasons for their fussing and feuding. They most likely didn't need a reason; they simply irritated one another. Heidt probably recognized in O'Toole an easy opportunity to bedevil Carney. Because, as Art angrily exclaimed, "Who ever heard of a band with two impersonators?"

The hiring of Ollie O'Toole convinced Carney that Heidt was planning to fire him. Heidt didn't help ease the tension. He pointedly ignored Carney while lavishing attention on O'Toole. The newcomer, a warm, friendly man, was embarrassed at finding himself in the center of the Carney-Heidt clash. He tried several times to assure Art that he wasn't after his job, but his peacemaking efforts failed.

Despite Art's constant stewing about his job, by the time we arrived in

Chicago for a three-week engagement at the Edgewater Beach Hotel the band still had two impressionists—or impersonators, as they were called in those days. Heidt still hadn't said a word to Carney, probably relishing the opportunity to make the band's most carefree spirit sweat. Finally Art decided to have a showdown with Horace.

Heidt professed amazement at Carney's belief that his days with the band were numbered. He not only assured Art that no firings were contemplated, but confided that he had a great idea for an act. When we opened at the Cocoanut Grove the band would have a brand-new novelty number: a Battle of the Impersonators featuring Art Carney and Ollie O'Toole!

Since he wasn't being fired, Art was convinced that our boss had deliberately set out to torment him. And he was suspicious of Heidt's sketchy plans for a new act. But Heidt wasn't kidding. Again demonstrating his genius as a showman, he found a way for a band to utilize two impersonators. The Battle of the Impersonators turned out to be a great act. It remained one of the big hits of our shows until Carney left the band a couple of years later. And once Art's employment worries were dispelled he and Ollie O'Toole became good friends.

It wasn't just the O'Toole situation that caused Carney to be on edge during our Chicago engagement. To my amazement I discovered that Art also had romantic problems. We were sitting in the St. James bar, across the street from the New Lawrence Hotel where the band was quartered, when Art broke a moody silence to announce that he was in love.

"So what's new?" I laughed. I couldn't muster much interest in Art's amorous mooning. I had my own problems to worry about. "Are you trying to tell me that you fell for that woman in Milwaukee?" I asked. I was talking about a practical joke someone had played on him while we were performing in Milwaukee. They had sent him a hooker as a "gift."

"Don't be stupid," Carney snapped. "Although I've got to admit that got me to thinking."

"What's that supposed to mean?" A philosophical Carney was hard to contemplate.

Art was impatient with my refusal to lend a sympathetic ear to his troubles. "I mean I've been thinking about my girl back home . . . about Jean."

I had met Jean Myers, the girl from Mount Vernon who dated Art regularly during our stays in New York. She was something special— attractive, lots of class, quiet, refined, very proper, and a nondrinker. Art had known her since their school days in Mount Vernon, but I never suspected that it was a serious romance. It was impossible for me to imagine Art being seriously in love. And Jean didn't impress me as Art's type. I said so.

Art agreed that it was a strange romance. He knew there were great differences between them. He loved boisterous fun, partying until dawn, the freewheeling life. Jean was a completely opposite personality—a girl who disliked partying and drinking, who preferred a serene, orderly life. Yet they loved one another and wanted to get married. Still, they were fearful of taking the big step.

"I don't know what to do," Art sighed. "I'm tired of playing around. I want a home and family, but I keep hesitating. I can't give up show business, and I'm not sure that Jean will ever be able to adapt to it. I don't want to make a mess of our lives."

As close as we were, as much as we hung around together, Art and I had never realized that we had such similar problems and feelings. Art was aware of my long-distance romance with Gracie and had helped me write letters to her. But it wasn't until that afternoon that we realized we both faced the same plight. Each of us in his own way was reluctant to ask a girl he loved to take a chance on what might be a bad marital risk.

Art asked me what I thought he should do. It occurred to me that as a man who couldn't cope with his own problems I wasn't exactly qualified to offer advice to the lovelorn. But I gave what I hoped was wise counsel. I advised him to telephone Jean, tell her how much he loved her, and ask her to please take a chance and marry him.

Art pondered my suggestion briefly and then said that was just what he was going to do. But he didn't have enough change for the long-distance phone call to New York. So I emptied my pockets and we came up with enough coins for a three-minute call. That was all the time Art needed. He returned on the run, gleefully hugged me, and said, "She'll marry me! As soon as I can get home!"

Always delighted when one of the bachelors in his band got hooked, Heidt gave Carney time off to return to New York for the wedding. In fact, with a spare impersonator on the job, he told Art to enjoy a leisurely honeymoon and rejoin the band in Los Angeles.

I viewed Art's marriage with mixed feelings. I was happy for him, but saddened at losing the roomie and trusted "seeing-eye" who had helped me navigate through many perilous shoals. Art's marriage plans also made me feel more than ever the emptiness of my own personal life.

On the day Art left for New York I headed for the New Lawrence Hotel bar with Charlie Goodman as soon as the band finished its final performance of the evening. Like me, Charlie was among the band's dwindling numbers of bachelors, and we were determined to hold a "wake" for our departed comrade. Charlie and I had told other band members about our plan, so as the evening wore on we were joined by various Musical Knights in toasting in absentia our matrimony-bound buddy and recounting some of his—and our—more memorable escapades.

Among the late arrivals were trumpet player Jimmy Troutman and his fiancee. Jimmy was one of the more recent additions to our band. His fiancee, Mary Ann Mercer, had been a vocalist with Vincent Lopez in the late twenties. She was gone by the time I joined Lopez several years later, but even then she was an intriguing topic of conversation among the musicians.

During the twenties Mary Ann Mercer, a beautiful girl with an exceptional blues delivery, seemed to have a great future. But she vanished one day in Chicago. No notes, no phone calls, no trace. Even more baffling, police in the Windy City seemed strangely reluctant to push an investigation. As Lopez once reflected, it seemed as if the cops knew where she was but didn't want to get involved.

And then, several months later, Mary Ann showed up suddenly in New York wanting to resume her job with Lopez. She was as talented as ever, but she adamantly refused to talk about her vanishing act. It was personal, something she wanted to forget, she said. Lopez wouldn't buy that. Always suspicious of women and their behavior, he refused to take her back, and she went with another band.

That night at the New Lawrence bar, as talk about Carney's marriage led to gossiping about other big-band romances, I summoned the nerve to ask Mary Ann Mercer about her long-ago disappearance. I knew I was rattling old skeletons in the closet, an action that might anger Jimmy Troutman. But I was unable to restrain my curiosity. There had been talk in the Lopez band, I told her, that she had fallen in love and fled with her boyfriend to some secluded rendezvous.

Mary Ann's laugh was brittle and bitter. "Some rendezvous!" she said. "Anyhow, it's all ancient history, so why bring it up?"

I expected Jimmy to blast me for my nosiness. Instead, in a soft, compassionate voice, he told Mary Ann it might be a good idea for her to talk about her ordeal after keeping it bottled up for so many years. "I'm sure there's nothing to worry about anymore," he said.

So Mary Ann told us the story. While singing with the Lopez band at a Chicago hotel in 1929 she had been romanced by a young and handsome customer—a slick-haired, dark-eyed Rudolph Valentino type with a red Packard coupe, an endless supply of money, and a smooth line. One night he talked her into driving with him to Indiana for a secret justice-of-the-peace wedding.

But Mary Ann soon discovered that her Romeo was a hoodlum connected with the Capone mob. In addition he turned out to be insanely jealous. He couldn't stand the sight of other men admiring her from the dance floor as she sang, and he demanded that she quit the band. When she refused and threatened to walk out on him he locked her in a suite in Chicago's Eastgate Hotel.

Mary Ann was imprisoned in that downtown hotel for more than two months. The telephone had been removed. Burly thugs guarded her door around the clock. Other than her husband the only person she ever saw was an elderly waiter who brought her meals and cleaned the rooms.

Her imprisonment finally ended when her husband was gunned down during the hijacking of a shipment of liquor at Cicero. Before they let her walk out of the hotel, however, the mobsters told her in explicit language what would happen if she ever talked about her weeks of captivity.

"That's why I never said anything even when it cost me my job with Lopez," Mary Ann said. "I was afraid to talk . . . afraid some triggerman would come calling."

Art's "wake" turned into an all-night affair. We talked until the bar closed, and then a few of us continued the gabfest in my room at the New Lawrence until dawn. There was a lot of reminiscing that night, and a lot of memorable tales were retold, but none of them could equal Mary Ann Mercer's.

Art Carney's marriage brought to an end our wild days as the Heidt band's hell-raising room-mates. Jean Carney, Art's new "roomie," joined the band on its tours, hoping with wifely concern to reform her rambunctious mate. Charlie Goodman took over as my room-mate and "seeing-eye." It became a friendship that lasted through the years, long after the Heidt band folded. I even served as Charlie's best man when the right girl finally came along and led him to the altar.

Horace Heidt professed to be greatly relieved when Charlie became my roomie and companion. With good reason, Horace was always fearful that Carney and Lowery would get into trouble. Carney and I seemed to have a talent for upsetting our boss. Charlie may have been more reserved than Art, but he was also a dedicated man-about-town. He always knew the really good restaurants, and he was always acquainted with a city's most interesting offbeat bars. Like a gifted fisherman stalking the wily trout, he had an unerring instinct for spotting the haunts of fascinating people.

Charlie did have one great weakness. He was an incurable romantic, a nice guy who truly believed women should be placed on a pedestal. Most women, of course, didn't want to be placed in such a precarious position, and as a result Charlie seemed to be forever involved in frustrated romances.

Once, after Heidt formed Donna and the Don Juans, a singing group that included Goodman, Charlie developed a grand passion for lovely Donna Wood. It was another of Charlie's one-sided romances. But this time it almost had disastrous repercussions.

On network radio in those days the biggest headache was what was known as "repeat broadcasts." Every network broadcast had to be made twice, because tape had not yet been perfected. Say a show went on the air at 9 P.M. for East Coast and Midwest listeners. At 11 P.M. the same show had to be rebroadcast for listeners in the Rocky Mountains and Far West. During this boring two-hour delay between broadcasts musicians frequently drifted away to nearby bars. On occasion this caused severe production problems.

On this particular night, about an hour before the second broadcast, Donna Wood came to me with a problem. After the first broadcast Charlie had renewed his wooing, and Donna had told him off in rather harsh language.

"Now I can't find Charlie anywhere," Donna cried. "I know I hurt his feelings, and he's out drinking somewhere. You've got to help me find him."

Donna and I flagged down a cab and for the next half hour made a frantic tour of midtown bistros. Finally we found Charlie at Steuben's bar across the street from the Palace Theater. Fortunately he hadn't had too much of a head start, and we had him back with the band, ready to sing, when we went on the air at eleven. Charlie soon got over his infatuation with Donna and went on to some other unrequited love affair.

It was about this time that Charlie introduced me to one of the most talented and unforgettable musicians I've ever known. It was a Monday night in Chicago, a night off for the band. Charlie and I were finishing a fabulous steak at some unimposing restaurant in the stockyards district when he said he simply had to introduce me to the world's greatest pianist. He wouldn't tell me who he had in mind. He flagged down a cab, gave an address, and we rode in silence into the heart of the city. At last the taxi pulled up in front of a honky-tonk south of the Loop.

"What kind of a dive is this?" I grumbled as Charlie led me into the dark, smoke-fogged tavern.

"Quit griping and listen," he replied.

All at once a silence settled over the barroom as a piano player launched into "Ain't Misbehavin'." I'd heard a lot of memorable pianists in my time;

Vincent Lopez and Frankie Carle were hard to beat. But I'd never before heard the piano played with such magnificent improvisation. And hearing it in a place like this boggled the mind.

I pulled Charlie up short at the end of a long bar. At the far end of the room I could faintly make out the glow of a spotlight, no doubt focused on the piano player. "Who in the world is that?" I whispered in Charlie's ear.

"Be patient," Charlie hissed. "I'll introduce you."

When the piano at last fell silent and the customary tavern noise started up again, Charlie told me the pianist with the magical touch was Art Tatum.

"I never heard of him," I said. "But whoever he is, wherever he's from, he's one of the greatest pianists I've ever heard. How come he's playing in a place like this?"

Charlie explained that for several years Tatum had been playing for whatever tips he could scrounge in joints around Chicago. His local fame had spread, but his professional career remained stalled. Fate had played a dirty trick on Art Tatum: he was both black and blind.

In his wanderings around Chicago, Charlie had only recently heard of Tatum. He had visited the bar and chatted with the pianist. When Tatum learned that Goodman was with the Heidt band he had a favor to ask. Could Charlie bring Fred Lowery into the bar some evening for a visit?

"Is it because I'm blind too?" I asked Charlie.

Charlie didn't know. All Art Tatum had said was that he'd heard me whistle on radio and wanted to talk with me. Maybe, Charlie suggested, Tatum wanted to know if I could tell him how a blind person could make it in show business.

As it turned out, Art Tatum didn't ask for any advice. I think he was just lonely and wanted a chance to talk with another sightless musician— someone who could understand his problems. After we were introduced, Tatum asked me to sit beside him on the piano bench and share the beers admiring customers were constantly dispatching to the piano. I remained in that seat until the bar closed, utterly charmed by the variety and quality of Tatum's repertoire, by the humorous line of patter with which he regaled his audience, and by our conversation during intermissions.

I still half-expected Tatum to ask me to help him get a big-band job or do a surprise guest appearance and whistle a few numbers. Nothing of the sort ever happened, either during the time at the piano or during our subsequent tour of after-hours jazz joints. He just wanted to talk, to share experiences.

We talked a lot about our school years. Tatum had attended the Ohio School for the Blind in Columbus. Like me he had resisted all attempts to discourage his ambitions for a musical career. Like me he had met with much frustration and many rejections. He hadn't been as fortunate as I in overcoming the prejudices against blind performers but probably the real reason for his lack of recognition was the color of his skin.

I asked if he was bitter. Art Tatum pondered my question. Not really, not anymore, he said. He had lots of scars, but he'd finally made peace with himself. He no longer struggled for that elusive big break. "I'm happy working these bars and cutting a few records," he said. "I don't need the aggravation of the big-time rat race. I'm making enough . . . all that I need. As long as I've got a piano to play and somebody to listen, I'm satisfied."

One thing was certain. Tatum certainly had somebody to listen. The bar remained crowded throughout the night, and each time he began to play a hush settled over the place. Tatum was also a master showman. He maintained a constant flow of chatter, and whenever the waiter deposited foaming steins of beer on the piano Tatum's right hand would dart out with astounding accuracy and fetch the latest delivery of suds without groping. While his left hand continued pounding out the rhythm he'd drain the stein, plop the empty back on the piano top, and finish the number without missing a beat. I'm sure newcomers to the bar were positive that Tatum could see, that his blindness was just an act.

Tatum's skill at cajoling the customers into generous tips was equally impressive. A large cigar box was placed at the end of the piano nearest the dance floor. It bore a sign reminding patrons that the only pay the piano player received was the money they gave him. The sign was unnecessary, because between numbers Tatum was constantly reminding the crowd that "the clinkin' and clankin' of half-dollars is mighty pretty music to my tired ol' ears!

"Ain't nothin' more satisfying, brothers and sisters," he'd continue, "unless maybe it's the rustlin' of paper money falling into my cigar box." In closing his pitch he'd remind everyone that "it ain't right to drop anything smaller than two bits in my box 'cause I gotta strain too hard to hear a penny, a nickel, or a dime drop!"

Whenever Tatum's sharp ears detected the sound of small change rather than the clank of a half-dollar or the reassuring rustle of paper money he'd cry out for all to hear, "Hey there, brother, don't be a cheap skate! Show your chick you're a classy guy, a big-time spender!" More often than not that exhortation produced at least a fifty-cent offering in Tatum's cigar-box depository.

That night was the beginning of a long friendship. Even though a year or more might pass between our meetings, whenever I dropped in at whatever bar or club Art Tatum was playing I'd get a warm welcome from my favorite piano player. And we'd usually end up doing the town, laughing a lot, and sometimes crying into our beer over life's injustices.

It's sad to realize that Art Tatum spent so much of his life playing piano in nondescript places, scrounging a living on tips solicited through an Uncle Tom routine. But wherever he played Art brought beauty and humor with him, enriching the lives of those who listened. And he hasn't been forgotten. As the years passed, Tatum did achieve significant fame, if not fortune. The records he cut are now classics. Today, long after his death, his genius is widely recognized. Will somebody please drop a half-dollar in the tip box? The clankin' of the silver is mighty pretty music!

I was reminded of Art Tatum's genius some years ago when I was privileged to appear on a broadcast with André Previn. Oscar Peterson, the great black pianist, was one of the featured artists. During rehearsals I told Peterson of my friendship with Art Tatum. In turn, Peterson recalled how Tatum had unknowingly influenced his life.

Peterson was a reluctant musical prodigy, always trying to avoid tiresome practice at the piano in favor of more casual and fun-filled pursuits. Finally his father bought a baby grand, hoping that its presence in the house would encourage his gifted son to practice. But the boy still balked.

"My father tried all sorts of reasoning, but I wouldn't listen," Peterson recalled. "Then one day he brought home an Art Tatum album and asked me to play it. I did, and the music was tremendous. My father agreed. When I asked him who Art Tatum was he told me he was a black pianist who was also blind. Just realizing that a man with that kind of a handicap could develop such fantastic artistry inspired me. After that I didn't need anyone to prod me into practicing. Art Tatum was all the inspiration I needed!"

Chicago and the music of Tatum were memories several weeks old when the band arrived in Los Angeles in September. After another tiring cross-country tour it was exciting to be back for a long stay at the Cocoanut Grove. However, the prospect of appearing in a movie was even more exciting—especially after we learned that Jimmy Stewart, one of Hollywood's newest stars, and Paulette Goddard, the town's current target for spicy gossip, had been signed for the "Pot o' Gold" movie.

We weren't sure what kind of roles we would play until Jimmy Roosevelt dropped in during rehearsal at the Grove one afternoon and said we would be used mainly for background and music with just a few close-ups to lend a touch of authenticity to the "Pot o' Gold" aspect of the plot. The story, as related to us that afternoon by the president's son, employed the typical boy-meets-girl, boy-loses-girl, boy-finally-wins-girl-back pattern the studios cherished. It involved a dance band living in a large boardinghouse operated by an eccentric couple, portrayed by Charles Winninger and Mary Gordon. One of the "Pot o' Gold" winners, played by Goddard, turns up at the boarding house to collect her prize money. Here she is spotted by a shy young band member, played by Stewart, and they fall in love at first sight. From that point the movie meandered rather witlessly through all manner of improbable situations as Jimmy won, lost, and rewon the girl.

We were on the MGM set every day once shooting began even though our services were rarely called for. Except for Larry Cotton and Art Carney, making what proved to be the first of many movies, actors took the roles of any band members who had speaking parts. The real-life Musical Knights were used only for long-range shots of the band at work plus a few fleeting close-ups.

Carney was the regular "Pot o' Gold" announcer when we were broadcasting the show from somewhere other than New York or Hollywood, and Larry always ran the wheel. The fact that they had the biggest movie roles entrusted to members of the band rankled Horace, who only rated a couple of brief episodes. Even Frankie Carle, who got to demonstrate his famous hands-behind-the-back piano playing, received more exposure. I didn't fare any better than Heidt. Other than sitting on the bandstand, my sole appearance before the cameras came during a scene in which Cotton sang "Do You Believe in Fairy Tales?" In that sequence I whistled eight bars of the song, enough to give me perhaps thirty seconds as a movie star.

As things turned out it was just as well we didn't get a lot of exposure in the movie. *Pot o' Gold* turned out to be one of the worst flops ever produced. It was universally panned by the critics and was quickly pulled out of circulation because the studio bosses were afraid it would destroy the promising career of Jimmy Stewart. Later, the studio brought *Pot o' Gold* out of mothballs, retitled it *Jimmy Steps Out*, and rereleased it. Still later it began to appear on television's late-late-late shows, the proper burial ground for such a turkey.

Even before work on the movie began, there had been a big change in my life. After learning that the band would be based in Los Angeles for several months of performances, my sister Minnie Lee and her five-year-old daughter Carol Ann had traveled all the way from Tulsa to help me establish some kind of semipermanent residence. From my recent letters and her conversations with Gracie, Minnie Lee was certain that the unending cross-country tours and my free-wheeling life-style had left me emotionally exhausted and depressed, and she thought having someone around to cook and look after things for awhile would be a boost to my spirits.

She couldn't have been more correct. It was a generous thing for her to do, and it was equally generous of her husband Glenn Brown, who operated a service station in Tulsa, to let her do it. So Minnie Lee and Carol Ann and I found a large, comfortably furnished apartment in Hollywood for $85 a month and prepared to set up housekeeping. My new "home" was on the third floor of the St. George Apartments, just a block from the NBC Studios at Hollywood and Vine.

It was a strange new life for me. I luxuriated in the unaccustomed domesticity. I had someone to take care of tasks like laundry and dry cleaning, someone to prepare home-cooked meals, someone other than Horace Heidt and my friends in the band to worry about me. Most of all, I guess, I was fascinated by the introduction of a child into my life.

Little Carol Ann was a joy—a bright, impish girl who even at her early age was exhibiting an excellent ear for music. She was forever coaxing me to whistle or to teach her songs and giggling delightedly when I made up silly lyrics for popular tunes. Before long she was attending rehearsals with me, sitting beside Frankie Carle at the piano or perched on Horace's lap as he supervised the Musical Knights from the sidelines. Her favorite in the band was Larry Cotton. "I could just listen to Larry forever and ever," she confided to me—a feeling which, though she didn't know it, she shared with lots of bigger girls around the country.

Within a few weeks I was becoming thoroughly domesticated. What's more, I was liking it. I even began to go marketing with my sister and Carol Ann. I discovered there was great fun to be had in food stores, although I'm sure I was a pest both to the clerks and the budget-conscious Minnie Lee. I was forever knocking merchandise off the shelves or walking into displays of packages or canned goods as I rummaged about with Carol Ann trying to pick out our favorite delicacies.

Then disaster struck. As we left the apartment bound for the market one day, Carol Ann skipped blithely down the long hallway in a race to get to the rickety elevator ahead of us. It was a game she played, reaching the elevator first so she could punch the button before we got there. But something was awry with the elevator's mechanism this time. Carol Ann pushed the button, the car rose, and the door opened. But the elevator continued on to the next floor, and my niece stepped unknowingly into the empty elevator shaft.

Minnie Lee and I were still some distance down the hall when we heard

Carol Ann's terrified scream, loud at first and then fading into a deathly silence. "My God, what's happened?" Minnie Lee cried. She began running, calling her daughter's name. I groped my way slowly down the hall, cursing my faulty eyesight.

My sister reached the open doorway, peered down the shaft, and saw her daughter's body sprawled in the subbasement elevator pit far below. She was screaming hysterically when I reached her side, but she had the presence of mind to push me away from the open shaft. "Carol Ann's fallen down the elevator," she sobbed. "Dear God, my baby's hurt. Help her, Fred, help her!"

Fortunately several neighbors were at home in adjacent apartments and heard the screams and cries. Two of them helped Minnie Lee and me scramble down the steep flights of stairs to the basement. Others summoned the apartment manager and the building custodian who had the key to the door to the elevator pit. Another telephoned for an ambulance.

In the elevator pit we found Carol Ann alive but unconscious. Miraculously, one leg of her bell-bottomed slacks had caught momentarily on a steel projection, breaking the full force of the fall and saving her life.

Carol Ann was gravely hurt—several broken bones, a ruptured spleen, and other internal injuries. She was rushed to Children's Hospital where, after emergency surgery, she hovered near death for a number of days before beginning a slow recovery.

It was a nightmarish time. Minnie Lee and I spent long hours at the hospital keeping a prayerful vigil at Carol Ann's bedside. At home, when the phone rang we were slow to pick it up, afraid it would be dreadful news from the hospital. And my sleep was constantly broken by chilling dreams in which I relived the terror and futility I had felt when the accident happened. I would dream about Carol Ann's screams, and about clutching a stranger's hand during a frantic dash down stairs I couldn't see. Never before or since have I felt the loss of sight so sharply. Never before or since have I so deeply regretted my blindness.

Carol Ann was hospitalized for two months. It was an emotional and fearful time of waiting for doctors' reports as our hopes rose and fell like the tides. It was also, in those days before hospitalization benefits, a crushing financial burden. Minnie Lee's husband sent as much money as he could muster, and I emptied my savings. Still we fell behind in meeting the soaring medical costs. But Horace Heidt came to the rescue with a $600 loan that got us out of hock.

Horace also made sure I had enough free time in the band's busy schedule to share the long hours at the hospital with Minnie Lee. I was at the hospital so much I began to feel like a member of the staff. I got to know the doctors, nurses, and orderlies on a first-name basis. And to ease the tedium of waiting I entertained young patients with my whistling and off-key singing. Art Carney and Ollie O'Toole often joined me on these rounds through the wards, sending the kids into gales of laughter with their silly impersonations and outlandish tales.

Before long I found a new reason to spend as much time as possible at Children's Hospital. The attraction was a slender, dark-haired young lady named Betty Wilson, one of the team of nurses assigned to the intensive-care ward in which Carol Ann was housed for so long. Betty was a devoted nurse, a warm, good-humored woman who spent hours each day helping Carol Ann fight her way back to an active life. More and more I found myself chatting and joking with Betty. We shared a common concern for my niece's welfare, but beyond that we discovered that we liked many of the same things, laughed at many of the same things, believed in many of the same things. What started out to be a casual acquaintance quickly developed into friendship and then blossomed into romance. By the time Carol Ann was released from the hospital and Minnie Lee prepared to take her back home to Tulsa for further convalescence, Betty and I were engaged.

My sister had watched my romancing of Betty Wilson with obvious disapproval. She had said nothing, no doubt hoping it was just a passing fancy. But when I broke the news that we were engaged, Minnie Lee erupted angrily. "But, Fred, you're already engaged!"

I had wrestled with that problem repeatedly, and I admitted that I didn't know what had happened to me. I was in love with Gracie and in love with Betty, and I didn't know how to get off the horns of this dilemma. I just didn't know what to do.

I kept asking myself how I could turn away from Gracie after all these years. Yet Betty was now in my life, and sooner or later I knew I'd have to tell Gracie something. But not right away. I rejected Minnie Lee's suggestion that I put an end to my romance with Betty before I got in any deeper. "I've got to think about it," I procrastinated. "I've got to have time to figure things out."

Actually I'd already figured out a great deal. Betty Wilson had entered my life at a time when I knew my sister would soon be returning to Oklahoma with Carol Ann. In just a few months I'd grown accustomed to having a home and family, even if it was a family of live-in kinfolks. Now I wanted to hang onto this newfound happiness with a home and a wife of my own, and my doubts and fears be damned. Gracie was far away and wanted a

229

guarantee. Betty was close at hand and willing. I was following the course of least resistance.

Confronted by my stubborn refusal to make a decision, Minnie Lee—as I later learned—indulged in a typically feminine conspiracy. She telephoned my favorite cousin Elsie White, the playmate of my childhood in the Piney Woods, and told her of my predicament. Would Elsie please hurry out to Los Angeles and try to reason with her bullheaded, love-sick brother?

Elsie White came to visit me in my Hollywood apartment the day Minnie Lee and Carol Ann left for home. But Elsie wisely delayed a few days before discussing my dual romance. She waited until the evening when I escorted her to the Cocoanut Grove for her introduction to Hollywood night life. There, at a table for two, my cousin went to work during intermissions. She didn't argue, plead, or scold. She just attacked my most vulnerable spot, my sentimentality.

As we sipped the champagne I'd ordered to prove I was a big shot, Elsie began talking about the good old days in Texas. She recalled Gracie's schoolgirl crush on me and our romance and engagement shortly before my departure from Dallas for Manhattan. She recalled how faithful Gracie had been even though she'd heard reports about some of my escapades. She reminded me that Gracie was still waiting for the telephone to ring, hoping it would be me, eager to assure her that I was ready for marriage.

"Dammit, Elsie," I replied, "she knew I wanted to marry her. I told her so. But she wanted to be guaranteed that I had no fears of marriage. And I couldn't truthfully say that."

Elsie patted my hand sympathetically. "Fred, you and Gracie are hung up on words that have no real meaning. The truth is that Gracie is probably just as scared of marriage as you are. Most folks are, I guess. Most folks must wonder if they're doing the right thing as they walk down the aisle. But they go ahead and take a chance, and things generally work out okay."

"Maybe so," I admitted. "But what am I supposed to do? I can't seem to convince Gracie of that."

"I don't think you've really tried very hard. I think Gracie would say yes right away if you'd just tell her in real plain Piney Woods language that you want to get married, that you don't want to hear any more reasons why you should wait."

Never once during our talk had Elsie mentioned my engagement to Betty Wilson. She didn't have to. By talking about old times, about Gracie's love and patience, about the doubts and fears she no doubt felt too, Elsie had made her point eloquently. And I finally made up my mind.

230

The next day before rehearsal I stopped by the hospital and asked Betty Wilson to join me for coffee in the cafeteria. I didn't try to sweet talk my way out of the unhappy situation. Even though I knew I might be vulnerable to a breach of promise suit, a favorite legal device of jilted women in those days, I told it like it was. I told Betty about my long engagement to Gracie Johnston, about the fears of marriage that had delayed our wedding, and about how she had come along at a critical moment in my life.

"And now you've thought it over and want to break our engagement?" There was pain but no anger in Betty's voice.

Yes, I admitted, that was what I wanted. I told Betty I was sorry—sorry I had hurt her. Certainly she was not at fault. But it was better to end it now rather than mess up three lives.

Betty Wilson didn't protest. Perhaps she too was relieved. Perhaps she too was beset by fears and doubts about marriage. She didn't say. She just kissed my cheek softly, murmured good-bye, and walked out of my life. I never saw her again. I only hope she found the happiness she deserved.

When I arrived at the Grove that afternoon I headed for the nearest telephone booth and placed a call to Dr. Sherwood's office in Tulsa. Gracie answered the phone.

There was an awkward pause, and finally I blurted, "I guess you've heard about my troubles out here." Gracie admitted in frigid tones that she had.

"Well, that's all done with now."

"What's that supposed to mean?"

"It means that I've just put an end to my foolish engagement to. Betty Wilson. I've told her that it's all over . . . that it was a mistake."

"Well," Gracie said noncommittaly, "I'm glad you've at least got something straightened out."

"Is that all you can say?"

"What more is there to say?"

Gracie's aloofness was understandable. It didn't take much imagination to realize it wasn't very flattering to have your fiance end up engaged to a second girl. But I was becoming impatient with the verbal sparring, and Gracie's terse response triggered an angry, frustrated outburst.

I told Gracie bluntly that I had narrowly escaped a terrible mistake—a mistake for which we both were to blame. I had been at fault because I wouldn't take a positive stance. And she had been at fault because she insisted on happy-ever-after assurances. We both had been fools, afraid to take a chance, afraid to follow the urgings of our hearts.

I feared I would only succeed in aggravating Gracie's anger. I would probably become the only man in history to lose two fiancees in one afternoon. But I plunged ahead. I told Gracie that I was tired of waiting, tired of my lonely existence, tired of just dreaming about a home, a wife, and a family.

"Dammit, Gracie," I raged, "I know I'm no bargain. And I'm not going to tell you I don't have any doubts about marriage, because I'd be lying. As a matter of fact, I reckon you've got some doubts too. But if we love each other we sure as shootin' ought to be willing to take a chance. I don't want any more waiting. Either we get married right away or we forget about each other. That's all I've got to say!"

There was a long silence at the other end of the line, and I was positive that it was all over. Then, in faraway Tulsa, Gracie giggled in the kind of girlish glee I had known and loved so long ago.

"You're such a ninny, Fred Lowery," she said. "Why did you wait so long to tell me how you really feel? Of course I'll marry you! I'll be out in Los Angeles with you as soon as I can get things settled here!"

There was a lot more conversation, and when I finally hung up I sat there in the phone booth trying to collect my dazed senses. Whatever the future might hold, I mused, there would never be another day like this one.

And then I added out loud, "I certainly hope there won't."

Chapter 17

On the evening of December 20, 1940, Morgan Beatty of NBC—the Walter Cronkite of radio in those days—announced during his network broadcast that "Fred Lowery, the famous blind whistler of the Horace Heidt orchestra, is no longer a swinging bachelor. Fred and Gracie Johnston, his sweetheart from the Piney Woods of East Texas, flew from Los Angeles to Las Vegas today for a quiet wedding ceremony in a quaint little chapel. I guess that gambling Nevada town is a good place to take a chance on love. . . ."

Beatty's words echoed loudly in the honeymoon suite of the Frontier Hotel. Gracie gasped. She had been impatient when I insisted on turning on the radio for the newscast before we left for our wedding dinner. She was obviously puzzled by her bridegroom's irrational behavior, and that puzzlement deepened a few minutes later when she heard the news of our marriage broadcast from New York City.

I roared with laughter at my bride's astonishment and pretended to be hurt when she observed that she hadn't realized what a big shot she had married, that she couldn't understand how we rated mention on a national news program. Besides, why did Beatty have to be so flippant about a very special occasion?

After teasing Gracie a bit I confessed that I had played a joke on her. I knew Morgan Beatty, had met him at one of Clara Bell Walsh's parties, and we had become good friends through the years. I had telephoned him the previous day and told him of my marriage plans. He had suggested it would be great fun to surprise Gracie with an announcement of our wedding on his newscast.

"Well, it sure did surprise me!" Gracie grumbled. "It's also going to surprise my folks and a lot of other people I know, hearing about my marriage for the first time on the radio!"

It seemed that Gracie had told her family and friends only that we planned to wed. She had kept our marriage date a secret because she knew her parents would insist on a fancy wedding, while both of us wanted a simple ceremony with no frills. She had planned to telephone her parents the day after the wedding. But now the news had been broadcast from coast to coast, and she knew she'd have a lot of explaining to do and a lot of hurt feelings to soothe.

"You just wait, Mr. Big Shot," Gracie said. "I'll get even with you one of these days!"

Gracie didn't have to wait very long for her revenge. We were eating in the dining room of the Frontier the next morning when Jimmy Stewart stopped at our table to say hello. He said he was in Las Vegas for a few days of relaxation and happened to see us when he came down for breakfast.

I was flattered that Jimmy had stopped to say hello and delighted to have the unexpected good fortune of impressing my bride with an introduction to a genuine Hollywood celebrity. I invited him to join us. He accepted, and in my excitement I introduced the new Mrs. Lowery as "my friend, Gracie Johnston."

I was much too occupied with showing off my talents as a genial host to realize I had committed such a dreadful gaffe. Gracie said nothing until Jimmy Stewart finally departed after a pleasant breakfast devoted to a stimulating serving of the latest Hollywood gossip. Then she exploded.

"Fred Lowery, I'll never talk to you again!"

Gracie's tone made it clear that although I had been married less than twenty-four hours I had already managed to get myself in the doghouse. But I didn't have the foggiest notion of what I had done.

"Don't try to kid me!" Gracie fumed. "You know perfectly well that you introduced me to Jimmy Stewart as a friend, and not as Mrs. Lowery!"

And Gracie fled from the dining room, leaving me stranded and dazed. I ordered another cup of coffee, certain she'd return soon. But she didn't. After two more cups of coffee I finally paid the tab and tipped a bellboy to help me find my way back to our room in the unfamiliar hotel.

The honeymoon suite was empty. Hours passed, and still no sign of Gracie. I was distraught and began to imagine all sorts of things. What a place for a marital spat, here in the notorious mecca of quickie divorces! I could imagine Gracie already consulting a lawyer, ending our marriage before it had even begun.

It was midafternoon when Gracie bounced merrily into our honeymoon suite laden with packages. She announced that she had been to the beauty shop for a permanent, facial, and manicure—the works. After that she'd gone shopping and paused in the hotel lobby to try her luck with the slot machines. After just a few spins she'd won a $25 jackpot. Wasn't that simply fabulous?

"Gracie," I exclaimed, "do you mean to say you've been having a ball around town while I've been sitting here torturing myself with thoughts about your seeing a lawyer to get a divorce?"

"Whatever gave you that idea?" Gracie's giggle was the epitome of amused innocence.

"What was I supposed to think?"

"Don't be silly, Fred! Why would I let a little thing like that upset me? It was a perfectly natural mistake. After all, you aren't used to having a wife to introduce."

That was all Gracie would say. Our honeymoon time was too short to waste on foolish quarreling, she said—which puzzled me no end since it had been she who had started the spat. Or had she? At that point I was too confused to really know and too eager to resume our honeymoon to care.

It wasn't until several years later that Gracie admitted she had seized on my *faux pas* as a chance to get even with me for the Morgan Beatty broadcast. It certainly was an effective chastisement. I never again forgot to introduce her as "Mrs. Lowery."

With the Christmas and New Year's festivities approaching, Horace Heidt had only been able to allow us a three-day honeymoon. I was due to report for rehearsal at the Grove on the afternoon of December 23, and we almost didn't make it. The day we were scheduled to leave was bright and clear in Las Vegas, but the American Airlines flight was grounded by a blizzard in Salt Lake City.

Airline flights in those days were still considered a secondary means of transportation, with limited passenger service. But even though we were the only Los Angeles–bound travelers American got me to the Cocoanut Grove on time. They wheeled a plane out of the hangar just for us and flew us back to Los Angeles. We were the only passengers. The only other people aboard the big plane were the pilot, copilot, and two stewardesses. It was a wonderful way to end a honeymoon.

We returned home anticipating that we'd have plenty of time alone to get settled in the cozy one-bedroom furnished apartment Gracie had rented before we left for Las Vegas. But we didn't see much of our love nest during that holiday season, for as soon as we landed in Los Angeles we were swept up in a round of parties.

The highlight of the holidays was a Christmas Day wedding party Horace Heidt hosted for us in one of the Ambassador Hotel's private banquet chambers. The large room was festooned with holiday decorations, and gifts were piled under a lighted Yule tree. All of the band and all the band wives were on hand to welcome Gracie to the "family." The party inspired Horace to create another of his myths; on the "Pot o' Gold" broadcast a couple of days later he announced that Gracie and I had been married on Christmas Day.

"Why on earth did you say that?" I asked Heidt after the broadcast. "You know perfectly well we were married on December twentieth."

"There's absolutely nothing to get excited about," Heidt nonchalantly assured me. "What difference does it make? I just thought Christmas Day was a lot more romantic! This is show business, pal, and we need all the romance we can get! That's what the public loves!"

For the second time within a few days Gracie received an anxious phone call from her bewildered parents in Texas. "What in the world is going on?" her mother asked. First they had learned from a news broadcast that their daughter was married in Las Vegas on December 20. Then on the "Pot o' Gold" program Horace Heidt had said we were married on Christmas Day—the very day Gracie had phoned to tell her parents how happy we were, getting settled in our own small apartment.

"Which report is true?" Gracie's mother asked. "Are you and Fred really married or just fooling everybody?"

Gracie tried to explain that Horace had simply changed the facts to suit his own fancy. The Johnstons, however, remained skeptical until I finally prevailed on Horace to telephone them and set the record straight.

After the holidays the Musical Knights embarked on one of the many road trips we would make that year. Except for a plush two-week engagement at the Top of the Mark in San Francisco it was a routine tour. But for Gracie it was a baptism into the rigors of the one-nighter circuit. As it turned out, she relished the traveling, the constantly changing scenes of strange cities and towns, and the new people we encountered. Although she had rarely ventured beyond Texas and Oklahoma before our marriage, Gracie discovered that, like most of the musicians, she was a gypsy at heart. It's fortunate that she was, for during the ensuing four decades she has been on the road almost constantly, touring with me wherever the booking agents have sent us.

That first tour as a married man was a completely new experience for me. Gracie and I joined the ranks of the band's married couples, a branch of Heidt's musical family that previously had been largely outside my orbit. To my surprise I discovered that husbands and wives can have fun too. In fact, they were just as enthusiastic a group of fun-seekers as the single men. From the first, I never had time or inclination to miss my bachelor days. I was much too busy introducing Gracie to the world I had lived in for so long, especially when the band arrived in Manhattan in the spring of 1941 for another lengthy engagement at the Biltmore.

With Gracie as my companion I once again found Manhattan to be the enchanted city of my earlier years, a city in which every block held new wonderment for both of us. Together we visited my favorite haunts— Charley's Tavern on Seventh Avenue; Hurley's and the Rainbow Room in the RCA building; Muller's Restaurant next door to Madison Square Garden; the St. Regis Roof; the great Italian restaurants on Mulberry Street; the Alamo on Forty-seventh Street, a hole-in-the-wall establishment that specialized in genuine red-hot Texas chili and icy beer; and the Pickin' Rib on Fifty-second Street, a favorite all-night hangout for musicians, perhaps because it was owned and operated by Benny Goodman's brother.

Looking back, I wonder how I found time to gad about town with Gracie during that interlude in New York. The band was busier than ever. We were doing two big broadcasts a week plus our regular dance programs at the Biltmore and matinee and evening performances at the Strand. Somehow, though, we always managed to find the energy to have fun whenever there was free time in the band's schedule. When we weren't prowling about town I was acquainting Gracie with my New York friends. We attended some of Clara Bell Walsh's Plaza parties and occasionally joined in one of her club-hopping safaris. We had dinner with Jere and Doris Buckley and with Irvin Taubkin and Morgan Beatty. We even got together a few times with Vincent Lopez, whose band was back at a familiar stand, the Taft. And during one weekend we were able to sneak out of town for the first of many rollicking visits to the Jersey Shore home of the Coltons—the family that had given me so much help and encouragement during my early struggles in New York. Their huge three-story home at 108 Sixth Avenue in Long Branch was a fabulous fun house, always peopled with a fascinating assortment of guests ranging from prizefighters trained by Dorothy Colton's brother Bill to politicians and artists.

Aside from the socializing, the band's 1941 stay in New York was marked by only one memorable happening. That was Heidt's acquisition of a new vocalist—a good-looking, cheeky kid named Gordon MacRae.

It's funny how things sometimes happen in show business. One minute a guy's a nobody, then by some lucky fluke he gets discovered, and before you know it he's a star. For example, if George Jackson, one of the Heidt band's small army of vocalists, hadn't paused on the way to rehearsal at NBC one day for a visit to the men's room, Gordon might never have graduated from his page-boy job.

As Jackson later remembered it, he rushed into the john and came to an abrupt halt when he heard someone singing "South of the Border" in a most melodious voice. He investigated and discovered it was a tall, broad-shouldered, pink-cheeked youth in an NBC page's uniform. The kid was standing at one of a long line of fixtures as he soulfully warbled the lament of a Yankee tourist who is rejected by a lovely Latin lady "down Mexico way."

As George Jackson positioned himself at the adjoining fixture the young singer realized he had an audience and faltered a bit in the chorus. "Say, kid, you've got a real nice voice," George remarked in a neighborly fashion.

It was quickly evident that modesty was not one of the rest-room vocalist's vices. He said he didn't have a *nice* voice. He was a helluva singer and a great talent.

"Then what are you doing working as a page?" George asked, suddenly hoping to deflate the monumental ego he had encountered.

"You've got to start somewhere," the kid answered. "And NBC is where the action is."

Further conversation at the washbasins disclosed that the "helluva singer" was named Gordon MacRae. He was nineteen and had come to New York from Syracuse a few months previously because he was sure he could make it big as a vocalist. He also admitted that he hadn't been singing in the john in a sudden outburst of musical inspiration. He sang just about every time he went to the men's room at the studio, hoping someone important might wander in and be struck by his voice.

Jackson later admitted he was impressed by Gordon's talent but put off by his brashness. Still, he knew that Heidt was looking for a tenor for the Don Juans quartet, preferably a handsome young crooner who'd be able to appeal to the bobby-soxer crowd that was being monopolized by a skinny newcomer named Frank Sinatra with the Dorsey band. So he invited the singing page boy to accompany him to rehearsal and meet Horace Heidt.

After listening to MacRae sing two numbers Heidt hired him, even though the kid confessed that he couldn't read music. Actually, Horace didn't have time to shop around. Tenor Eddie Jones, ill with tuberculosis, was leaving the band to enter a sanitarium. As it turned out, he was destined to spend his last days there. It was a critical situation because Donna and the Don Juans were one of the band's main attractions.

Gordon MacRae turned in his braided page boy uniform immediately and reported for work. Even though Jones was still with the quartet Gordon didn't loaf. When it came to music he was a hard, devoted worker. He spent a week practicing the quartet's repertoire and taking lessons from Donna in reading music. By the time Jones left, Gordon was ready to join George

Jackson, Charlie Goodman, and Jim O'Brien in the Don Juan harmonies.

Gordon MacRae turned out to be a fine talent. He also possessed an abundance of boyish charm and sex appeal that drove the bobby-soxers wild. However, he was extremely cocky and boastful. A lot of big-band performers were guilty of self-admiration to some degree. Like Gordon, they knew they were good and were seldom hesitant in letting the world know it. But Gordon was also jealous, nosy, and inclined to play politics. And he tried overly hard to maintain the image of an irresistible lady-killer, even after he married Sheila Stevens, an eighteen-year-old drama student. The long and nerve-grating sound of Gordon meticulously clearing his throat before singing became his trademark and earned him the nickname "Cruds" MacRae.

By the time we ended our Biltmore engagement and boarded the train for Baltimore on the first leg of a lengthy whistle-stopping return to Los Angeles, Gordon was an accepted member of the Don Juans and had a frenzied following of teenyboppers. Already he was pressuring Heidt for more solo spots and more money.

Baltimore provided a couple of that tour's highlights. At the Hippodrome Theater Horace decided to display his talents as a juggler. Through the years he had tried his hand at a number of things, from singing to playing various musical instruments to tap-dancing. All of his attempts at artistic performance had failed, but still he sought some specialty in which he might excel. During his college days he had been a skilled juggler, a reflection of his athletic prowess. For several months he practiced diligently, developing a routine in which he finally was able to keep seven saucers in the air at one time. In Baltimore he decided he was ready for a live audience.

At the opening of that night's show the curtain rose, the band played, and Horace strolled to center stage and began his act. Soon the whirling flow of brightly colored saucers mesmerized the audience—two, three, four, five, and then six saucers spinning in orbit at the same time. It was a masterful performance. But in his concentration our leader failed to notice that he was edging ever closer to the front of the stage. His act was nearing its climax and the launching of the seventh saucer when disaster struck. Horace lunged across the footlights and plummeted ten feet into the orchestra pit with a crash that touched off the evening's greatest explosion of applause.

Horace miraculously emerged from the pit with nothing but his dignity injured. Muttering to himself, he stormed backstage where his anger erupted in a long and profane tirade. But the theater manager arrived to congratulate him on the magnificent pratfall that had provided the comic finale to his act. It was the last time Horace attempted juggling, at least on the stage. He returned to safer pursuits, like making money.

While we were in Baltimore I took Gracie to the doctor when she began complaining of a nagging pain in her side, a visit that ended with the doctor patiently explaining that before the end of the year I was due to become a father.

Gracie was elated by the doctor's report, but I was stunned. I had considered that fatherhood was a status I might attain on some vague tomorrow. Now, to my surprise, that tomorrow was at hand. I was proud and happy, but my happiness was tempered with worry. Fears about my ability to cope with the responsibilities of fatherhood were still in my mind. But I pushed those fears aside and treated Gracie to a venison dinner at Miller's restaurant, an old-time Baltimore establishment that featured wild game. By the time dessert was finished I was too engrossed in celebrating the idea of becoming a father to be afraid.

The next day, though, I found something else to worry about. We were far away from California with a lot of rough touring ahead of us. I couldn't expect Gracie to continue the trip in her delicate condition, no matter how much I had come to depend on her. She'd have to leave immediately, either for our apartment in Los Angeles or the home of her parents in Jacksonville, Texas.

Gracie heard me out patiently, then told me I didn't know what I was talking about. That "delicate condition" talk was a lot of nonsense. Having a baby was no big deal, at least not for the first six or seven months. As the time drew near she'd go to her parents' home so our baby could be delivered by the family doctor she trusted. But until that time she was staying with me.

I put up an argument. But, as I was rapidly learning, arguing with Gracie once her mind was made up was an exercise in futility. I reluctantly gave in, and Gracie continued with us all the way to Omaha. By then everyone was sick of travel—everyone, that is, except Gracie. For a woman who was in the serious process of hatching a new generation of Lowerys, Gracie was certainly savoring life on the open road.

By the time we reached Omaha in late September, however, even Gracie thought it was time to get ready for the big event, so she returned to her parents' home in Jacksonville to await the arrival of the baby. She didn't have long to wait. We were still playing the Orpheum Theater in Omaha on October 8 when I received a phone call from Gracie's excited father in

Jacksonville. He congratulated me and told me I had just become the father of a healthy six-pound, four-ounce baby boy. Mother and son were just fine.

Horace Heidt was delighted to hear the news. He had been sharing my prenatal jitters, as he was about to become a father too. The Heidt baby was due in December, but Horace's wife Adeline had remained with the tour like Gracie. However, she was curtailing her night life, which gave Horace a chance to get out with the boys. He suggested we have a night on the town to properly celebrate the birth of my son.

"I'll pick up the tab this time, and you can treat when my kid arrives," Horace suggested.

By the time that night's last performance ended, Larry Cotton, Ollie O'Toole, Art Carney, Charlie Goodman, Ralph Wingert, and trombonist Jimmy Simms had joined the party. It was a great idea, but we encountered a major stumbling block. Omaha in those days was not a very swinging town. We prowled around the city for about an hour, but every night spot was either closed or closing. They really rolled up the sidewalks early. Finally we went back to our hotel for our own private party.

We spent the night in Horace's suite waxing philosophical and solving all of the weary world's problems. We gossiped, discussed wives, children, and sex. Then we got around to selecting a name for my son. The first name, I declared, was already decided. It was going to be Fred. But the second name was still up in the air. A number of suggestions were made, but I rejected all of them. Then in a moment of sentimentality, after a discordant rendition of "My Buddy," I asked Larry Cotton if he'd be my son's godfather. Larry accepted, and that gave me a brilliant idea.

"I'll name him Fred Larry Lowery in honor of his godfather," I proclaimed.

"You can't do that," Larry protested.

"How come?"

"Because Larry isn't my real name."

"No big deal," I replied. "What's your real name? That'll be okay with me."

Larry Cotton paused and then finally admitted that his real name was Lawrence Maurice. "I never liked it. That's why I go by the name of Larry," he said.

"Hell's fire!" Heidt exclaimed. "Call the kid Horace. It sure beats Lawrence or Maurice!"

I wasn't impressed. At that point in the evening it sounded fine to me. My son's name, I announced, would be Fred Maurice Lowery. And that's what it was. In later years my son agreed with Larry Cotton. He thought, and still does, that no helpless baby should ever be stuck with Maurice, not even as a middle name. There was only one name that he came to dislike even more intensely. That was the nickname "Scooter" which Gracie gave him because of the way he scooted around in his crib before he learned how to walk.

After Omaha, the band moved on to Kansas City for a week's engagement and then on to Memphis for another short stay. Our next scheduled stop was a weeklong run at the Metropolitan Theater in Houston. Larry Cotton and I detoured through Jacksonville on our way, and I got to meet my son for the first time. He was two weeks old.

I had never been one to enjoy cuddling infants. The thought of handling a squirming, burping baby that I couldn't see terrified me. I was afraid I would drop or mishandle a creature so small and delicate. But once Gracie placed young Fred in my arms I forgot my fears. My fingers traced and etched into my memory my son's face, his button nose, his body, fingers, and toes. All of the accessories were in place and pleasingly formed. I was warmed by a deep sense of pride and love and thankfulness—a feeling of wonder at what Gracie and I had produced. Then I asked the question that had been haunting me.

"The baby's eyes . . . how are they?" I inquired apprehensively.

"His eyes are fine," Gracie assured me. "He's a splendid, healthy baby, and he's the spitting image of you!"

I was flooded with relief and joy. I wasn't particularly impressed by the news that the baby looked like me since I didn't know just what I looked like. But I was elated that this tiny, newborn Fred Lowery would grow up seeing the world in which he lived. It was a priceless gift that I could appreciate, even though I knew my son most likely would take it for granted.

Houston was the band's last engagement before returning to California for a six-month stay, and Gracie said she and the baby would be ready to head for the West Coast as soon as we finished our week at the Metropolitan Theater. So, at the tender age of three weeks, little Fred began the first of many long journeys he would make with us. He made this one in a wicker bassinet.

As the train rattled along the tracks toward Austin, I realized that many years before, as a lonely, frightened boy, I had ridden this same railroad on my way to the School for the Blind. It had been my first step into the mysterious outside world. Now I was a man, taking my family out of the same Piney Woods I had left so long ago.

Despite the usual hardships, all members of the band had survived the long tour in reasonably good health except Ollie O'Toole. As we arrived back in L.A., he limped off the train on crutches, still shaken by a narrow escape from serious injury at the hands of an angry mob of bar patrons.

We had been playing a weeklong engagement at the Michigan Theater in Detroit when, one night between shows, O'Toole and a couple of other Heidt bandsmen scurried around the corner to the Paddock Bar for refreshments. En route Ollie was gripped by inspiration. Wouldn't it be great if he were to dash into the bar doing his Hitler routine? It would be really funny to see the startled looks on the faces of the customers, one of his companions agreed.

Ollie needed no further encouragement. He combed his hair over one eye in the führer manner, pasted on the little black mustache he always carried for impromptu performances, and turned up the collar of his coat around his scrawny neck. He rushed into the Paddock shouting an incoherent tide of Germanic-sounding nonsense, a verbal routine he had developed by listening to and imitating a recording of one of Adolf Hitler's speeches.

The results of O'Toole's dramatic entry were electrifying, but not exactly what he had anticipated. The bar was crowded with servicemen—soldiers, sailors, and marines who, although America still was not in the war, had been pulled away from their homes and families by Hitler's militaristic activities. These men didn't find Ollie's act amusing. As several of them later told police, they thought Ollie was a Nazi sympathizer making fun of America's fighting men.

Before Ollie realized what was happening the servicemen mobbed him—punching, kicking, cursing, and ripping his clothes to shreds. By the time the police arrived to restore order Ollie had a broken arm, a broken nose, fractured ribs, a fractured ankle, and several teeth missing. He spent the rest of that week in a Detroit hospital and accompanied us on the remainder of the road trip looking like a wounded survivor of Dunkirk.

But the Paddock Massacre, as we kiddingly called it, didn't intimidate Ollie. Once he recovered he continued his Hitler impersonation wherever we went. In fact, due to the time he lavished on perfecting and expanding this routine, Ollie's ersatz German accent became so convincing that in later years during his long movie career he always seemed to show up in war movies cast as a pompous little Nazi officer.

Our touring had also taken us back to the Edgewater Beach Hotel for a two-week run. And this time I was the one who had ended up as fate's unsuspecting target.

One night, while I was whistling "The Flight of the Bumblebee," a moth flew into my mouth just as I was gulping an intake of air after a particularly long and complicated passage. The results were devastating. It was one of the few times in my career that I wasn't able to continue a number to completion. I forgot all about music, all about everything except the bug that was flopping about halfway down my throat. I choked and wheezed and gasped, clinging to the microphone to keep from falling.

Heidt and the rest of the band—and the audience too—didn't know what had happened. They thought I was having a heart attack or a seizure of some kind. Heidt pulled my hands off the mike and pushed me down on the floor. A doctor in the audience arrived, loosened my collar, held my wrist, and began taking my pulse. By that time I had finally swallowed the pesky moth and was beginning to recover my breath. I sat up and asked for a glass of water.

"What's the matter, Fred? What happened?" Heidt asked anxiously. "You got chest pains or feel dizzy?"

After gulping down the water that somebody had fetched for me I managed to explain. "A bug flew in my mouth and I nearly choked. But I'm okay now."

Heidt's sympathy index plunged abruptly to zero. Horace was not one who liked to squander life's gentler emotions. "Good grief!" he muttered. "Here I thought you were having a heart attack, and it was just a bug! You've got a helluva nerve, Lowery, scaring me that way!"

Misfortune struck again a few nights later. I was whistling "Indian Love Call" as background music for one of the show's dancers, a girl named Wiletta, who was presenting her interpretation of an Indian harvest dance. Wiletta's number followed an animal act in which a horse with a brightly costumed rider pranced about the stage performing a variety of trick steps and jumps. As usual, after the curtain fell on the horse act, stagehands hurried out with buckets and shovels to police the stage. On this particular evening, however, they were careless.

The routine for Wiletta's Indian dance called for me to gradually increase the tempo of my whistling as she entered the final moments of her performance. Everything was going fine. Wiletta whirled, leaped, and darted about the stage. Then her foot landed on a horse dropping. She skidded wildly across the stage and crashed headlong into me at the microphone. The force of the collision catapulted both of us back into the band.

Fortunately nobody was hurt, although two chairs were smashed and a trombone dented. Wiletta didn't lose her temper or her sense of humor. She pulled me to my feet, made sure I was okay, and led me back to the

244

microphone. Standing there with me facing the snickering audience, Wiletta calmly shook the residue from her foot and announced, "Just you wait till I get my hands on Tonto!"

That brought the house down. The audience stood and cheered the gutsy little dancer. When the tumult ended I began to whistle and Wiletta once again went whirling into her dance, this time with greater care.

Back in Los Angeles we resumed our usual hectic schedule—twice-weekly network broadcasts and another long run at the Cocoanut Grove. Gracie and I now relocated to a larger apartment with little Fred, and I renewed a red-tape battle with the Selective Service bureaucracy that had started a year earlier.

In October of 1940 I had joined all the male members of the band and millions of other American men in registering for the newly activated military draft. I showed up one day at the designated office with Larry Cotton for what I thought would be a quick, routine interview that would inevitably result in my summary rejection.

It didn't turn out that way. Larry and I and a number of other prospective soldiers were seated on one side of a long table. Across from each of us was a Selective Service worker equipped with pencil, eraser, and a lengthy government form. My inquisitor, a matronly lady with a no-nonsense voice, delved into all sorts of personal matters. She asked for details about my birth and my parents, my marital status, whether I had any children, whether I had a criminal record, where I worked, what kind of work I did, where I lived, the condition of my health, whether I had any military experience, and all manner of other questions. But never once did she ask about my eyesight.

When the inquiry ended the lady put her pencil aside and observed that I certainly seemed to be a fine, healthy candidate.

"You forgot something," I hastened to point out. "You forgot to ask me about my eyes."

The interviewer observed that she didn't need my help in telling her how to do her job. There was no need to ask foolish questions when it was perfectly obvious that I was a healthy, vigorous, draftable male specimen.

"Madam," I replied, "I have been blind since childhood. I attended the School for the Blind in Texas. I possess only one-percent vision."

"Nonsense," she retorted. "You're just like a lot of other fellows I interview, trying to find a way to avoid being drafted!"

I decided there was only one way to convince her I was telling the truth. I removed my glass eye and placed it on the table.

The doubting lady was horrified but convinced. "I believe you!" she cried in dismay. "Just put that hideous thing back where it belongs!" And she made a hasty notation on the bottom of my form indicating that I was blind.

At that point I figured my business with the Selective Service was ended. The military may have had its share of shortsighted leaders, but it certainly didn't need any unsighted soldiers. But shortly after the band returned to Los Angeles, I received notification that I had been classified 1-A and should begin getting my civilian affairs in order preparatory to being drafted.

Once again I had to wage my own private war with the bureaucracy. On the first of several visits to Selective Service headquarters in Los Angeles I discovered that whoever had transcribed the data from the original questionnaire had failed to see the notation about my blindness. My official draft form indicated only that I was in good health. What's more, the draft-board people refused to consider the possibility that their records might be in error. Even when I again removed my artificial eye to prove my point they wouldn't retreat from their decision. They were not qualified to judge medical matters, they stated. I would continue to be classified 1-A and would have to report for a physical whenever I was directed to do so.

Several stormy sessions produced the same results. So one morning I found myself reporting for a physical with perhaps a hundred other disgruntled draftees. Larry had accompanied me, and he tried to convince the people in charge that I was blind and that it would be a waste of everybody's time for me to submit to the lengthy examination. But his plea also was summarily rejected. He was directed to a nearby waiting room, and the physical began. Luckily one of the first examinations was the sight test.

One of the technicians conducting the test ordered me to read the eye chart.

"What chart?" I asked.

"The chart on the wall, dummy!"

"What wall?"

"Okay, buddy, quit horsing around," the technician snarled. "We don't have time to play games!"

When I informed the irate tester that I couldn't see the chart or the wall because I was blind, he summoned a doctor. "You'd better be telling the truth," he warned, "or you're going to be in big trouble!"

The doctor conducted a brief examination. "How in the hell did you end up 1-A?" he asked.

I told the doctor of my frustrating experiences, and as he stamped a big REJECTED on my draft papers he muttered, "God help us, the whole world's gone mad!"

Judging by the headlines in the daily newspapers, the doctor's observation

246

was right on target. Since the spring of 1940 Hitler's armies had swept across Europe with little opposition. Norway had fallen, then the Lowlands, Belgium and France. More than 300,000 British troops had been evacuated at Dunkirk, falling back to their small island kingdom. Planes of the Luftwaffe had followed them, bombing airfields, coastal defenses, and then London. The Balkans and Crete had been seized, and Rommel's tanks were rumbling across North Africa, threatening the Suez. Russia had been invaded, and in the Orient Japan had signed an Axis Pact with Germany and Italy, establishing a "new order" designed for world domination.

America was still neutral, but more and more men were in uniform, more and more military bases were being opened, and more and more factories were working around the clock. Most people were convinced that tragic times were upon us.

I was never able to carry out my side of the bargain and treat Horace to a celebration when his baby was born. It wasn't that I was unwilling. The reason was Emperor Hirohito and his Japanese warplanes. Harriet Hildegarde Heidt was born on December 7, 1941.

It started out like any ordinary serene Sunday morning in southern California. It was a warm, sun-bathed December day with just a touch of crispness in the air, the kind of day that charms the winter tourists and spoils the natives. Gracie and I were having a late, lazy breakfast beside an open kitchen window. A soft breeze filtered through the curtains.

Across the parking lot below our window, in another apartment complex, a radio was playing. At first the harsh, excited voice of the announcer only vaguely intruded on our conversation. Then slowly words began to register—"Pearl Harbor . . . Japanese . . . sneak attack . . . Pacific fleet destroyed . . . barracks in flames . . . Honolulu strafed . . . hundreds or thousands killed . . . declaration of war . . ."

"What in the world is that?" Gracie asked in a hushed, frightened voice.

A sense of dread suddenly came over me. I tried to brush it off, to calm Gracie's alarm. It sounded like another of Orson Welles's wild broadcasts, I suggested, not really believing my quick fabrication.

There was a hammering at the door. Gracie responded, and George Jackson and his wife Edie who lived in the adjoining apartment rushed in. George was furious, almost incoherent in his rage. "Those rotten Japs," he stormed. "They'll all be rotting in hell by the time we're finished with them!"

"Whoa, buddy," I said. "Calm down! What on earth is going on?"

"Haven't you been listening to the radio?" Edie Jackson asked. "The Japanese have attacked Pearl Harbor!"

Gracie hurriedly turned on our radio, and the four of us huddled in shocked silence at our kitchen table listening to the tale of horror unfold. It was like listening to the end of the world. And in a way it *was* the end of the world—at least as we knew it.

George and I had to dress and report to NBC for a Sunday "Fitch Bandwagon" broadcast by early that afternoon. It was a network program hosted by our friend Dick Powell and his wife June Allyson. Edie and Gracie, carrying little Fred in her arms, accompanied us to the studio. They were afraid to stay home. The entire city was in a state of panic after hearing rumors, broadcast on the radio between reports from Hawaii, that another attack by the Japanese was feared, this time on Los Angeles. Japanese submarines, battleships, and carriers had reportedly been sighted off our coast. All military units were on alert, manning antiaircraft guns, radar posts, and shore artillery and guarding utilities, defense factories, airfields, docks, and other vital installations against sabotage.

The panic was also evident at the studio. Radios were tuned to the constant flow of reports from Honolulu and local defense officials. Rumors were traded and magnified. NBC officials and Dick Powell debated whether or not the show should be canceled, but nobody could make a decision. It didn't seem decent to broadcast music and jokes at a time like this. Still there was the old battle cry that the show must go on. June Allyson, sniffling with one of her perennial colds, finally became exasperated.

"For heaven's sake," she snapped, "let's quit talking and get the show on the road. It seems to me the American people could use some cheering up today!"

June's logic was accepted, and preparations were initiated to get the program on the air. There was one problem. Everyone was present except Horace Heidt. Nobody had heard from him.

"Maybe a Jap saboteur got him," some clown in the band suggested. No one laughed. It wasn't funny. About that time the studio phone jangled. It was Horace calling from Cedars of Lebanon Hospital. Adeline had just given birth to a little girl. Everything was fine. He'd get to the studio as soon as he could break away. Meanwhile, go ahead with the show.

Horace finally reached the studio as we were winding up the broadcast. He was enraged—at the Japanese and at his wife. "You might know it," he fumed. "There's thirty-one days in December, and my wife has to pick the worst day in our history to have a baby! How is my daughter ever going to be able to celebrate her birthday on such a horrible day?"

After the broadcast most of us assembled in the Radio Room, a bar across from NBC where the Nat King Cole trio was performing. Nat had joined us for a few drinks when it was announced that a blackout would be in effect that night throughout southern California. A curfew had also been ordered. Anyone out on the streets after dark without official authorization would be arrested.

"There goes the old ball game!" Nat sighed, getting up from the table to help close the bar.

The rest of us trooped silently into the dusk, hurrying to get home before the curfew, wondering what lay ahead for the country, and also wondering what happens to the music-makers and troubadours in times when there's nothing left to sing about.

Chapter 18

There are those who insist that the big-band era died at one specific time or another. I don't subscribe to that view. The curtain did not drop suddenly; it fell so gradually that those who were deeply involved in the music of the times never noticed until the end was upon them. Like vaudeville the big bands died slowly, not with a bang but a whimper.

The war years, of course, had a drastic impact on the bands. Many musicians went off to war. Some, like Glenn Miller and George Jackson, never returned. Gasoline rationing and the military's demand for railway service restricted travel. The large hotels, resorts, and nightclubs cut back on entertainment. Still, a surprising number of bands survived and, after the end of hostilities in 1945, enjoyed a brief revival. But that ended too. There were two newly emerging forces the big bands couldn't counter: the boom in home entertainment created by television and the change in musical tastes toward rock and roll.

The war soon began to thin the ranks of the Musical Knights. At times it seemed as if our bandstand was equipped with a revolving door—familiar faces leaving, new faces arriving. Through the years Larry Cotton, Ralph Wingert, George Jackson, Art Carney, Jimmy Troutman, Charlie Goodman, and others entered the military. Henry Russell, a devout Jehovah's Witness, was a conscientious objector, and the government finally ordered him to leave the band and work in a defense plant.

Paul Dudley, the longtime producer of Heidt's and other radio shows, enlisted and was assigned to serve as producer with Maj. Glenn Miller's army orchestra in England. Late in 1944 the big Miller band was scheduled to fly to Paris to stage a series of Christmas holiday shows, but the flight was repeatedly canceled because of bad weather. Impatient over the delay, Miller decided to fly to Paris ahead of the band to make arrangements for the opening show. He asked Dudley if he wanted to come along. But Dudley had several urgent business details to take care of, so he declined. On December 15, Miller and a pilot took off from Bedford, England, in a small plane. The plane disappeared in dense fog over the English Channel. It was never heard from; no wreckage was ever found. Glenn Miller became one of the war's mysterious casualties.

The war started a desperate scramble among bandleaders for talented musicians. Heidt even went so far as to run an ad saying he would meet any other salary offer for quality sidemen. So as the old Heidt members left, new musicians arrived. Some stayed, while some soon departed to be replaced by other sidemen who had found themselves jobless as more and more bands folded. During the closing years of the war a number of talented musicians served with the Heidt band. Several, like saxist Tex Beneke and trumpeter Shorty Sherock, later formed their own bands. Others, like drummers Hack O'Brien and Frankie Carlson, bass saxist Joe Rushton, trumpeter Charles Parlatto, and Benny Goodman's pianist Jess Stacy, went on to other bands in later years.

Larry Cotton was the first of the Musical Knights to enter the service after Pearl Harbor—a departure that foolishly flared into a break in his long friendship with Horace. It was a break that was not healed until many years later.

Not only was Larry good friends with Heidt, he was popular with everyone in the band except Gordon MacRae. A mutual dislike existed between the two singers almost from Gordon's first day with the organization. Gordon made little effort to conceal his jealousy. He felt he was the better singer and resented Larry's star status. Cotton in turn was angered by Gordon's verbal sniping and let it be known that he viewed the youngest member of the Don Juans as pushy, obnoxious, and overrated.

Gordon was never a threat to Larry Cotton's position in the band. Cotton was a talented, veteran performer. He was our premier solo vocalist, our big recording star, and a tireless promoter of the band's records among the nation's disc jockeys. With Horace spending an increasing amount of time off the bandstand Larry frequently served as conductor and master of ceremonies. He was also in charge of the band's complex logistical problems—the chartering of trains and buses to meet our sometimes insane travel schedules. In short, Larry was Heidt's right-hand man, someone Horace could depend on to handle every aspect of our operation.

It was this dependence, I'm sure, that caused Heidt to act irrationally when the draft board sent Larry an induction notice. The prospect of losing his "man for all seasons" spurred Heidt into frantic action. He was certain that the band and America's music-loving public needed Cotton more than Uncle Sam. For several months our leader succeeded in getting the induction deferred. But finally it became apparent to all of us except Heidt that Cotton's call to military duty could not be delayed much longer.

At last Larry accepted a lieutenant's commission in the Air Force. Horace was outraged when he heard the news. In one of his perverse moods he declared that Larry was deliberately deserting the band in a time of need. He stubbornly refused to consider the possibility that his friend was taking the best of two unpleasant alternatives. He even rejected Larry's explanation that as a vigorous, able-bodied man he was embarrassed to continue in a soft, high-paying civilian job at a time when so many Americans were fighting and dying on far-off battlefields.

But then Heidt did seem to relent a bit. As the time for Larry's departure neared, Horace arranged a going-away party for him at the Radio Room lounge. Larry and the rest of us welcomed this as an indication that the fussing and feuding was over. But we were mistaken. Heidt had merely set up the party so he could launch a parting shot or two at the man who had incurred his unreasoning wrath.

Horace didn't have much to say at the party until he was called on to make a few remarks. We all expected the usual jokes and sentimental tributes. Instead Heidt made a terse announcement. Effective at once, he said, Gordon MacRae would take over as the band's top soloist. We were stunned—we had expected Charlie Goodman to get the promotion. Heidt had delivered what was tantamount to a slap in the face by naming the one man that Cotton would most dislike as his replacement on the bandstand.

That proved to be just the first step in Heidt's plan to get even with Cotton. Since Horace had organized the party we expected him to pick up the tab. After all, Larry Cotton had played a long and vital role in the band's success. Horace did pick up one tab. He paid for his own dinner and drinks, then walked out without a word to his friend. The rest of us pooled our money to pay for Larry's party. Even Nat King Cole, who provided the entertainment for the evening, chipped in.

Larry was deeply hurt, but he tried to view Horace's spiteful behavior calmly. He figured it was just another of the silly snits in which our boss indulged at times of extreme frustration, something he'd get over in a few weeks. But Horace didn't relent. For some reason perhaps unknown even to himself he couldn't abide the thought of forgiving Larry for trading his Musical Knights tuxedo for an Air Corps uniform.

A few months later during an engagement in Oklahoma City, the band broadcast its Thursday night Tums program from station WKY. Larry Cotton was home in Oklahoma on leave at the time, and he came to the studio to touch bases with his old friends. With Larry sitting in the studio audience several of us urged Heidt to let him sing a number during the program. We said it would be a nice touch, a sure hit with the national radio audience, and a valuable reminder that men from the big bands were doing their bit in serving their country. Heidt angrily rejected our pleas. He didn't even mention Larry's presence during the broadcast.

After the band finished its dance program at the Skirvin Towers, we got together with Larry for a party at the hotel. Everyone was there except Horace Heidt and Gordon MacRae, which probably prevented bloodshed since Cotton was both drunk and mad. He let everybody know that after the way the "Old Man" had bad-mouthed him, humiliated him, and ignored him, he wanted nothing more to do with Heidt. In fact, he said, he hoped Heidt would be drafted "and get his worthless butt shot by the Germans or the Japs."

A local radio announcer heard Larry's tirade and reported it back to Heidt with considerable colorful embroidery. After that Larry's name really was a dirty word as far as Horace was concerned. It was only years later, during the Heidt band's nationally televised reunion, that the two onetime friends finally shook hands and agreed that their feuding had been ridiculous.

Eventually Horace also parted company on a sour note with another of his longtime stars. This time it was Art Carney. Unlike Larry Cotton, however, Art was responsible for his own downfall.

It happened in Chicago on one of the occasional tours the Heidt band made during the war years. We were scheduled to do the Tums broadcast from a studio in the Merchandise Mart. After rehearsal Art and I decided to have a couple of cocktails and dinner in one of that huge building's restaurants. The "couple of cocktails" evolved into several double Manhattans. When the third round was served I ordered steaks and coffee for both of us. However, while I ate Carney scarcely nibbled at his food. Instead he indulged in two more doubles.

Despite his incredible diet of cocktails undiluted by any sobering food, Art seemed in surprisingly good shape as we headed back to the studio for the start of the broadcast. His steps were steady, his voice firm and coherent. He appeared admirably ready for his singing and impersonation routines and for his regular Thursday-night job as announcer for the Tums program.

Inside the stuffy, overly warm studio, however, Art's condition deteriorated rapidly. After the band's opening fanfare he stumbled up to the microphone and started his regular commercial pitch—a spiel that called for him to spell out $T . . . U . . . M . . . S$ over the air. He didn't get very far.

"Ladeeees an' gennulllmum," he began, "Tums for the tummy! That's spelled . . ." He paused as he struggled to remember how to spell the product name, then plunged ahead once more. "That's spelled *T . . . M . . . L . . .* No, dammit, that's not right. *T . . . U . . . M . . . L . . .* Oh, the hell with it!" Admitting defeat, Art turned away from the mike and made his uncertain way back to his chair on the bandstand.

Somehow the show carried on with a few hasty substitutions as the indisposed Carney slumped in his chair. I doubt if his flub had any deleterious effect on the sale of Tums. In fact I'm sure it brought a spark of unexpected humor into millions of American homes. But there was no laughter in the executive offices of the manufacturer of Tums. Officials of the firm were on the telephone to Heidt early the next morning screaming for Carney's scalp.

Although Heidt and Carney were involved in countless clashes over the years, Horace admired the handsome, feisty Irishman's quick wit and talent. He was outraged by Art's latest escapade and bitterly blamed him for endangering a big account, but he tried to resist the pressures of the sponsor. Several stormy days passed before he caved in and agreed to fire Art. When Heidt approached Carney to give him the bad news Art beat him to the punch. He quit. A few weeks later he enlisted in the army. He served in the infantry and was wounded in action shortly after being shipped to the battlefront in Europe.

Gordon MacRae was another Musical Knight who managed to beat Heidt to the punch. Even though he had promoted Gordon to Larry Cotton's soloist spot Heidt was far from enchanted by the young singer's pompous airs. And he was especially displeased by Gordon's aversion to the tedious but important hours spent in practicing and rehearsing.

During his early days with the band Gordon had worked endlessly to learn the routines and perfect his singing and music-reading. But once his job was secure he quickly adopted the attitude that there was just no way to improve on perfection. He became the laziest performer in the band. He complained constantly about everything imaginable, from overwork to the tempo and interpretation of arrangements. He ducked rehearsals whenever he could, showed up late for others, and was forever disrupting things with temperamental outbursts. His attitude infuriated Heidt and sparked a continuing series of disputes between the two. Heidt, of course, made no attempt to soothe the tenor's easily bruised ego. In fact he delighted in finding ways to puncture it.

Sheila MacRae was always egging her husband on to complain because I was getting top billing on the marquees and lobby posters. But Heidt never bowed to the MacRaes' pleas that he be given the same billing Larry Cotton had received.

"Lowery's just a two-bit whistler," Gordon once complained to Heidt. "How come he rates bigger billing than me?"

"For one thing, kid, Fred's been around a lot longer, and he's earned that kind of billing," Heidt replied. "Besides, if I gave you top billing you wouldn't be able to find a hat to fit your head!"

Heidt's favorite target, however, was MacRae's image as a bobby-sox idol. A classic incident occurred at one wartime matinee at the Palace Theater in Cleveland. When Horace, Charlie Goodman, Ralph Wingert, Frankie Carle, and I arrived by taxi from our hotel for the afternoon show at least fifty teenyboppers had trapped Gordon at the theater entrance screaming for autographs, for kisses, for bits of clothing, for locks of hair, and other favors. Gordon was bellowing for help.

At the fringe of the mob scene Sheila spotted us and hurried over. "My God, do something!" she cried, "Those girls are nuts! They're going to tear Gordon to pieces! You've got to do something. Call the cops or something!"

Horace, using tactics from his football-playing days, bulled his way into the crowd of frenzied females and emerged seconds later with a disheveled MacRae in tow. Safely inside, Gordon forgot his momentary fright and began boasting about his irresistible sex appeal. "That ought to prove who draws the crowds," he crowed. "Those dolls just can't leave me alone!"

Like the rest of us Sheila didn't appreciate her husband's self-adulation. Angered by his rhapsodizing, she flounced out of the theater. When Sheila ignored his cries to come back Gordon scurried after her. But when he stuck his head out the stage door an even larger crowd of bobby-soxers squealed with delight. Gordon popped back into the safety of the theater. "See what I mean?" he told Heidt. "Those chicks go crazy when they see me!"

Horace had heard enough. With tongue in cheek he told MacRae to take the afternoon off. "Sneak out the stagehands' door and find Sheila," Heidt said. "Treat her to dinner and a movie and get yourself out of the doghouse."

Getting excused from a theater performance was a rare privilege, and Gordon accepted Heidt's offer without pausing to wonder why the boss was being so generous. He rushed out before Heidt could change his mind. But apparently it soon dawned on him that this was a Saturday—the day he always received the adoration he deserved. Those were *his* fans waiting for the theater to open, and if he wasn't on the bandstand all of those wonderful teen-agers would be deprived of his music. He hurried back into the theater and breathlessly informed Heidt that he'd suddenly realized this was a Saturday matinee, the one appearance of the week that he simply couldn't miss.

255

Horace pretended amazement. "Why in the world should you worry about missing a Saturday matinee?" he asked. "There's no reason for you to hang around, man. Take the afternoon off and enjoy yourself!"

Gordon quickly protested. No matter how much he'd enjoy having a free afternoon he just couldn't disappoint all the kids who had been waiting to hear him sing. It would break their hearts if he wasn't on the stage.

"Don't be silly, Gordon," Heidt said. "I'm sure all those pretty girls will survive. You take the time off like I told you."

"But who'll be here to keep them happy if I'm gone?"

Heidt assured Gordon that the entire band would be on stage—that Fred Lowery, Charlie Goodman, Frankie Carle, and a lot of other splendid music-makers would be on hand to cheer them up.

"But that's not me! I'm the guy they want to see and hear!"

"Baloney!" Heidt laughed. "Those kids follow all the bands. It's not just you they're wild about. They've got all kinds of idols . . . Frank Sinatra and Perry Como, Benny Goodman and Harry James, and a lot of others. They just get a bang out of getting together, hollering and swooning and jumping around like crazy. If we dressed a gorilla in a fancy suit and stuck him in front of a mike those nutty kids would still scream and screech and cry and dance in the aisles, just the same as when you sing."

By then Gordon was beginning to get the idea that Horace was having fun at his expense. Still he tried to set the record straight. "Those kids are Gordon MacRae fans," he insisted. "And when you claim they're ready to cheer any old musician it's ridiculous."

"No it isn't," Heidt countered. "You take yourself too seriously, Gordon. Get out of here like I told you. We'll take care of your fans today!"

Gordon MacRae left the theater again, mumbling to himself. No doubt he realized he'd been jazzed into a corner by his boss, and he probably soothed his ego by telling himself it was just another score he'd settle with Horace Heidt some day.

It took a while for Gordon to get around to settling the score with Horace, but when he did it was a special occasion. We were playing at the Strand in New York at the time, and Adeline Heidt had arranged a surprise birthday party for her husband after the final evening performance. However, hours before the party Gordon delivered his own surprise, a surprise that put an end to the Heidt festivities before they began.

The band had assembled for the matinee performance when MacRae showed up later than usual. When Heidt flew into one of his preshow tantrums, berating his soloist for his tardiness, Gordon angrily interrupted.

"Cut the lecture, Horace. I've got a few words to say to you, and it can't wait!"

A hush settled over the room. Something out of the ordinary was obviously brewing. Only the very foolish, the very drunk, or the very mad talked to the terrible-tempered Heidt that way. It was quite possible that Gordon MacRae's intemperate outburst was the product of all three factors.

Heidt didn't explode as we expected. He seemed to realize that something serious was bugging Gordon. He suggested they get together after the show for a private heart-to-heart talk.

"Nuts!" Gordon replied heatedly. "I don't want a private talk. This is something I want the whole band to hear!"

Gordon then launched as brutal a verbal assault as I'd ever heard. Not even in his most vitriolic moments had Heidt ever equaled it. Our leader sat silent and stunned as Gordon thundered on. We never did learn what triggered the singer's attack. Perhaps he had just reached the breaking point. In any event he called Heidt a phony, an untalented oaf who was making millions off the talents of others, an overbearing loudmouth who hogged all the glory while his musicians and singers did all the work.

"You're a cheap skate, Heidt!" Gordon roared. "You pay us peanuts, and you've got the nerve to criticize us, to belittle us. You . . . a clown who can't play any instrument, who can't read a note!"

I'd had my differences with Heidt. I'd done my share of griping. But he was no ogre. As cantankerous and contrary and inconsiderate as he could be at times, he still had done a lot for all of us in the band. And despite Gordon's wild claims he certainly wasn't cheap. Our band was one of the best-paid in the business. So I spoke up. Actually I had to shout to be heard over Gordon's tirade.

"You're out of line, Gordon, and you know it. You've got to admit Horace took you out of a page boy's monkey suit and made you a star. What's more, he's paying you and the rest of us damned good money. The Old Man does a heck of a lot he doesn't get credit for!"

Gordon brushed aside my defense of Heidt. "You can sit on this bandstand the rest of your life, Fred . . . sit here until your pucker falls off. I don't care. I'm going to make something of myself. I've had it! I quit!"

Heidt suddenly found his voice. "The hell you do, you ungrateful brat!" he screamed. "You're fired!"

On that harsh note Gordon MacRae walked away from the Heidt organization and headed for the greener pastures he dreamed of. The stormy scene dampened our mood for partying. Horace went back to the hotel in a towering rage, and Adeline wisely canceled his birthday bash.

Despite such unhappy interludes as the breaks with Larry Cotton, Art Carney, and Gordon MacRae, the war years weren't all gloom and dissension for the Musical Knights. For one thing, as the war continued we did less touring and almost no one-nighters. We did accept some long engagements in major cities and we also played a number of military bases and army and navy hospitals.

Our work at NBC gave me a chance to get to know several big-name stars who appeared regularly on programs originating in the network's Hollywood studios. John Barrymore's dramatic hour on NBC preceded the Heidt broadcast, and we became friends. I was fascinated by Barrymore's tales, by his irreverent views on life, and by his amazing capacity for alcohol. One evening as we were having a drink in his dressing room he remarked that we were a lot alike.

"How so?" I asked.

"Because we're both always blind!" he laughed.

At the time Barrymore was in deteriorating health. He scorned doctors' warnings that if he wanted to live he'd have to give up liquor. Frequently he seemed so drunk he couldn't possibly go on the air, but he always managed to make the broadcast. One time he decided he wanted me at his side while he was on the air. He refused to budge from his dressing room until some network flunkies fetched me. I arrived and accompanied Barrymore into the broadcast studio, wondering how he could possibly perform. However, once he was set at the microphone with the script of the play he seemed to sober up in an instant. His diction was perfect, his emoting superb. He never faltered, never flubbed a line. Yet when I returned to his dressing room with him before the Heidt broadcast began he once more seemed stoned.

Of all the stars performing at NBC in Hollywood my favorites were Bing Crosby and Bob Hope, not only because they gave me opportunities to perform on their shows but because they were fun to be around, real pros with no pretensions. Bing Crosby and I had of course met years before when I was with the Lopez orchestra. When we first encountered each other in Los Angeles Bing remembered how he had knocked me off the bandstand at Saratoga Springs. At NBC we had adjoining dressing rooms, and one evening before Bing's "Kraft Music Hall" broadcast I knocked on his door.

As usual Bing was friendly and relaxed. We chatted briefly. Then, sensing that I was nervous, he asked, "What's on your mind, Fred?"

I had come to Bing's dressing room with the idea of asking to be on his show, but I wasn't sure how he'd take it. "I hope you won't think I'm being pushy, but I've got an idea that I think is pretty good." Hastily I explained that since Bing was a pretty fair whistler we could work up a couple of duets for his program.

Without hesitation Bing agreed. "How about a week from tonight? Can you make it?" I could, and Crosby announced during that night's program: "Fred Lowery, the king of whistlers, is going to be a guest on next Thursday's program. He's going to try to teach me how to whistle!"

At the "Kraft Music Hall" rehearsal the following week the producer handed Bing and me the typed scripts for a skit that would precede our whistling duet.

"What in the devil is this?" Crosby asked. When he learned that dialogue had been prepared he exclaimed with disgust, "How do you expect Fred to read a script? We don't need this." Ignoring the producer's dismayed protest, Bing ripped up the script. "We'll ad lib our way through the skit," he said.

Before the evening broadcast Bing and I discussed the general outline of a nonsensical routine. On the air everything went smoothly. We made up the dialogue as we went along, traded puns, and resurrected several ancient jokes. Then, with the accompaniment of John Scott Trotter's orchestra, we whistled our way through "In the Mood." Later I whistled a solo, "Holiday for Strings." I think the show was well-received, since it led to several return performances on the Crosby program.

My whistling duets with Crosby were followed by an invitation to make a guest appearance on a "Hall of Fame" broadcast emceed by Bob Hope. Bob told me it was a command performance in response to letters from GIs overseas and in the States requesting that I be invited to whistle. On that show I whistled three numbers and joined Hope in several comedy routines. It was great exposure.

One of the most serious problems for the bands during wartime was the sharp limitation of profitable playing dates. With more and more men and women going into either the military or defense industries there was a shortage of manpower for nonessential businesses, including entertainment. A number of nightclubs closed their doors for the duration, and even the larger hotels curtailed their wining, dining, and dancing operations. Only the long, guaranteed dates in large cities were profitable, and there was wild, cutthroat competition for those jobs. With gasoline rationed, transportation was a constant headache, especially in southern California where distances between home and bandstand were formidable. In the

Heidt band we formed car pools. Our Buick sedan, chauffeured by Gracie, was usually bulging with nine or ten musicians.

Despite the commuting inconveniences our band was luckier than most, for in one of his shrewd deals Heidt acquired a huge ballroom that gave us a permanent and profitable base of operations. The deal began to incubate in the autumn of 1942 when we were booked into the Trianon Ballroom in South Gate, a suburb of Los Angeles. We soon discovered that the Trianon was a gold mine. Owned by a onetime gambler and Prohibition-era bootlegger named Jimmy Contratto, the Trianon was situated across the street from a mammoth Firestone Rubber Company plant that employed thousands on a round-the-clock operation. Every night the place was jammed with a heavy-spending mixture of defense workers, soldiers, sailors, and marines.

During that first engagement at the Trianon Horace Heidt undoubtedly indulged in considerable musing, sizing up the house each night, listening to the merry tune of jingling cash registers, and computing the constant flow of alcohol between bar and customers. A few months later, after we'd returned to the Trianon in the spring of 1943, Heidt announced during rehearsal one day that he had just purchased the ballroom and hired Contratto to continue as manager. We tried with no success to get details from Heidt. As usual he was reluctant to discuss his wheeling and dealing. But he did admit that it was "a heck of a deal!"

It wasn't until three years later in a *Time* magazine piece on Heidt's expanding business empire that we learned what had transpired. Here's what *Time* reported in its September 16, 1946, issue:

"[In 1943] Heidt guessed that a profitable urban Los Angeles ballroom, the Trianon, could be bought by catching the owner off guard with enough ready cash.

"Heidt sold his annuities, put $200,000 in thousand dollar bills in pocket, called on the owner, a onetime gambler named Jimmy Contratto.

" 'Mr. Contratto,' said Heidt, 'have you ever thought of selling this place?'

" 'To tell you the truth, I haven't,' answered Contratto, 'but I suppose if some joker walked in and put $150,000 in cash on this table, I'd sell it to him lock, stock and barrel.'

"Heidt reached into his pocket and began counting out thousand-dollar bills. Contratto's jaw dropped. 'I have $45,000 worth of liquor in the cellar,' he demurred.

" 'I assume, Mr. Contratto,' said Heidt coldly, 'that you are a man of your word.'

"Heidt kept on counting out the bills—150 of them. When he finished, he took out an envelope and wrote a bill of sale on the back of it. Contratto signed it; Heidt hired him as his manager. In a year, the ballroom netted a profit equal to the sale price. . . . This year Heidt will do a business of $566,000 in the Trianon . . ."

There was never a dull moment at the Trianon. Every night was like New Year's Eve on Times Square. The establishment opened at 7 P.M. and closed at 2 A.M. every day of the week. It was constantly packed with humanity, even on Sundays, and the clientele danced, romanced, and spent money like there was no tomorrow.

It certainly wasn't the atmosphere or the prices that drew the customers. The Trianon was a large, drafty, barnlike structure with few amenities, and whatever decor it possessed was strictly schlock. Its menu was limited and of dubious quality and its drinks costly. But at a time when Los Angeles was a major defense center and a "jumping-off place to eternity" for soldiers heading for the war in the Pacific it was a convenient playground, a rough-and-ready joint where a guy and his gal could live it up and forget the war for a few hours.

Scarcely a night passed without several fights or even a Pier 6 brawl. One evening a factory worker was knifed to death right in front of the bandstand by the jealous husband of the woman with whom he was dancing. The band took a recess until police arrived and removed the body. Then we returned to the bandstand, the music resumed, and the dancing continued.

It was also at the Trianon that Horace Heidt narrowly missed becoming one of the ballroom's grim statistics. Henry Russell, Charlie Goodman, and I arrived early one afternoon to rehearse a new arrangement we were planning to record. We had the ballroom to ourselves, and our music echoed in the vast emptiness. Russell was trying to smooth out a rough passage on the organ as Goodman hummed along when I heard a door slam and footsteps clatter across the dance floor.

"Who can that be at this hour?" I asked.

Goodman turned and spotted the newcomer, calling him by name. It was one of our former musicians, and Goodman's voice echoed his surprise. "Where on earth have you been keeping yourself? It must be at least a year!"

It had been more than a year since we last saw this ex-Musical Knight. Heidt had fired him during a gig in Dallas after one of the man's notorious lost weekends. It had been a nasty scene—one that we in the band hadn't expected, because this musician had been with Heidt for years. His loud, braying laugh, his sentimental Irish ballads, and his wild tales had become

261

band traditions. Despite his heavy drinking and constant wenching Horace had always forgiven his trespasses.

Suddenly all that changed. After one relatively short spree with no arrests and no tavern brawls, Heidt berated him unmercifully in front of the entire band, called him a hopeless, incompetent drunk, and fired him. Our friend had been shocked. He said nothing until he was leaving, then at the door he turned and shouted, "You're a rotten jerk, Heidt! I hope you rot in hell!"

We never learned what caused the sudden break. Of course, there were rumors. But about the only thing we knew for sure was that it wasn't caused by our associate's binge.

In any event, he showed up unexpectedly at the Trianon that afternoon. He seemed at first to be the same old guy—drunk, boastful, loud, and as full of blue gags as a burlesque comedian. But after a boisterous reunion we learned that he hadn't come around just to talk about old times.

"Where's Heidt?" he suddenly asked, cutting Charlie Goodman short in the middle of a juicy bit of band gossip.

Goodman explained that it was early, that Horace and the rest of the band wouldn't be straggling in for a couple of hours.

"I've got plenty of time. I'll wait." The former bandsman flopped down on a chair. "I've got a surprise for Heidt, and I want to give it to him personally."

"What kind of surprise?" Goodman asked.

Our friend pulled a pistol from his jacket pocket and began waving it wildly. "I'm gonna kill the lousy creep!" he shouted. He emphasized his homicidal intent by pulling the trigger. The gun roared, and a bullet smashed into the ceiling. "I've got a lot more left, and I'm gonna use 'em all on Heidt!"

"Sweet Jesus!" Goodman cried. "Put that gun away before somebody gets hurt!"

"Ain't nobody gonna get hurt but Heidt," our maniac crooned, patting his pistol lovingly. "This little ol' gun is gonna take care of Heidt!"

Although I could barely detect our ex-sidekick sprawling on one of the bandstand chairs, it didn't take 20-20 eyesight to know what was going on. Even in his most lucid moments of sobriety he was a nervous, unpredictable, quick-tempered man. He was big, strong, and rough—not the type to be easily disarmed. And the gun, the senseless shooting, and the murderous threats provided frightening evidence that we were dealing with an irrational mind.

"Don't do anything foolish," I pleaded. "Shooting Horace isn't going to solve anything. It's only going to get you in terrible trouble. Give us the gun before it's too late."

Our friend took no heed of my words. He just mouthed new and profane

262

versions of the old threats and fired another shot into the ceiling, probably to prove that he meant what he said.

Henry Russell, a soft-spoken and deeply religious man, had been quietly listening to us trying unsuccessfully to reason with our friend. At last he must have decided that a higher power would have to be consulted. Henry left his seat at the organ and pulled a chair up close, ignoring the threatening pistol. He didn't plead or threaten or ask for the weapon. Instead, in a calm, soothing voice, he began to talk of God's mercy, of the hope for salvation, of Christ's compassion for all men and His sacrifice on the cross. And he began to pray for our friend's deliverance from evil. He asked God to save the man from the ultimate sin of murder. He asked God to touch his heart with understanding and love, to cast out the bitterness and hate. He asked God in His mercy to lead our friend back to the paths of righteousness and faith.

Except for Henry's soft voice a silence settled over the ballroom. A feeling of awe, of reverence, pervaded that tawdry palace of pleasure. The violent threats stopped. By the time Henry ended his prayer I could hear our friend sobbing quietly. Meekly, without being asked, he handed the pistol to Henry. He brushed away the tears and embraced each of us in turn.

"Thank you, Henry," he said, his voice hoarse with emotion. "Thanks for the prayer . . . for helping me regain my senses." He paused, groping for words. "You know, I haven't had anybody pray for me since I was a kid!"

He walked slowly back across the dance floor. At the door he turned for a final word. "I don't think I'd have shot Heidt. I don't think I'd have had the nerve. I just talk big and bad, that's all." Then he pushed through the door and walked out of the Trianon. To my knowledge no one in the band heard from him after that strange afternoon when Henry Russell's prayers, voiced from a ballroom bandstand, were answered.

After his successful Trianon deal in 1943, Heidt systematically acquired a variety of properties. He bought farms, vacant lots, apartment houses, commercial buildings—a restaurant in Beverly Hills, a hotel in Palm Springs, and the Nevada Biltmore Hotel in Las Vegas. Most of these properties were in the red, crippled by wartime restrictions, when Horace bought them. But he seemed gifted with the Midas touch. All his investments turned around and became big money-makers.

Quite likely Horace's success in business was attributable to the same formula he employed with his musical enterprises. He hired professionals to run the show and stayed mostly in the background, making policy decisions and indulging his flair for promotion. I suspect, however, that in the hardheaded business world he didn't engage in the temperamental outbursts, the sudden inspirations, and the stubborn grudges that marked his artistic endeavors. When really big bucks were involved Horace played it cool.

By 1945 Heidt was probably the wealthiest of all the big-band leaders, and getting richer with each passing month. His mushrooming fortune had started with music and the phenomenal success of "Pot o' Gold," but most of his money came from his commercial investments. Apparently it was this flood of profits from enterprises outside the world of music that began to stir the interest of Jules Stein, president of the Music Corporation of America. This gigantic talent and booking agency handled the Heidt band and had a contract under which it received 10 percent of Heidt's musical earnings. Stein, however, wanted a bigger piece of the pie. He demanded 10 percent of *all* of Heidt's earnings, not just the music profits.

Heidt told Stein to get lost, but MCA's boss went to court and, based on the wording of his contract with Heidt, won the case. Heidt appealed the ruling and lost. In the end, though, he outfoxed Stein.

Unfortunately for the Musical Knights, Heidt's outwitting of Stein was achieved at the cost of our jobs. In the spring of 1945 Horace found a loophole through which he could avoid sharing profits with MCA. The answer was simple. If there was no band to provide services for, MCA would have no legal claim to fees from Heidt. So Heidt broke up the band he had headed for nearly a quarter-century, an action that left Stein holding a contract with a nonexistent organization. As for Heidt, he couldn't perform as a musician or bandleader until 1947, when his contract with MCA was due to expire.

When he folded the band in 1945 Heidt retired to his rambling glass-and-brick home in the San Fernando Valley, an elegant five-acre hacienda with two large swimming pools, a half-dozen guest cottages, and pens for the prized turkeys and tropical birds he raised as a hobby. From the secluded comfort of a large office in his home he began the full-time management of his businesses. He even found time to expand the Horace Heidt School for Stammering, a project dear to his heart. As a young man Heidt had suffered from a speech impediment but had somehow managed to correct it. As he became more affluent he founded the school, hoping to help others overcome similar problems.

It was at his home on Magnolia Boulevard that Heidt first informed Gracie and me that he was disbanding the Musical Knights. It had been a terribly difficult decision, he confided as we sipped after-dinner brandy and coffee. He had devoted a big part of his life to the band. He looked upon it as his family, and the thought of breaking it up was devastating. Yet there didn't seem to be any other answer.

However, Horace hurried to assure me that there would be no jobless blues for the Lowery family. He had dreamed up a great act for me to put on the road, one that eventually could bring in a lot more money than the $450 a week I was making with the band at the time. It would be a whistler-singer act teaming me with Dorothy Rae, one of the band's lovely vocalists.

Heidt said he had already lined up a month's engagement for us at the Palace Theater in Dallas at $750 a week, plus another four weeks at the Metropolitan in Houston. And he had arranged for a reliable talent agency, General Artists Corporation, to take over our management and bookings after the Dallas job.

It sounded great, I told Heidt, but there were two things that bothered me. First, how could we be sure that Dorothy would want to join the act? And also, why was he going to all this trouble to get me settled?

"I've already talked to Dorothy, and she's delighted with the idea," Heidt said. "As for why I'm doing it, I happen to like you and feel responsible for you. Also, I'm not doing it for nothing."

Heidt explained that, in return for helping Dorothy and me get started and backing us with his prestige and his contacts, he wanted a 5 percent fee off the top on all our bookings.

"But remember, Fred," he said, "if the time comes when you feel I'm not really earning that fee you can discontinue it and I won't complain."

It sounded like an equitable deal to me. Certainly I felt obligated to Horace for his help in forming my own act and for the six years I had performed with his band. Besides, I was apprehensive about starting out on my own. I'd never had to handle bookings and all the other business details involved in running a show. So I welcomed Horace's offer and accepted the 5 percent price even though I knew the talent agency would be taking another 10 percent for the same sort of services.

A few days after that meeting at Horace's home, the curtain went down on the Musical Knights. We played our last dance program on a Saturday night at the Trianon. The only change in the evening routine was our musical sign-off. Our finale was "Auld Lang Syne," a number we customarily reserved for New Year's Eve. But this was a special occasion. I whistled the initial passages, and then the entire band rose and sang Robert Burns's haunting refrain.

It was a melancholy night. After the last of the boisterous crowd had vanished the Musical Knights remained in the Trianon laughing and crying and remembering. As we drank our farewell toasts that night I'm sure we all realized that this was more than the parting of friends, the end of a job. Somehow we knew that the glory days we had shared were past and would not come again.

Chapter 19

The years with Heidt had been eventful, stimulating, and rewarding. In retrospect, I realized just how successful they had been, and how rich in good times and good fortune. I couldn't help but mourn their passing. However, I was consoled by the realization that Gracie and I were more fortunate than many members of the band. We owned a comfortable home in North Hollywood, purchased with royalties from my records. We had a respectable savings account. Our young son, now three and a half years old, was thriving. And I at last had my own show, was my own boss, with a pert, pretty songstress as my partner.

Dorothy Rae was a skilled, talented performer. She had been singing professionally since she was sixteen and for the past two or three years had been part of the Heidt band's Sweet Swingsters. Dorothy and I quickly developed a solid musical routine that mixed solos and duets and a repertoire ranging from classical to pop to country and western ballads. We started out in Dallas and Houston making $750 a week. By the time we arrived at Loew's State on Broadway a few weeks later the General Artists agency had boosted our weekly take to $1,500. Eventually, as our reputation grew and our popularity flourished, our act received as much as $2,500 a week. Out of that came Dorothy's salary, expenses for transportation, hotels, food, clothes, and the double talent fees paid to General Artists and Heidt. When all that was paid, I pocketed the balance.

After sending Heidt his fees for eighteen months I decided I had adequately repaid our former boss for his help. We hadn't heard from him for months. He no longer offered advice or assistance in obtaining profitable dates. He hadn't even written to acknowledge receiving my payments. It was time, I felt, to notify him that I was putting an end to his 5 percent fee. Horace reacted with an angry outburst. He denied having told me that I could discontinue the fee whenever I felt he was no longer earning it. Instead he insisted he owned 5 percent of my act, with no services required to collect the money. Horace called me an ingrate and threatened to sue, but he never carried out that threat; attorneys advised him he didn't have a case. He carried a grudge against me for several years before he suddenly renewed our friendship.

Dorothy and I kept our act on the road until June 1949, performing with various bands and staging our own shows at theaters and nightclubs throughout the United States, Canada, and Mexico. After Dorothy quit the act to get married I worked another five years with three other singers. Despite the rigors of constant touring my years on the road were rarely marred by boredom. It was an exciting nomad life.

Gracie and Scooter joined Dorothy and me on the tour right from the start. Our young son took to the gypsy life like a veteran and seemed to love the constantly changing scene. At first we traveled by train, but after the Christmas holidays that first year we switched to our sedan. However, the sedan was too cramped, and in 1946 we bought a nine passenger DeSoto station wagon.

Since we were never home, Gracie and I let a couple live in our North Hollywood house rent-free just for taking care of it. On rare occasions, Gracie and Scooter would leave the tour for a short visit with relatives. At those times Dorothy and I traveled by train or bus—and once by taxi. Our train from Youngstown arrived in Pittsburgh one crisp autumn day. We were bound for a weeklong engagement at the Eastman Theater in Rochester, New York. To our dismay we discovered that we faced a four-hour layover before we could catch a train to Rochester. We were exhausted, so I impulsively decided to splurge. I hired a cab to drive us from Pittsburgh to Rochester—an excursion that cost me $350, including meals and refreshments for the driver and his girlfriend, who accompanied us. As it turned out, we more than made up the cost in free publicity. UPI somehow found out about our taxi ride, and we were met by a bevy of local and national reporters when we arrived. The story made NBC's "Nightly News." After that adventure, Dorothy bought her own car.

Early in the touring Gracie and I decided that Los Angeles wasn't an ideal place to maintain our home. It was too far removed from the East, the Midwest, the South, and the Plains States in which most of our bookings were concentrated. But we liked the feeling of having a "home base" even if we never saw it. Finally we rented our San Fernando Valley home to Norm Van Brocklin, the star quarterback of the Los Angeles Rams, and bought a new house in Park Ridge, a Chicago suburb. There we felt we could enter our young son in school; Gracie could stay home and I could have a centrally located base to tour from.

During my years with the bands I had always had a "seeing-eye" like Art

Carney, Charlie Goodman, or Bobby Lytle, plus others who pitched in to help me. Someone else handled travel arrangements, schedules, hotel reservations, bills, bookkeeping, meals, and other necessary chores. Now that I had my own act I really needed Gracie's help. So after a year of struggling and trying to handle things on my own, Gracie and I decided that if the act were to continue she and Scooter would have to join Dorothy and me on the tour again. We sold our Park Ridge home after Scooter's first year in school. Actually, he had been placed in the second grade because of his advanced reading skills and all the background he had picked up on tour.

Our first engagement after that decision was at the Circle Theater in Indianapolis, en route to a tour in Dixie. On the road we formed a two-car caravan. Our big station wagon was packed with luggage and Scooter's toys and books. In fact, it was so crammed with our belongings that Nita Walker, a young lady we had employed as a full-time baby-sitter, had to ride in Dorothy's car. This arrangement continued until Dorothy Rae left the show to marry Ted Woodruff, a grandson of the founder of the Bigelow carpet company. After that, we dispensed with our traveling baby-sitter to make room for Leslie Roberts, our new vocalist, who didn't have a car.

Until bookings for our kind of music became increasingly scarce in the mid-fifties, Gracie, Scooter, and I—and Peggy, the German shepherd we acquired as a watchdog and pet for our son—were on the road almost constantly.

Today when I look back on those years I marvel at Gracie's patience, devotion, and—most of all—stamina. For me, touring was a way of life I had long been accustomed to. But it was also a life-style I could not handle alone. I couldn't drive. I couldn't find my way about strange cities. I couldn't make my way through busy airports, railway depots, or bus stations without encountering endless problems. I couldn't even cope with numerous business details involved in being the boss of my own act. So Gracie gave up her domestic tranquillity. She was my full-time chauffeur, logging an average of 50,000 miles a year. She took care of the shopping, the laundry, the servicing of the car, the planning of travel routes, and a myriad business chores. And she also had the responsibilities of caring for and educating a somewhat precocious son who had inherited the headstrong Lowery temperament.

Fortunately, like Huckleberry Finn floating down the Mississippi on a raft, Scooter—or Fred, as he now preferred to be called—relished the vagabond life. Even the odd sort of schooling he received appealed to him. The family car became his classroom, the tumultuous backstage environment of countless theaters his campus, a campus peopled by all sorts of wonderfully gifted and frequently eccentric show people. Young Fred was educated by his mother as we traveled from city to city, from show to show. Using the home-study courses developed by the Calvert School of Baltimore for children who for various reasons couldn't attend regular school classes, Gracie taught our son all of the essential disciplines, from reading, writing, and arithmetic to history, literature, and a smattering of the general sciences.

Fred stayed on the road with us until he entered the eighth grade in a Chicago private school. The quality of Gracie's one-pupil mobile classroom was evidenced by our son's scholastic achievements in later years. He graduated from high school as an honor student, attended Butler University in Indianapolis for a year, then transferred to Bryant College at Providence, Rhode Island, where he graduated *summa cum laude* after serving as president of the student senate. Later he received his master's degree in business administration from North Texas State University before embarking on a career in marketing.

The decade we spent traveling with our own act had little of the carefree spirit that had marked my years with Lopez and Heidt. Socially we had an ever-widening circle of friends wherever we went, but there was none of the wild partying of the thirties and forties. After long years of making whoopee society seemed to be sobering up. Even Clara Bell Walsh's bashes were more sedate. Gracie and I attended her last party—a somewhat subdued but lavish affair in 1957 celebrating her birthday and the 50th anniversary of her tenancy at the Plaza. Hundreds of people from all walks of life showed up to quietly honor the aged "First Lady of the Plaza." It was the last time we saw Clara Bell. She died a few months later, and to me New York never again seemed so bright.

During my decade of touring I appeared frequently as a featured attraction with some of the dwindling number of big bands, including Stan Kenton, Shep Fields, Lawrence Welk, Guy Lombardo, Artie Shaw, Phil Harris, Frankie Carle, Fred Waring, Tony Pastor, Ted Weems, and Joe Reichman. But for me at least some of the old zest was gone. Where once there had been no worries beyond today, the main concern now was tomorrow. The responsibilities of a family and keeping my own career on track were paramount. Music still had its magic, but it was also a highly competitive business. In the old days I had joined with others in deriding Horace Heidt's serious and sometimes grim approach to music-making. Now I at last could understand his hardheaded attitude, his dedication to making a buck.

But those years between 1945 and 1954 still had some memorable moments. At the State Theater in Hartford, Connecticut, our whistler-singer act had been booked to work with Jane Russell, a large and sexy young actress who was on tour to build up her screen image. Jane was astonishingly voluptuous. The only other woman of my acquaintance who could possibly come close to rivaling her silhouette was my vocalist Leslie Roberts, a Florida girl I had hired after Dorothy Rae gave up her career for marriage.

At the close of rehearsal before the opening night's performance, Jane Russell summoned me to her dressing room. She simply adored my whistling, she said, but she would not under any circumstances appear on the same stage with Leslie Roberts. Leslie would have to sit on the sidelines during this two-week run, contract or no.

So that's the way it was in Hartford. Leslie enjoyed a paid vacation, and I ended up with Jane Russell as my vocalist. Jane was a lovely person— warmhearted, sensitive, and intelligent. At the end of our Hartford engagement she asked me to continue on tour with her, but I declined since it would have meant firing Leslie.

I remember the time in New York when Matty Rosen—one of Broadway's most memorable old-timers, who was credited with discovering Jack Benny on the vaudeville circuit—booked my act for a profitable engagement at the Palace Theater. While still there I received an invitation to perform in a Carnegie Hall concert benefiting the Lighthouse for the Blind. It was a high honor to be asked to appear on such a prestigious stage, and it was gratifying to be able to help the Lighthouse cause. Beyond these considerations, however, I had a very personal reason for welcoming the invitation.

A few weeks earlier Deems Taylor of the *New York Times*, the dean of America's music critics, had devoted an entire column to deriding the art of whistling. It was a freakish oddity, he said, a highly suspect form of music that certainly had no place in the nation's concert halls. He said that at best it was a commonplace music meant only for bird-call acts, dance-band flourishes, and the privacy of one's own bath.

Taylor's column never mentioned me, but I took it as a personal affront. I felt that the Carnegie Hall appearance would give me a chance to counter the bad press. I took great pains with my performance and resurrected several classical numbers from my early training with Peggy Richter. The next morning, in one of his infrequent apologies, Deems Taylor praised my performance as "magnificent." He even said that after hearing me perform he realized that whistling could be developed and perfected to an art form.

I remember one of several tours with Stan Kenton's band. We were playing the RKO Theater in Boston when one of Stan's musicians, a talented sideman named Muzzy Marcellino, asked me to teach him how to whistle. During the rest of that tour I gave Muzzy lessons at $25 a session, and he developed rapidly. To my knowledge he did little or no whistling for the Kenton band, but when he headed a combo on Art Linkletter's "House Party" he began to whistle professionally. Later he did considerable background whistling for movie sound tracks.

I remember the tearful scene after Claire Stewart appeared with me for the first time at the Capital Theater in Washington. I had hired Claire in Kingsville, Texas, after Leslie Roberts left the act to return to her Florida home. Claire was a sweet eighteen-year-old blonde who had been singing on station WFAA's "Early Birds" program—the same Dallas radio show on which I had performed nearly a quarter of a century earlier. She had a pleasant voice and an angelic, girl-next-door appearance. I thought she gave an adequate performance during our debut in the nation's capital, but *Variety* didn't agree. For one of the very few times, that bible of show business panned my act severely. Their critic said it was the first time in memory that Fred Lowery had appeared on stage with "an untalented amateur—a pretty girl lacking even the faintest trace of sex appeal."

Poor Claire Stewart was devastated by the review. She sobbed hysterically, threatened to kill herself, and refused to eat for several days. Never in my entire life have I seen a person so completely distraught. Gracie and I worked desperately to console her and restore her normally saucy temperament. Gene Ford, the manager of the Capital Theater, helped. He called Claire to his office and assured her he still had confidence in her talent, that she looked like a delightful little angel on the theater's massive stage. He gave her some tips on how to conquer her stage fright and warned her that some critics enjoyed tearing apart a performer even when they knew it was a nerve-wracking first-time appearance in a major theater. After that fatherly pep talk Claire cheered up, and the show went on.

Claire was part of our act for less than a year. Her parents, Bart and Connie Stewart, were our friends, and we had promised them we'd take care of her, but she was awfully young and impetuous. She finally decided to return home to Texas.

Our next vocalist was Catharine Toomay. She was singing at a nightclub in Winnemucca, Nevada, when I hired her. She was a delightful, mature young woman with a fine voice and a compelling stage presence. She was chaperoned by "Mom" Toomay, as we called her—a vigilant parent who made our touring tasks immeasurably easier.

Mom Toomay was an inspiration to all who knew her. Although she was sorely crippled with arthritis she never missed a trip. She was a cultured woman with a wonderful sense of humor. Mom was the daughter of a University of Colorado professor, a well-educated woman who had spent most of her adult life traveling with her lecturer husband. After his death she joined her daughter on the entertainment circuit. When she and Catharine joined our "caravan," Mom promptly adopted us as part of her family. She was a wonderful companion for Gracie and a thoughtful friend for young Fred during our long tours, telling him all manner of stories and helping with his schooling.

On one trip Mom Toomay was literally a lifesaver. Gracie and young Fred were visiting the Johnstons in Texas, and I was traveling with Catharine and her mother on a tour with Frankie Carle's orchestra. After closing a show in Tyler, Texas, about midnight, we had to leave immediately for a date in Wichita, Kansas. It had been a tough tour, and Catharine and I were exhausted. I was able to get some sleep, but Catharine had to drive. Sometime during the night I was awakened by Mom Toomay's loud warning, "Catharine, if you insist on driving eighty miles an hour, for heaven's sake keep your eyes open!"

Later I learned that Mom Toomay had jolted her daughter out of a doze just in time to avoid crashing into a concrete bridge abutment. Shortly afterward, when we stopped for gas, the service station attendant told us that three people had been killed the previous night when their car smashed into that same abutment.

Catharine Toomay was a part of my act during the dreary Korean war years. During that time we made a number of visits to military hospitals where we tried to bring a bit of diversion to the lives of wounded soldiers, sailors, and marines. As I had during World War II, I concentrated on the wards with patients who had lost their sight.

It was frequently a shattering emotional experience talking with these young men who suddenly had to face life blind, to try to penetrate their bitterness and despair with words of inspiration and encouragement, with wise counsel and good humor.

At the Sawtelle Veterans Hospital in Los Angeles I spent perhaps fifteen minutes talking to a young soldier still in his teens who had been blinded by shrapnel during the fighting at Inchon. The doctors had told me in advance that he was their most desperate case. He couldn't come to grips with his blindness. He wanted to die. As I talked I couldn't determine whether the young man was listening or if he had tuned me out. He said nothing as I talked about the problems and hurts he would encounter and how he might overcome them. He remained silent as I discussed my own experiences and those of other blind people. Finally he spoke.

"Mister," he asked, "how long have you been blind?"

"Since I was about two . . . so long ago I can't remember having my sight," I said.

"Then how do you get off telling me how I should adjust to blindness? How in the hell do you know anything about adjusting? Being blind is the only life you've known. But guys like me, we've had our sight all our lives and then bam! A shell explodes and we're in the dark forever and ever!"

I admitted that he and many, many others who lose their sight in their youth or adult years through accident or disease had agonizing adjustments to make. "I know it's got to be tough, losing your sight so suddenly," I said. "I can only imagine the terrible shock. Like you said, blindness is all I've ever known. But you've got to remember one thing."

"What's that?" the soldier asked.

"At least you have had the blessing of perfect sight. You've had a good, long look at the world and its beauty. You know what colors are truly like. You have seen the faces of your loved ones. You've seen your own face. You've seen movies and television and baseball games and pretty girls. At least you've had that privilege. People who have always been blind live and die in a world they've never seen. And that, young man, can be mighty tough too!"

Silence hung momentarily over the ward as I ended my impulsive sermonizing. Then the young man's hand groped for mine. "Mister," he said quietly, "I hope to God you'll forgive me. I've been lying here feeling so sorry for myself I couldn't imagine how others can be hurt. I'm ashamed of myself!"

After that we had a long discussion about blindness and about life in general. When I left he promised he'd really work to overcome his sudden handicap and make something of his life. Somehow I have a hunch that he worked out his problems. He seemed like a gutsy kid once he shed his shell of self-pity.

I did so many things, had so many experiences in those fading days of the big-band years. There were recording sessions with Les Paul and Mary Ford, a remarkably talented couple who taught me how to do a "multiple" — to whistle a duet with myself. This technique paid good dividends when I recorded "When I Grow too Old to Dream" as a multiple for Columbia Records. I appeared on the "Perry Como Show," reviewing my acquaintance with the "singing barber" I'd first met in a Pittsburgh theater years before. I suffered the insane practical jokes of the Three Stooges during an engagement in Cincinnati. I did another Lighthouse for the Blind benefit in Hollywood where I performed with Jack Benny, Eddie "Rochester"

Anderson, Bob Hope, Dorothy Lamour, Bing Crosby, Fred Astaire, George Burns and Gracie Allen, and a number of other great stars.

And I recorded "The High and the Mighty."

By mid-1953 only a few of the original big bands survived, reflecting a continuous decline in available big-time bookings. The large ballrooms of the major hotels were being converted to banquet and convention business. More and more Americans were flicking on their TV sets for entertainment, and this stay-at-home trend cut drastically into motion-picture attendance, a fact that dealt a fatal blow to the live shows the larger movie houses had traditionally featured.

In addition to all this, popular music was undergoing sweeping change. Such disciples of the feverish rock 'n' roll sound as disc jockey Alan Freed and his "Moondog Rock 'n' Roll Party" and bandleader Bill Haley and his "Crazy, Man, Crazy" reflected the changing tastes in the music market.

Confronted with sharp cutbacks in bookings, Catharine Toomay and I put our touring on a part-time basis. To help bolster my income I joined with arranger, singer, and songwriter Maury Laws in a record-promoting business. Maury and I took over an office in an overage New York building on West Forty-sixth Street, an office in which composer Gordon Jenkins had written his classic *Manhattan Towers Suite*. With such a noted tenant in its past our office was sure to bring us luck, Maury claimed. He was right, for it was in this office that Maury wrote all the original music for "Rudolph the Red-Nosed Reindeer," a TV Christmas production that brought him fame and fortune. And it was here that I agreed to a deal to make a record that turned out to be one of the all-time best sellers.

I was in the office one afternoon when the phone rang. It was Leroy Holmes, one of several arrangers with Vincent Lopez during my years with the band; he was now an arranger and conductor for the MGM Music Company. Leroy excitedly told me he had discovered a terrific new tune composed by Dmitri Tiomkin, a song based on a current best-selling novel, *The High and the Mighty*.

"I've heard of the book, but not the song," I said.

"Not many people have," Holmes enthused. "But the word's going to get around fast. This song's a surefire winner, and we can turn out a smash hit if we can get it out in a hurry before one of the big labels grabs it."

I was puzzled. When a record company sets its sights on a tune with great potential it usually goes shopping for a well-known vocalist. "It sounds great," I told Leroy, "but why are you calling me? Remember me, Leroy? I'm Fred Lowery . . . a whistler, not a singer."

Leroy Holmes chuckled. He'd been saving the punch line. Fred, I forgot

275

to tell you. There's no singing in this number. It's all orchestra and whistling."

I was elated. A tune written exclusively for whistling is a rarity to be treasured. I asked Leroy when he could arrange for rehearsals to begin so I could spend a few days with the orchestra memorizing the number.

"Sorry, Fred," Holmes said. "We don't have time for any lengthy rehearsing. Like I told you, we've got to really run with this tune to get on the market first. We're cutting the record tomorrow. I'll pick you up in the morning and take you to the studio."

I told Leroy he was insane, that nobody could produce a professional record that fast, especially a brand-new number. I said it would be impossible for me to memorize a complex arrangement and record it in one session with a strange orchestra.

Leroy Holmes just laughed. "Sure you can, Fred. I know you can do the job, or I wouldn't have called you. Don't worry about it!" And he hung up before I could voice another word of protest.

The next morning, in a cab headed for the recording studio on Twenty-third Street, Leroy whistled the number over and over for me. He wasn't much of a whistler, but at least he gave me some idea about the music. In the studio I discovered that I would be supported by a forty-seven-piece orchestra. I also learned that I would have the first eight bars to myself with no musical background.

I was dismayed by the magnitude of the memorizing job that faced me, and so was the producer when he discovered I was blind and unable to read the carefully prepared score. However, we went to work. The orchestra, conducted by Leroy Holmes, played the entire number repeatedly— including my eight opening bars of solo whistling—until I felt I had the arrangement fairly well in mind. Then we began recording. After what seemed an eternity, our thirteenth cutting sounded perfect. We closed shop, and six days later the record was released for public sale and jukebox distribution across the nation. It was an amazing production effort—one week from recording to distribution.

Within a month "The High and the Mighty" had soared to No. 1 on the lists of all the trade magazines. It held that glorified position for fourteen weeks and sold millions of records. It was one of the all-time recording gold mines—but not for me. I was paid a flat fee of $50 for doing the record, or about $4 an hour for the time involved in producing the hit.

A few weeks after the record was released Broadway columnist Walter Winchell reported that "Fred Lowery, the famous blind whistler of the Big Bands, received *only* $25 for recording one of the greatest hits of all time,

'The High and the Mighty.' " It was Leroy Holmes who made the big money, Winchell concluded.

This accusation stirred a furious rebuttal from Holmes. He hadn't made a fortune on his arrangement of "The High and the Mighty," he protested. He was just an employee of MGM, an arranger and conductor for the company, and he had received only his regular salary for his part in making the hit record. Besides, he indignantly told reporters, Fred Lowery had been paid $50, and not the $25 claimed by Winchell.

When this controversy flared into print it generated all sorts of priceless publicity for me, including a highly complimentary review in *Newsweek* magazine, an article that credited my whistling with making "High and Mighty" such an amazing overnight success.

The publicity gave my flagging career new life. My booking agent, who had been evading my phone calls, suddenly became my buddy once more. Columbia and Decca Records, with whom I had been affiliated for years, again began to seek me out for new recordings. I was also asked by MGM to whistle two new arrangements, "Tara's Theme" from *Gone With the Wind* and "Unchained Melody." I even heard from Horace Heidt for the first time in several years. He contacted me in New York during an engagement at the Palace Theater and, after asking me to help him organize a Heidt band reunion, put me on the trail of a new enterprise, whistling commercials for radio and TV.

A few days later Enoch Light, a former bandleader whose music had been featured at New York's Algonquin Hotel, got in touch with me. He too was in the record business. He had made a new arrangement of "The High and the Mighty." He assured me he had altered it enough from the MGM original to avoid a lawsuit. Would I be interested in doing the whistling for this version? I said I would—if the price was right.

When he said $75, I figured I might as well take the money and reap whatever publicity the new record generated. After all, it was $25 more than MGM had paid me. Soon I had two versions of "The High and the Mighty" on the market. Enoch Light's version never made the charts, but it did enjoy respectable sales and brought me a new flurry of good reviews. In fact, the great success of Dmitri Tiomkin's tune and all its attendant publicity fueled a lot of interest in a movie production incorporating the song. Based on the plot of the novel *The High and the Mighty* by Ernest K. Gann, the 1954 movie starring John Wayne and Robert Stack was one of Hollywood's first airline disaster thrillers. Ironically Muzzy Marcellino, my former pupil, was hired to whistle the movie version of the song that won an Oscar that year.

"The High and the Mighty" had been at the top of the charts for several months when I had to fly from New York to Los Angeles for the television show featuring the reunion of the old Horace Heidt band, the reunion for which Heidt had enlisted my aid.

It was shortly before Christmas, and the plane was crowded with preholiday travelers. I was traveling alone; Gracie and Scooter were at the home of her parents in Texas where I would join them for the holidays after the telecast. As our plane came in from the east over the mountains and the passengers began to prepare for disembarking at the Los Angeles air terminal, I paid little heed. Gradually I became aware that it was taking an unusually long time for the plane to make a landing. For some reason we seemed to be circling over the city and its sprawling suburbs. Then the pilot's voice sounded over the public address system.

In cool, precise language he informed us that the plane had encountered mechanical problems. The landing gear had stuck midway in the lowering process. The crew was trying to correct the problem. Meanwhile the plane would continue circling over Los Angeles until its supply of fuel was exhausted—a precautionary move designed to prevent a fire or explosion if we had to make an emergency landing. Would everybody please stay calm.

The pilot's urging for calm was futile. His announcement touched off a wave of alarm. A few women fainted, others screamed and cried. Some passengers prayed and others asked frantic questions no one was qualified to answer. And some just sat silently, no doubt wondering as I was what cruel turn of fate had put them on this flight, wondering if the end was near and what lay beyond.

My brooding was interrupted by one of the stewardesses. She asked me if I would accompany her to the cockpit; the pilot wanted to talk with me. Mystified by this unexpected summons I meekly grasped the girl's hand and followed her up the aisle.

The pilot said he had been looking over the passenger list, hoping he'd spot the name of somebody from show business. "Your name was familiar," he said. "You're Fred Lowery the whistler, aren't you?"

"I am," I said, still bewildered.

The pilot explained that he had heard me whistle on radio broadcasts and at the Cocoanut Grove. "I've also heard your record of "The High and the Mighty," he said. "I know it's an awful lot to ask at a time like this, but could you whistle it for us over the public-address system?"

"I'll be happy to do anything you ask. But what's it supposed to accomplish?"

278

The pilot said he hoped some entertainment would help ease the tension, help take everybody's thoughts off the danger.

"How big a danger is that?" I asked. "What are our chances if we have to attempt an emergency landing without wheels?"

"Not so good," the pilot grimly replied.

Having received those gloomy tidings I began to whistle, trying to ignore the plane's radio as it crackled with terse advice from the control tower. For what seemed an eternity I whistled "High and Mighty" for the plane's passengers and crew. At one point the plane began bouncing erratically in rough air. Suddenly there was a loud thumping noise, like the falling of a heavy object. The pilot and copilot shouted with joy and relief. The turbulence apparently had jarred loose the stuck landing gear and the wheels had dropped into place. A few minutes later we landed safely, flashing past ambulances and fire trucks lining the runway.

I left the big plane with the crew. As we parted inside the terminal the pilot pumped my hand and observed that heaven must been tuned in on my whistling.

"All I can say, Fred, is that somebody upstairs sure likes you!" The pilot turned and walked away, never realizing that he and I and all those other people had been involved in a true-life version of a movie that would soon be packing theaters across the country.

Chapter 20

In recent years there has been a renewal of interest in the big bands. Numerous albums from that era bearing the names of now-legendary band-leaders of long ago have been resurrected and reissued.

More and more hotels and nightclubs are featuring big band revivals. It is gratifying in a way, but of course it isn't the same. It's much like the special historical parks around the country that re-create the way our pioneer ancestors once lived—or perhaps the way we think they lived. The log stockades, the crude cabins, the homespun clothes, and the primitive furnishings of those historical parks may be authentic replicas, but there is no way to duplicate or bring back those frontier days. So it is with the big band revival. The music, the instruments, and even the colorful costumes may be accurately reproduced, but there is no way to recapture the spirit and special flavor of those times.

It is sad for us old dinosaurs to realize that the music we made now endures only in our memories and on the old, flawed records we cut so long ago. It is also sad to realize that the bouncing bobby-soxers and their hepcat swains are now sedate grandmas and grandpas bemoaning the wild ways of their grandchildren.

But are today's children really worse than the youngsters of past generations? I don't think so, and I may rate as an expert on the subject. Since 1960 Gracie and I have traveled in every state of the Union except Alaska and Hawaii entertaining and talking with boys and girls in public and private schools and colleges.

We have been on the road thirty-two weeks a year averaging fifteen shows a week. That adds up to more than 10,000 schools we have visited and literally millions of children who have listened to our music—much of it the music of the past—and often astounded us with their courtesy, their good will, and the penetrating intelligence of their questions.

Our experience tells us that the children of today are no better and no worse than the youngsters of yesterday. They may have some different values, different temptations, different interests, different heroes. But they are basically the same as young people have always been.

Like so many changes in our lives our involvement in school tours was almost accidental. It was a phase of show business we had never heard of, and one which I'm sure I would not have taken seriously as I searched for new and promising fields of entertainment during the spring of 1954.

One thing was certain at the time. Despite the success of "The High and the Mighty," our whistler-singer act was pretty much finished. There simply weren't enough profitable bookings for touring. Besides, Catharine Toomay's husband John McMullen, a Detroit insurance executive, was becoming impatient with their separations. Finally Catharine gave up her singing career to become a full-time wife, and I turned my attention to my record business. It was producing a good profit for me and my associate, the multitalented Maury Laws. After several years we had attracted an impressive clientele headed by two superb instrumentalists, Hugo Montenegro and Don Henry.

But Gracie and I were becoming disenchanted with New York. Old friends had left or died. Manhattan itself was losing the charm that once had fascinated us. By the mid-fifties it was becoming a dirty, disruptive, violent city—not an ideal place to live and bring up a son unless you were blessed with the kind of wealth that could shield you from an increasingly unpleasant environment.

The grimmer aspects of New York life extended even into the record business. Payola had become the name of the game. More and more of the big-name disc jockeys were demanding payoffs for pushing a record, and these under-the-table payoffs were becoming an essential ingredient in a record's success or failure. There were also increasingly distasteful pressures from underworld types moving in on the industry.

One day I was visited by a strong-arm thug who suggested that a New York mob boss wanted my office to push a certain popular female quartet's records as a favor for one of his Chicago pals who was playing house with one of the group's singers.

"What if I don't choose to play ball?" I asked.

"That would be a very foolish decision," the messenger growled.

When he departed after a few more warnings and demands, I telephoned Gracie. It took us only a few minutes to decide that despite its profits we'd had enough of the record-promoting business. We decided to settle in the Midwest, back in Chicago where I had become involved in making whistling commercials for 7 Up, Hires Root Beer, Duncan Hines, and Philip Morris. I knew it was a gamble for a family man to walk away from a thriving business. But despite some qualms I felt that the whistling commercials and record royalties would give me a comfortable financial base while I tried to develop new connections.

We entered our son in a Chicago private school for his eighth grade studies, his first exposure to a regular school since the second grade. Meanwhile I signed with a Chicago talent agency, and soon found myself working club dates in a five-state midwestern region in addition to radio and TV commercials and records for two companies—Decca and Word Records of Waco, Texas.

My longtime friend Norvell Slater of station WFAA in Dallas first introduced me to Jarrell McCracken, the founder of Word, Inc., a producer of inspirational and sacred music records. My first album, *Fred Lowery Whistles Your Gospel Favorites,* a record I cut at the WFAA studio with Texas pianist-composer Kurt Kaiser, was exceptionally successful. That led to a contract that has continued through the years and resulted in other best-selling religious albums, such as *Abide With Me, Precious Memories,* and *It Is Well With My Soul.*

The flow of club dates helped bolster my income, but there was one problem. I was doing a solo act, and that required employing a housekeeper to tend to young Fred while Gracie accompanied me on the road. Again my blindness created complications that required a sighted person's help.

Fortunately that problem was soon resolved. Early in my regional touring I was booked into LaRue's Supper Club in Indianapolis, a fashionable Hoosier night spot where Catharine Toomay and I had appeared several times. While having dinner one evening with Harley Horton, the owner of LaRue's, I told him of the difficulties Gracie and I were experiencing in trying to cope with the responsibilities of parenthood and the demands of touring.

Harley said he had a solution. He offered me a long-term contract to serve as the host of his supper club, a contract that would allow me ample time for whatever outside activities I might want to undertake. The pay was excellent, and there was an important added advantage. The job would give us a home base in a clean, friendly midwestern city, a place where we would settle down with Fred during his high-school years. I told Gracie about the offer, and she agreed that I should take the job. We sold the house we had bought in Chicago and bought one in Indianapolis.

I had been at LaRue's only a few months when I got another exceptional opportunity. Bob Ohleyer, the manager of radio station WISH, a CBS affiliate in Indianapolis, offered me a job as disc jockey, a position that wouldn't interfere with my duties at LaRue's. In fact the club benefited too, for Ohleyer soon came up with a plan to broadcast my show live from the first-floor lounge of LaRue's, which had been renamed The Whistlestop. By this time my show had evolved from platter-spinning and chitchat to a two-hour music-talk program in which I interviewed club patrons and visiting celebrities. Through the years my talk-show guests included just about every important person who stopped in Indianapolis—writers, artists, "500" race drivers and other sports figures. And of course there were many show business people—longtime friends like Mary Martin, Bob Hope, John Wayne, Jimmy Stewart, and Art Linkletter.

We remained in Indianapolis, and at the Whistlestop Lounge of LaRue's, for five years, until Fred had graduated from Shortridge High School and was established in his studies at Butler University.

Once Fred entered college Gracie felt less concern about joining me on tours. With the freedom I enjoyed at LaRue's and in my radio-show commitments, I began accepting out-of-town club dates again. I found it invigorating to get back at least part time to the excitement of life on the road. However, I gradually discovered that the pace of one's younger days cannot be continued forever. After a while I began to feel the strain of combining my work at LaRue's, my radio show, and my recording sessions with the intermittent club tours. Besides, more and more of the club dates were in smaller cities and towns. The big, profitable bookings were going to rock groups.

On a rain-drenched night, as we headed for a week engagement in Fort Lauderdale, Florida, our station wagon was hit head-on by a driver trying to pass three other cars on a narrow, winding highway south of Columbus, Georgia. Gracie was unhurt, but I was hospitalized briefly with cuts on my face. What worried me most, however, was a cut on my lip. I was frantic about how this might affect my whistling. But when it healed I found that I could whistle even higher than before!

In all of our long years of traveling it was our first accident. When we returned to Indianapolis, we agreed that we had to stop the club tours. Like it or not, we had to recognize that the years were catching up with us. We could no longer handle so much.

Even then we knew it was only a matter of time until we would have to move on. Television was cutting deeply into nightclub revenues, and it was becoming apparent that even such a long-established place as LaRue's would eventually have to turn to the new music to attract the younger generation. The same impact was evident at WISH. My problem, in contemplating the future, was not easily answered: Where could a middle-aged blind whistler with no gift or stomach for rock find a market for his talent?

That question was answered for me by one of the educator guests who appeared on my radio show. He told me of an agency in Chicago that was devoted exclusively to booking entertainment for school assemblies across the nation. "You won't get rich at this kind of work, but you won't starve," the educator said. "If you like traveling it's great. And it's rewarding work because you have the opportunity to be a good influence, an inspiration for young people."

I was curious and decided the opportunity might be worth investigating. I decided to go to Chicago to talk with S. E. Paulus, director of the School Assembly Service. Paulus said he was a longtime fan of mine dating back to the Vincent Lopez days. "But," he cautioned, "you'll still have to audition before we can accept you as a client."

"What kind of an audition?" I asked.

"You'll have to appear before a high-school assembly," he said. "A screening committee will be present to determine whether or not your act and your personality are suitable for young audiences." The committee, he said, would be comprised of school administrators, teachers, parents, high-school students, and representatives of School Assembly booking agencies from all over the country. As he put it, "The judges will be the people who are closest to this very special audience."

A few weeks later I was scheduled to appear at a Chicago high school and given explicit instructions to present a twenty-five-minute program—no more, no less. I was one of some fifty acts booked into that school during the weeklong auditions, and I was one of the lucky ones to be accepted by the screening committee, getting an A-plus rating.

Before I left Chicago I met with Paulus. He congratulated me and said I would be receiving a contract in a few weeks. Then in a more serious vein he warned Gracie and me, as he did all the other entertainers on the school circuit, that we would be confronting "some nasty situations."

"These kids will be the toughest audiences you've ever faced," Paulus said, echoing the views of my friend Art Linkletter who once told me that youngsters were the most demanding fans and the hardest to please or fool.

Paulus went on to say that there were many serious problems in the nation's schools and warned that he expected them to worsen. "Our boys and girls today too often are undisciplined," he said. "They're bitter, disillusioned, spoiled, angry, impatient, restless. We've got drug problems

284

and sex problems and a lot of other ugly things you folks may have to cope with on a face-to-face basis."

Paulus paused, puffed on his pipe, and then continued. "That's the bad side of the coin. But there's a good side too, and it's a lot more important. These youngsters by and large aren't bad. They're just growing up in a bad time. Despite their rebellious actions and their angry, bitter words, they want guidance and inspiration. They want help in finding themselves . . . help in finding a purpose and a meaning in this unhappy world."

That was the last time I saw Paulus; he died shortly after the auditions. But through the ensuing years—years in which we've used several booking agencies—his parting words have remained etched in my mind.

For more than two decades Gracie and I have visited campuses in cities, towns, villages, and remote rural areas in forty-eight states, and we've been through many tense, stormy times. We've faced situations we could never have imagined. We've been bombarded with all manner of questioning from young audiences and searched our hearts for the right answers. Through it all we have tried to follow Paulus's wise advice: to be friends with the youngsters, to be truthful with them, to try to help them face their problems with love, patience, and understanding.

It's been difficult at times, and frustrating, but our faith in youth has always been justified. Our son is no exception. He and his wife Astrid have made a success of their impetuous young marriage after his first year in college. They have a fine home in Houston and three wonderful children, John, Julie, and a third-generation Fred Lowery. Perhaps because he was exposed for so long to our chaotic show business life-style my son chose a business career. He has a responsible executive position and is also working on his Ph.D. Astrid got her B.A. degree from the University of Houston and is now working on her master's. Gracie and I consider ourselves blessed, although we sometimes wonder how in the make-believe world of our lives our son managed to grow the roots for such a mature, responsible life.

Our faith has also been justified by the lives of many of the children we have entertained and talked to. The fiery young rebels, the mixed-up kids we met on the campuses in our early years on the school tour have for the most part become responsible citizens and parents, with perhaps a deeper sense of compassion and awareness of the world around them than their parents and grandparents possessed.

On today's campuses the fires of rebellion seem more subdued, although the youngsters still typically question the ways of their elders. As a onetime young rebel I can appreciate their feelings. I can also sympathize with the challenge of adapting to a rapidly changing world with its bewildering shifts of values and its complex political, social, economic, and spiritual conflicts. Today's youth faces extreme stresses and strains, pressures and temptations. But they will take it in stride, because youth always does.

Our life has been good, but not always easy—especially for my Gracie who year after year has handled all the details of our tours. Since the day we left Indianapolis after closing my career at LaRue's and station WISH we have had our share of good times and bad times, laughter and tears, hopes and fears. We've been involved in other serious accidents. Once in North Dakota after I slipped on an icy sidewalk and shattered my left arm Gracie had to drive twenty miles through a blizzard to get me to the nearest doctor. Then we had a 140-mile ride in an ambulance to the nearest hospital in Grand Forks. The blizzard closed the highways and it was six days before we could get back to our motorhome. We've survived tornadoes and suffered through floods, heat waves, ice storms, and all the other discomforts and perils that beset the highways and byways of America. During the summer months we have transplanted our roots back to our native soil of the Texas Piney Woods. There in Jacksonville, not far from the village where I was born, we now have our home, to which we retreat whenever we can find the time.

During a return to Texas in May 1967, while visiting in Austin with Thurman Dobbins, my boyhood friend at the Blind School, I got a phone call from Harry Crozier, a well-known political reporter who had covered the Texas legislature for years. Crozier said Lieutenant Governor Preston Smith had asked him to invite me to perform before a session of the state senate. "Smith says the senate's been in session so long it needs somebody to wake them up," Crozier said. "He figures your whistling can do the job."

A couple of days later Dobbins and I, sporting identical gray suits and stetsons for the occasion, set out for the state senate chambers chauffeured by Gracie. Thurman's wife Nimmie had a dental appointment that day, and we had arranged to pick her up en route so she could watch the performance.

On the way to get Nimmie we stopped for gas, and Thurman asked Gracie to lead him to the service station's rest room. When they returned I asked for the same assistance. Again Gracie made the rest room trek, this time helping me. As we returned to the car we overheard one of the station attendants remarking to another, "Lordy, lordy, did you see what I just saw?"

"What's that?" the other attendant asked.

"Well, this woman that just went by . . . she's got two blind husbands, and she dresses 'em both alike!"

We were still chuckling about that incident when we arrived at the senate

286

to find an honor guard waiting to escort us into the inner sanctum of Texas politics. Inside the chamber the entire senate stood as we were led to the rostrum where the lieutenant governor introduced me as "our former page boy who has made whistling a fine art in America."

For the next half hour, without any accompaniment, I whistled for the Texas senators—whistled all the old-time favorites from my days on radio with the "Early Birds." As I whistled I could remember the young, spry, ambitious Fred Lowery, eagerly running errands for the politicians who had ruled that chamber so long ago. When I finished the members of the senate I once had served gave me a standing ovation and a plaque. It was a day never to be forgotten by me and Gracie, the "woman with two blind husbands."

There are so many good memories from our years of entertaining the nation's school children. The best of those memories is summed up by an eloquent story written by Rex Redifer of the *Indianapolis Star* in December 1980. Rex had covered one of my performances at an elementary school in Anderson, Indiana. Here is what he said:

". . . Watching, one had a certain sense of apprehension as the couple assembled an austere setting for their program. There was a tape recorder, which Gracie operated, a speaker and a microphone. That was it. It was rather spare fare for children accustomed to daily television, where the wonders of the world are brought into their living rooms with the click of a switch. How would the youngsters react to this blind performer and his wife? It was hardly on the scale of *Sesame Street.*

"After a short introduction, Fred took the mike, stepped forward and began to whistle.

"First, there were looks of bewilderment; then disbelief and finally awe showed in the faces of the children.

"This was not something they were used to, nothing they had seen or heard before.

"Fred Lowery has a rare and beautiful talent—he is probably the premier whistler of his generation, and 51 years in show business has not dulled the edge of his skill.

"Although the children were fascinated by this unexpected and entirely new (to them) performance, it was just a beginning. Fred is not simply a whistler. He is a personality, a multi-talented man with a totally engaging way. Joking, kidding, lecturing—within 10 minutes he had completely captivated the audience with a delightful array of imitations, bird calls and beautiful renditions of songs, the likes of which these youngsters had never heard before.

287

"Obviously as delighted with his audience as they were with him, he invited two of them up to whistle a song with him. By that point, Fred Lowery was no longer an unknown old blind man from the past who did this weird thing—whistle. He was as fresh and new as his young audience—as much a kid as the delighted youngsters he was entertaining.

"Between selections, Fred dispensed an array of upbeat philosophy, bantered with Gracie, encouraged the children to overcome handicaps, setbacks and feelings of doubt. It was a show with a subtle message presented with humor, compassion and understanding. Strangely, the children understood. . . . By the end of that 45-minute performance, Fred Lowery had become a friend of everyone in that small gymnasium.

"And that is his secret. He does not see with his eyes; he sees with his heart, his wisdom, his talent and his understanding of human nature. In the space of 45 minutes, Fred had allayed the natural discomfort people have with the handicapped; had broken through the generation gap; had won the total affection of a group of strange children, and had filled that gray, gloomy afternoon with whoops of delight and laughter. . . ."

Coming from a reporter—and a music reviewer for a major American newspaper who had met me and heard me perform for the first time—Redifer's story was most gratifying. Of course, all my audiences aren't so receptive. I have occasionally been booed and hissed, and once police had to be called to maintain order. Another time at a junior high school in South Carolina a youngster in the audience shouted, "We've had a lot of crummy shows, but yours is ridiculous!"

For the most part, though, Gracie and I have been happily received. At a school in Hannibal, Missouri, where I closed the program by whistling "Amazing Grace" and "Tammy" with bagpipe music in the background, a number of the pupils cried—as I had wept years before at the School for the Blind when "Taps" was played to mark the end of World War I. At a school in Idaho a boy came up to me at the close of the performance and handed me a nickel. "Mr. Lowery," he said, "that's the best program we've ever had. I paid a whole quarter to hear it, but it's worth more. Here's a nickel tip. It's all I've got!"

Beautiful moments like these keep me going. When will I decide to retire? After a lifetime in show business I can't really say. Perhaps never. Certainly I've considered it on occasion, especially during the winter of 1978 when we encountered one of the coldest sieges in the history of the South. After an unusually stormy autumn and early winter in the plains states, Gracie and I had looked forward to a balmy after-Christmas tour in the milder climes of Dixie. Instead we were constantly plagued by snow, sleet, and ice storms that stalled our large motorhome for days at a time. On that thoroughly miserable tour 60 percent of our bookings were canceled because of the weather.

At last, as Easter neared, Gracie and I decided to ring down the curtain on school tours. We headed back toward our home in Jacksonville. However, we made one stop en route for a personal appearance at a memorial program at Warm Springs, Georgia. As I received a flattering ovation from patients and medical personnel at the health center founded by Franklin Delano Roosevelt I recalled the time I had entertained the president and his First Lady in Washington. At that moment in Warm Springs it seemed a most appropriate way to end my long career.

But as the next autumn approached I fell victim once more to that old, familiar yearning to move on. Once again Gracie and I took to the open road in our home on wheels, heading for schools in the Wisconsin and Minnesota northland, our plans for retirement forgotten.

Sometimes in the years that have followed I have suspected that at heart I'm very much like my old bandleader boss Vincent Lopez—too deeply involved in music and the compelling call of show business to ever willingly make my exit.

I last heard from Vincent in July 1975. It was a nostalgic letter filled with wistful memories and shadowed by a vague premonition that the end of the road at last was in sight—a foreboding rooted in the numerological and astrological beliefs which had guided his long and lusty life.

At the time, Lopez was eighty years old and still leading a band, scrounging whatever jobs he could find in the Catskills in the summer and in Florida in the winter. It wasn't that he needed the money. He just couldn't face life in retirement. In his letter Lopez recalled his beginnings and his later years on the bandstand long after the glory days had faded. And for some reason he remembered a morning on one of our tours that I had long since forgotten.

The Lopez band was touring one summer somewhere in southern Ohio. We had been driving all night, and with the coming of dawn the driver stopped our bus on a wide bluff overlooking the Ohio River so the overage vehicle could cool off. The entire band scrambled off the bus to stretch their legs and enjoy the glory of the dawn. For some reason, as I sprawled lazily on the grassy shoulder of the highway, I was inspired to start whistling MacDowell's "At Dawning," a number I hadn't performed since my days with Peggy Richter.

"I don't know what it was, but your whistling got to me that morning," Lopez wrote. "As you know, I'm not a sentimental man, and it was one of the few times in my life that I broke down and bawled. I guess it was your whistling combined with the beauty of the dawn. Somehow I was overwhelmed by the realization of what a brief time we have on earth to enjoy life's beauties and wonders. . . ."

There was much more in his long letter, and I was touched at this aging musician taking a rare moment to putter about in the closet of his memories and share some of them with an old friend.

"Our paths crossed for some reason or other," he wrote. "Only God knows why. . . . And perhaps they will cross again, although the forces that control our lives tell me this cannot be. I only know now that I can never retire . . . that music is too much a part of me to ever let it go, to sit idly in the sun and await the last moment. Perhaps, Fred, it is the same with you. . . ."

As Lopez predicted, our paths never crossed again. Two months later, on September 20, 1975, Vincent Lopez died in a nursing home in North Miami Beach, Florida. He had continued making music up until a couple of weeks before his death.

Gracie and I had parked our motorhome for the night behind a school auditorium in a small Iowa farming community when we heard the news of Lopez's death on the radio. It wasn't a surprise, but still it was a shock.

For a long time I sat in silence—thinking not just of Vincent Lopez but of all the aging troubadours from the big-band days.

Then I remembered breathlessly arriving at the St. Regis Roof for the first time and hearing the inimitable sound of "Nola" being styled by Vincent Lopez at the piano. The refrain echoed clear and sharp in my memory, and instinctively—just as I had greeted the dawn so many years before—I started to whistle along with the music in my mind.

But no sound came. For once my whistle failed me, and I quietly wept for my friend and for those days forever past.

Epilogue

I suppose an autobiography should end with some kind of statement about life and the human condition. And I do have an observation to offer, for whatever it's worth.

There was a time when I liked to believe I had single-handedly met and overcome all the obstacles—a blind man who through sheer talent and commitment had become self-sufficient and risen, alone, above the limitations of his affliction. At the time when I believed that, I was the blindest of all. My stalwart independence was obviously only in my imagination.

Through the years I have come to understand that my striving to participate fully in the affairs of the sighted world has exacted a price from all those who have been close to me, because my participation in the world of sight has required their participation in my world of blindness. The names of those on whom I have had to lean and depend are legion. The fabric of my life is richly woven with their love and concern.

But I also know that my make-believe independence wasn't all bad, because if my spirit had not been sustained by that illusion I might have spent my life stranded in the dead-end streets of despair.

And aren't all of us in the same boat—trying to overlook or minimize our handicaps and flaws as we struggle to shape our lives to whatever pattern of excellence we aspire? We cannot escape whatever it is that afflicts us, but we can stand fast in refusing to let it distort or destroy our lives. And if along the way we miss a truth or two and do some whistling in the dark, those who love us will surely understand.